THINKING IN TIME

THINKING IN TIME

✳✳✳

AN INTRODUCTION TO
HENRI BERGSON

✳✳✳

SUZANNE GUERLAC

CORNELL UNIVERSITY PRESS
ITHACA AND LONDON

First published 2006 by Cornell University Press
First printing, Cornell Paperbacks, 2006

Design by Scott Levine

Library of Congress Cataloging-in-Publication Data

Guerlac, Suzanne.
    Thinking in time : an introduction to Henri Bergson /
Suzanne Guerlac.
        p. cm.
    Includes bibliographical references and index.
    ISBN-13: 978-0-8014-4421-0 (cloth)
    ISBN-10: 0-8014-4421-7 (cloth)
    ISBN-13: 978-0-8014-7300-5 (pbk.)
    ISBN-10: 0-8014-7300-4 (pbk.)
    1. Bergson, Henri, 1859–1941. I. Title.
    B2430.B43G76 2006
    194—dc22
2005032184

Cornell University Press strives to use environmentally responsible suppliers and materials to the fullest extent possible in the publishing of its books. Such materials include vegetable-based, low-VOC inks and acid-free papers that are recycled, totally chlorine-free, or partly composed of nonwood fibers. For further information, visit our website at www.cornellpress.cornell.edu.

| Cloth printing | 10 9 8 7 6 5 4 3 2 1 |
| Paperback printing | 10 9 8 7 6 5 4 3 2 1 |

In fond memory of my friend Scott Bryson

Contents

Preface   ix

Note on Translations   xiii

1. Bergson and Bergsonisms   1

2. From the Certainties of Mechanism to the Anxieties of Indeterminism   14

3. *Time and Free Will (Essai sur les données immédiates de la conscience)*   42

4. *Matter and Memory*   106

5. Channels of Contemporary Reception   173

6. Current Issues   197

Conclusion   212

Bibliography   215

Index   225

Preface

In *What Is Called Thinking?* Heidegger reminds us that there is no such thing as a mere presentation, or description, of a philosopher's thought of the kind I attempt here. Every account is also an interpretation. An exposition is also necessarily a reading.

Where does my interpretation of Bergson begin? With the selection of texts I have chosen to present, the *Essai sur les données immédiates de la conscience* [*Time and Free Will*] and *Matière et mémoire* [*Matter and Memory*]. I focus on these two works, not because they are Bergson's most famous books, but because they provide the best introduction to his thought. They present a rigorous account of the concepts of duration and memory crucial to all the philosopher's works, and they reveal most clearly what is at stake in his thinking. In the end, however, we do not read Bergson for useful concepts so much as for a process of thought—a thinking in time—that carries remarkable critical force. As Heidegger has suggested in *What Is Called Thinking?*, we can learn thinking only by unlearning what thinking has traditionally been. Bergson can help us do this.

Réapprendre à lire—to relearn how to read. This was the watchword of Mallarméan modernism. To turn to Bergson today requires relearning how to read his works. It is not a question of finding yet another master discourse to plug into a set of conventional intellectual habits or postures. No summary of Bergson's thought will be particularly useful. What counts is his practice of writing and the movement of his thought. This is why I have devoted the two central chapters of this book to reading through the *Essai* and *Matter and Memory*. To the extent that reading Bergson consistently challenges our assumptions and our habits of thought, to read Bergson is to relearn how to think—to think in time.

The first two chapters of this book situate Bergson's thought in its historical context. The goal is to provide the reader with conceptual tools that will enrich the appreciation of his texts. Chapter 1 presents a brief account of Bergson's career and of the emergence of various Bergsonisms that arose from the popularization of his thought. It also gives a short summary of Bergson's other major works. Bergson was an interdisciplinary thinker *avant la lettre*. Chapter 2 explores intellectual issues and positions pertinent to his thought. This chapter deals with questions of determinism and humanism that both derive from, and reinforce, tendencies in emerging fields of the social sciences such as experimental psychology and sociology. It also treats, in considerable detail, developments in the physical sciences that occurred during Bergson's lifetime. These have radically transformed the way we think about the world and make clear why the question of time is crucial to modernity. Bergson, trained in mathematics, took a keen interest in the developments of modern physics. This background is essential to an appreciation of the rigor of Bergson's thought and of the specific interest his thought might have for us today.

Chapters 3 and 4, the book's center, lead us directly into the movement of Bergson's thinking. Chapter 3 presents the arguments of the *Essai*, chapter 4 those of *Matter and Memory*. In each case I respect the development of Bergson's texts, and provide substantial extracts from them. It is important to read them closely. It is a question of following what the philosopher has called the *zig-zag* path of his preeminently strategic writing. There is no short cut—we have to take our time.

Chapters 5 and 6 concern the current reception of Bergson in the Anglo-American context. I have not undertaken a history of the French reception of Bergson (this would be another project). Instead I have tried to show what the lines of transmission of Bergson's thought are for us here and now, and why one might want to read him. Chapter 5 analyzes the return to Bergson currently under way. It addresses the impact of Gilles Deleuze on the contemporary reception of Bergson and discusses issues of structuralism and post-structuralism in this connection. This chapter also serves as a guide to contemporary perspectives on Bergson in philosophy, cultural studies, and new media studies. Chapter 6 considers contemporary issues that engage us with aspects of Bergson's thought, issues concerning virtual reality, artificial intelligence, and chaos theory (where questions of determinism and of the reversibility or irreversibility of time are very much alive). All of these raise questions concerning freedom and determinism and the limits between the human and the inhuman. They refer us to Bergson's distinctions between the voluntary and the automatic, the living and the inert, and to his analyses of qualitative difference, affect, and embodiment.

Unlike many commentators involved in the ongoing return to Bergson, I did not come to Bergson through Deleuze. At least not that I was aware of. I came upon Bergson by chance only to discover for myself the fundamental insight of Deleuze: Bergson offers an alternative to Hegel. Reading Bergson has opened up new ways of approaching various theoretical questions—especially issues concerning time and representation—left over from my prolonged engagement with deconstruction. It continues to inform my reconsiderations of modernism. In recent years, we have grown accustomed to philosophical language that is intensely self-conscious and rhetorically thick, often tragic in tone. It is enlivening to read Bergson, who exerts so little rhetorical pressure while exacting such a substantial effort of thought. The effort is well rewarded. Bergson's texts teach the reader to let go of entrenched intellectual habits and to begin to think differently—to think in time.

I am grateful for the Humanities Research Fellowship I received from the University of California at Berkeley in support of this project. I thank Keith Ansell Pearson for carefully reading the book manuscript and providing helpful suggestions for its improvement. I also thank Darlene Pursely and James Meyer for reading various pieces of the work in progress; Armando Manalo and Jennifer Gipson for their help in preparing the manuscript. I also want to thank Bernhard Kendler for his interest in this project, together with my editors at Cornell University Press, especially Herman Rapaport and Teresa Jesionowski. I appreciate their commitment to this project and the care they have taken with it. Their help has been invaluable. Last but not least I thank Stephen Sharnoff for his unflagging love and support.

SUZANNE GUERLAC

Berkeley, California

Note on Translations

All translations of *Essai sur les données immédiates de la conscience* [*Time and Free Will*] (1888) and *Matière et mémoire* [*Matter and Memory*] (1896) are mine and references are given both to published English translations of these works and to the French text as published by Presses Universitaires de France. Various issues of translation need consideration, among them that *Time and Free Will* is an unfortunate translation of *Essai sur les données immédiates de la conscience*. I will simply refer to this text as the *Essai* and anticipate that the reasons for my criticism of the English translation will become clear as readers work through the arguments. Another issue of translation concerns the word *esprit*. It can, of course, be rendered in English as *mind*, although this gives an overly intellectual value to the term. I have preferred, whenever possible, to leave the word in the original. The word *durée* also presents difficulties given that the English word *duration* tends to evoke a period of elapsed time considered retrospectively (bounded by time limits of a beginning and an end). This is not what Bergson had in mind. For this reason I have also left this word in the original as often as possible. At times I have summarized steps of Bergson's argument without citing the text; page references are usually given when this is the case, as a guideline. At times I have added contemporary examples to those given by Bergson; it should be obvious when it is my voice intervening and when I am attempting to voice Bergson's text directly.

Essai sur les données immédiates de la conscience (Paris: PUF, 1997) is hereafter cited in the text as *EDI*. Subsequent citations of this work will be given in my English translation and will refer to this French edition. In all cases, this page reference to the French edition will be immediately followed by a page reference in brackets to the comparable passage in the authorized translation of this work: *Time and Free Will: An Essay on the Immediate Data of Consciousness*, trans. F. L. Pogson (New York: Dover Publications, 2001).

As to *Matière et mémoire* (Paris: PUF, 1985), it will be hereafter cited in the text as *MM*. Subsequent citations of this work will be given in my English translation and will refer to this French edition. In all cases, this page reference to the French edition will be immediately followed by a page reference in brackets to the comparable passage in the authorized translation of this work: *Matter and Memory*, trans. N. M. Paul and W. S. Palmer (New York: Zone Books, 1988).

THINKING IN TIME

1. Bergson and Bergsonisms

> "The time has passed when time doesn't count."
> —PAUL VALÉRY, "La crise de l'esprit"

Time is an age-old question that has become a preeminently modern problem. Walter Benjamin characterized modern experience in terms of a new temporal horizon: the horizon of distraction and the experience of shock.[1] Paul Valéry diagnosed modernity in terms of temporal crisis.[2] More recently, Paul Virilio has analyzed the post-modern world in terms of a crisis of speed.[3]

At the turn of the twentieth century, Bergson urged us to think time concretely. He invited us to consider the real act of moving, the happening of what happens (*ce qui se fait*), and asked us to construe movement in terms of qualitative change, not as change that we measure after the fact and map onto space.

When we figure time as a line, or a circle, time stops moving. We inadvertently turn time into space. "Our ordinary logic," Bergson writes, "is a logic of retrospection. It cannot help throwing present realities . . . back into the past, so that what is . . . must, in its eyes, always have been so. It will not admit that things spring up, that something is created and that time is efficacious. It sees in a new form or quality only a re-

---

1. In the collection *Illuminations*, Walter Benjamin characterizes cinema as a medium in which the perception of shock "has been established as a formal principle" (175), and reception occurs "in a state of distraction" (240). See in particular "The Work of Art in the Age of Mechanical Reproduction," "On Some Motifs in Baudelaire" (in which Benjamin refers to both Bergson and Valéry), and "The Storyteller." *Illuminations*, ed. Hannah Arendt, trans. Harry Zohn.

2. Paul Valéry, "La crise de l'esprit," in *Œuvres complètes*, 1:1045.

3. See Paul Virilio, *L'art du moteur* and *Cybermonde: La politique du pire* (translated as *Politics of the Very Worst*).

arrangement of the old and nothing absolutely new. . . . To be sure it is not a question of giving up that logic, or of revolting against it. But we must extend it, make it more supple, and adapt it to a duration in which evolution is creative."[4]

Bergson thinks time as force. This is what he means by Real Duration. Western philosophy, he argues, has lost sight of this efficacy of time, the productive force it displays in the emergence of the absolutely new. As Heidegger might say, this is what remains forgotten, what has been "unthought."[5] Bergson puts it even more strongly. He suggests that our static conception of time is a defense against the heterogeneity of the real. He proposes that discursive thought is itself a biological adaptation, one that overlays the real and gives the world to us in certain ways for pragmatic reasons. It presents an immobile world for us to master, projecting our thought through a grid of space, thrown out, Bergson says, like a net to collect and organize the heterogeneous and dynamic real, so that we can better act upon it and take control of it.

What happens when we try to consider real movement intellectually? We find that our thought is not cut out for the task. Thinking in time, Bergson writes, will always be incommensurable with language, which crushes duration through its very iterative structure. We repeat the same word to name a variety of things at different moments, when, in actuality, nothing ever occurs in exactly the same way twice. Bergson is a philosopher of intuition in that he undertakes to grasp what discursive thought and mathematical symbols edit out: the productive force of time as it happens and the complexity of the real.[6]

However, mathematics and the philosophy of physics significantly informed Bergson's thought. "It was my mathematical studies," he reveals, "which stirred my interest in duration . . . at first this was no more than a kind of puzzlement at the value given to the letter t in the equations of mechanics."[7] Developments in modern physics, many of

---

4. Cited in Keith Ansell Pearson, *Philosophy and the Adventure of the Virtual: Bergson and the Time of Life,* 85, from Bergson's "L'intuition philosophique."

5. "It is time, it is high time, finally to think through this nature of time, and its origin, so that we may reach the point where it becomes clear that all metaphysics leaves something essential unthought: its own ground and foundation," Heidegger, *What Is Called Thinking?* trans. J. Glenn Gray, 100. Concerning the forgetfulness of being, see *An Introduction to Metaphysics,* trans. Ralph Manheim. Heidegger's notion of the *es gibt* comes closest to Bergson's conception of duration in the late essay *On Time and Being,* trans. Joan Stambaugh.

6. F.C.T. Moore uses this expression in *Bergson: Thinking Backwards,* 64.

7. Ibid., 59.

which occurred during Bergson's lifetime, render his project of thinking time concretely all the more compelling.

As the celebrated physicist Louis de Broglie has written, given the wave-mechanical model of matter (which de Broglie had affirmed by 1924), "the efficacy of time became evident and the notion of memory as an integral part of material existence much less paradoxical."[8] When the wave replaces the particle "as the ultimate constituent of the material universe," our conception of time necessarily changes. Time can no longer be thought abstractly, as "an accident of matter" construed in terms of particles. Time enters into the very substance of matter. It becomes concrete and mobile, "embedded in the substance of particular strata or regions of matter, each of which may exhibit its own tempo or duration." Time has become concrete. It has become substance. This is precisely what Bergson asks us to think through his elaboration of the real time of duration.[9]

Thinking in time, Bergson affirms, requires the breaking of many frames. It lets us recognize the obsession with space that orients Western philosophy, limiting what we can think. It also lets us think outside the framework of the dialectical elaboration of becoming and the force of the negative, which Hegel identifies with the power of consciousness, or of l'esprit.[10]

In the French intellectual context, the philosophy of Hegel swept through the intellectual world of Paris in the years leading up to the Second World War when political and cultural events played out the sharp ideological opposition between fascism and communism. Ever since Eric Weil and Alexandre Kojève introduced Hegel's thought to the French in the thirties—displacing that of Bergson, which had held sway throughout the twenties—it has been a question of various modes of response to Hegel—epistemological, ontological, linguistic, genealogical, semiological, and deconstructive. The Hegelian framework even structured de-

8. Cited by Andrew C. Papanicolaou, "Aspects of Henri Bergson's Psycho-Physical Theory," in *Bergson and Modern Thought*, ed. Andrew C. Papanicolaou and Pete A. Y. Gunter, 84.

9. Ibid., 84, 85.

10. Yirmiyahu Yovel, ed. with commentary, *Preface to the Phenomenology of Spirit* by G.W.F. Hegel. See also Georges Bataille, "Hegel, la mort ou le sacrifice," *Deucalion 5*, available in English as "Hegel: Death and Sacrifice," in *The Bataille Reader*, ed. Fred Botting and Scott Wilson, and Vincent Descombes, who writes, speaking of the reception of Hegel in France, "One word summarizes this new status of consciousness, negativity," *Le même et l'autre*, 36 (my translation). It is available in English translation as *Modern French Philosophy*, trans. L. Scott-Fox and J. M. Harding.

bates that concerned the *dépassement* of Hegel as well as the lively debates that concerned humanism and anti-humanism that were so central to the second half of the twentieth century. "In 1945, everything modern comes from Hegel," writes Vincent Descombes, whereas "in 1968, everything modern (Marx, Freud, etc.) is hostile to Hegel. . . . The difference between the two generations is in the inversion of the sign which characterizes the relation to Hegel. What doesn't change is the reference [*repérage*] itself."[11] The inversion of the sign, of course, is a dialectical gesture.

In French theory of the last few decades the impact of Heidegger's insight concerning the "unthought" of being (and of time) has been married to a post-Hegelian mode of thinking by figures such as Bataille, Blanchot and, at times, even Foucault and Derrida.[12] In the post-structuralist context this configuration of issues was elaborated in semiological terms. Even psychoanalysis, as we know, became linked to operations of language through Lacan. With Foucault, history became largely a matter of discursive formations. The semiological or discursive framework became the dominant model for analyses in cultural studies.[13] This has been the predominant framework of thinking over the last several decades.

Bergson enables us to return to questions associated with temporality, affect, agency, and embodiment that were bracketed within the structuralist/post-structuralist context. He invites, as one critic has put it, "a return to process before signification or coding."[14] Reading Bergson enables a reengagement with the concreteness of the real, with affect, agency, and even a notion of experience, without sacrificing the perspective that drove the critique of representation and of the unified subject of consciousness. The subject, in Bergson, is primarily a subject of action, not of present consciousness or knowledge. And this makes all the difference.

This is the subject we encounter in Bergson's first major work, the *Essai sur les données immédiates de la conscience* [*Time and Free Will*].

11. Descombes, *Le même et l'autre*, 24.
12. I am thinking, in particular, of Foucault's and Derrida's essays on Bataille; see Michel Foucault, "Préface à la transgression," and Jacques Derrida, "De l'économie restreinte à l'économie générale," in *L'écriture et la différence*. It is available in English as *Writing and Difference*, trans. Alan Bass.
13. See the very interesting analysis by Brian Massumi in *Parables of the Virtual: Movement, Affect, Sensation*.
14. Ibid., 7.

Bergson's first approach to duration is to explore inner experience—the sensation of qualities and affects—things, he argues, that cannot be measured. He defines the human nervous system as a center of indetermination and pursues the implications of our capacity to have experiences that escape the grip of a spatial logic that divides things up and measures them. He attributes metaphysical importance to affect and affirms free agency. He does so through the notion of duration, which, as we shall see, he derives from experience—the experience of waiting for sugar to dissolve in water, for example—and extends in relation to the mathematics of Riemann and a notion of multiplicity that cannot be reduced to number.

Bergson makes an argument for freedom against determinist thinking through this appeal to time. He establishes a horizon of immediate experience—pre-linguistic and qualitative.[15] In the *Essai*, Bergson appeals to experimental psychology in order to tease out what philosophy cannot think and, at the same time, challenges the discourse of clinical psychology from within.

The *Essai* establishes the fact of duration. This enables Bergson to investigate the existence of *esprit* in *Matter and Memory*. If *l'esprit* does exist, he suggests memory is the place to locate it experimentally.[16] *Matter and Memory* provides a theory of perception as contact and of memory as constitutive of what it means to know. "Memory," Bergson writes quite astoundingly, "is the point of contact between consciousness and matter."[17] Bergson challenges fundamental assumptions of the cognitive sciences, namely, that the brain generates representations and stores memories. Mental events, he argues, cannot be reduced to the neuro-chemical level. In this work, Bergson defines perception in terms of action, theorizes the virtuality of pure memory, and affirms that past time exists.[18]

---

15. The importance of Bergson for Merleau-Ponty should not be underestimated. Merleau-Ponty and Sartre were both steeped in Bergson, although both went on to take their distance from Bergsonism. See Maurice Merleau-Ponty, *L'union de l'âme et du corps chez Malebranche, Biran et Bergson,* available in English as *The Incarnate Subject: Malebranche, Biran, and Bergson on the Union of Body and Soul,* trans. Andrew G. Bjelland, Patrick Burke, and Paul B. Milan, and Jean-Paul Sartre, *Imagination.*

16. He writes that it is "in phenomena of memory" that "we claim to be able to grasp the *esprit* in its most palpable form." See *Matière et mémoire,* 77 (my translation).

17. Ibid.

18. He extends the reach of duration beyond consciousness to matter itself. *L'évolution créatrice* [*Creative Evolution*] will go on to theorize duration as productive force and time as what Pearson calls "the time of life." See Pearson, *Philosophy and the Adventure of the Virtual.*

Matter and Memory investigates the interactive relations between body and mind. Bergson displaces the conventional metaphysical dualism of matter and mind, shifting asymmetrically to matter and *memory.* This enables him to pursue a dialogue with clinical studies in experimental psychology, most notably studies of aphasia.[19] The emphasis on memory reorients the investigation of the mind/body problem in relation to time instead of space. This challenges a number of conventional assumptions concerning brain locations for mental functions and the importance of the contemplative gaze in perception. Consciousness operates as memory. Through a subtle analysis of relations between perception and memory, Bergson refines his analysis of the dynamic relations that exist between duration and freedom.

Bergson's best-known work is *Creative Evolution,* which we will not discuss at length in this study, but which the *Essai* and *Matter and Memory* prepare us for. This work returns to the question of duration introduced in the *Essai.* However, in the study of evolution, Bergson no longer considers duration exclusively from the standpoint of subjective experience. *Creative Evolution* extends the model of consciousness presented in the *Essai* (where it was linked to memory) to the world at large. Duration becomes synonymous with existence—with life as perpetual change and invention of novelty. "The living organism is a thing that endures [*l'organisme qui vit est chose qui dure*]."[20] Duration "means invention, creation of forms, continual elaboration of the absolutely new."[21] In this work, Bergson explores the limits of classical epistemology in relation to the experience of duration and investigates relations between philosophy and biology. Instead of applying conceptual frameworks borrowed from the physical sciences to account for evolution, Bergson proposes that we let the thinking of creative evolution (i.e., evolution considered as the invention of new forms and realities) inform our understanding of epistemology. Instead of taking concepts of thought as *a priori* categories, and attempting to think about the world in terms of this unchanging framework, Bergson proposes that we situate our own intelligence within the movement of evolution, in other words, that we consider questions of knowledge in relation to modes of evolutionary adaptation. Knowledge (what we can know and how we can know it) is viewed as an effect of evolutionary change. In

19. As F. C. T. Moore points out, Bergson was quite familiar with the work of Freud and Charcot on amnesia and aphasia, *Bergson: Thinking Backwards,* 5 n. 4.

20. *L'évolution créatrice,* 15 (my translation).

21. Ibid., 11.

order to conceive of evolution correctly, questions of epistemology must be considered together with questions of life. Duration becomes "the very foundation of our being and . . . the very substance of the things with which we find ourselves in communication [*le fond de notre être et . . . la substance même des choses avec lesquelles nous sommes en communication*]."[22]

This is a revolutionary gesture, as it reverses the hierarchy between epistemology and biology (or life and knowledge) and resituates intelligence as a limited part of the process of life. Intelligence (i.e., rationalism or instrumental reason) is viewed as a specialized adaptation of the mind in the service of useful action. Bergson holds that scientific objectivity may enable the mastery of inert objects, but it cannot think being as a whole, cannot make contact with life or the real. This will be the domain of philosophy and intuition. By delimiting intelligence as a mode of instrumental knowledge, Bergson relativizes it, thereby undermining its pretensions to universality and its preeminent authority.

Bergson, for whom creation (or the movement of evolution) is neither mechanistic nor teleological, envisages life as a contingent process of growth and change, as a positive movement of perpetual differentiation that invents new forms. He calls this the *élan vital*, proposing the term not as a concept of rational knowledge but as an image that invites us to think outside the mechanistic framework of the physical sciences and of static metaphysical categories. The *élan vital* is an image for the process of time as duration, that is, for time as force, the force that "pushes life along the road of time."[23] Evolution is not something that happens to life, Bergson proposes, it is life itself, a perpetually contingent movement of differentiation.

One of the most widely read works of Bergson, especially in literary and artistic circles, is the short essay on laughter, begun very early in his career, and published a number of years later. In *Le rire: Essai sur la signification du comique* [*Laughter: An Essay on the Meaning of the Comic*] (1900), Bergson analyzes laughter (or the comic) in relation to a wide range of cultural materials—vaudeville, the classical theatre, caricature, clothing and masquerade, as well as comic effects of language.

---

22. Ibid., 39. The notions of continuity and communication become important for Bataille's thoughts on the sacred in *L'érotisme*, available in English as *Erotism: Death and Sensuality*, trans. Mary Dalwood, and *L'éxpérience intérieure*, available in English as *Inner Experience*, trans. Leslie Ann Boldt.

23. Bergson, *L'évolution créatrice*, 104 (my translation). The *élan vital* is an image inspired by principles of thermodynamics.

In brief, Bergson's theory holds that the comic occurs when mechanism intrudes into the domain of the living. It involves something like the performance of a category mistake. We find it comic when mechanical gestures take the place of living ones, when automatic operations are inserted into the animate world. We might think of Charlie Chaplin movies, or of Lucille Ball trying to cope with the assembly line in the chocolate factory. Only a reader who is familiar with the body of Bergson's work, however, and who appreciates the rigor and seriousness of his thought, will recognize that the terms of Bergson's apparently casual analysis in *Laughter* are derived from the *Essai* and *Matter and Memory*. Only then does one perceive a joke on another level. The *Essai* argues against the application of mechanistic modes of thinking to living beings. *Laughter* not only makes such a gesture appear intrinsically ludicrous; it turns this gesture into the very essence of comedy!

At the end of *Laughter*, Bergson reflects on vanity, which, like serious literary figures before him such as Balzac, Flaubert, and Proust, he considers to be the highest form of the comic. Laughter has a social function. It serves to discipline anti-social behavior through intimidation and humiliation. Laughter, in this respect, is contrasted with art, since art invites a mode of direct contact with the real for Bergson.

Bergson will pursue social and ethical questions in his last major work, *Les deux sources de la morale et de la religion* [*The Two Sources of Morality and Religion*], which investigates the individual's sense of moral obligation. This is a question brought home by the First World War and the sacrifice of life it exacted in the name of moral obligation. Bergson approaches this question from the perspective of creative evolution. Whereas for Herbert Spencer transformism implied egoism, Charles Darwin held that altruistic actions were coherent with an evolutionary perspective. They were not only signs of a higher mode of development; they served the interests of collective survival. Bergson's study takes up these questions and enters into implicit dialogue with Émile Durkheim in a discussion of the difference between closed and open societies. The celebrated sociologist had not only been Bergson's classmate and rival at the École Normale Supérieure, he had become Bergson's official intellectual counterpoint in connection with the Sorbonne Dispute.[24]

24. See my *Literary Polemics*, chap. 7, and for a more detailed account of the Sorbonne Dispute, R. C. Grogin, *The Bergsonian Controversy in France*.

An explicit appeal to the social values of mystical experience in this study appeared to vindicate those who had criticized Bergson all along for being simply a mystic. And yet the title of this work, and the basis for the notion of closed and open societies, derive from scientific, not mystical discourse. They refer us to an opposition between closed and open systems in Sadi Carnot's theories of thermodynamics. This book is one of the most challenging, and least read, of Bergson's works.[25] It was completed nine years before his death in 1941.

Henri Bergson was born in Paris 1859, the son of a Polish musician. At age four his family moved to Switzerland where they lived, reportedly, on the Boulevard des Philosophes. The Bergsons returned to Paris in 1866. Four years later, the family moved to England, leaving Henri behind in Paris to pursue his studies of science and math.

In the early years of the Third Republic Bergson attended the École Normale Supérieure along with Jean Jaurès and Émile Durkheim.[26] In the early 1880s he took a position teaching in a *lycée* in Clermont-Ferrand, during which time he published a selection of texts by Lucretius. He also wrote his first major work, *Essai sur les données immédiates de la conscience*, which was his thesis, along with a text on Aristotle and the notion of place.[27]

By 1889 Bergson had returned to Paris where he taught at the Lycée Louis le Grand and, subsequently, at the Lycée Henri IV. A few years later he married the second cousin of Marcel Proust. Proust served as best man at the wedding. Bergson published *Matière et mémoire* [*Matter and Memory*] in 1896. That same year, he was appointed to the Collège de France where he held the chair of Greek and Latin Philosophy.

He published *Le rire* [*Laughter*] in 1900 and, in the same year, became *maître de conférence* rue d'Ulm. The following year he was elected to the Académie des Sciences Morales et Politiques; the year after that, he received the Legion of Honor. He published *L'évolution créatrice*

25. See Bergson, *Les deux sources de la morale et de la religion*, edited by Arnaud Bouaniche, Frédéric Keck, and Frédéric Worms, and for an excellent commentary, Frédéric Worms, *Bergson ou les deux sens de la vie*, in particular chaps. 3 and 4.

26. Philippe Soulez and Frédéric Worms, *Bergson: Biographie*, 1.

27. *Quid Aristoteles de loco senserit* (Latin thesis) published in French in *Mélanges* and in English as *Aristotle's Concept of Place*, trans. J. K. Ryan in *Studies in Philosophy and History of Philosophy*, 5:13–72. The notion of place, in Aristotle, is linked to theories of time as movement from one place to another.

[*Creative Evolution*] in 1907; it would become an enormous popular success. From this time on his classes at the Collège de France overflowed with students. Bergson received an honorary doctorate at Oxford in 1909. He was elected to the Académie française in 1914. Because of his extraordinary international prestige, he was asked to undertake diplomatic missions during the First World War, first to Spain and then, in 1918, to the United States of America.[28] He received the Nobel Prize for Literature in 1927 and died, at age 82, during the German occupation of Paris in 1941. A Jew who had become Christian in his beliefs, he refrained from converting to Christianity during the war, and out of solidarity with the victims of the Nazi and Pétain regimes, he officially registered as a Jew. His last work, *Les deux sources de la morale et de la religion* [*The Two Sources of Morality and Religion*], was published in 1932. He was granted an inscription in the Pantheon in 1967.

All in all, Bergson's life presents a profile of exemplary institutional success. His career as a philosopher, however, developed in the margins of the official university system. He was never hired at the Sorbonne.[29] He taught at the Collège de France, an institution of high intellectual standards, which, however, required that all lectures associated with its teaching be open to the general public. Bergson achieved enormous popular success in this context, often due to the emotional appeal of his ideas. But he did not have the equivalent of graduate students who might have become rigorous interpreters of his thought. Thus Bergson's philosophy—in principle open and nonsystematic—was easily borrowed piecemeal and altered by enthusiastic admirers.

Bergson's thought was disseminated into a variety of Bergsonisms, appropriations of his thought that occurred in relation to a wide range of ideological, esthetic, political, spiritual, and institutional agendas. It was adopted in bits and pieces and reshaped according to the ideological requirements, or practical needs, of the borrower. The German sociologist Georg Simmel was a Bergsonist, as were the revolutionary anarchist Georges Sorel and various Catholic modernists, Italian futurists, French Symbolists, cubists, and assorted literary modernists.[30]

28. See Philippe Soulez, *Bergson politique.*
29. Indeed, he will become pitted against Durkheim, the rationalist, in what will be known as the Sorbonne Dispute. See my *Literary Polemics,* 196; for a more detailed treatment see R. C. Grogin, *The Bergsonian Controversy in France.*
30. See Mark Antliff, *Inventing Bergson: Cultural Politics and the Parisian Avant-Garde,* A. E. Pilkington, *Bergson and His Influence: A Reassessment,* and Romeo Arbour, *Bergson et les lettres françaises.*

Bergson's influence extended beyond the French context. T. S. Eliot, among others, attended his lectures and introduced aspects of his thought into the British modernist context. Bergson was also enthusiastically received in the United States. William James, whose work Bergson admired and referenced, mediated the reception of his thought in America and in England. His Hibbert lectures (delivered at Oxford in 1909 and subsequently published as *A Pluralistic Universe*) urged his audience to read Bergson directly: "New horizons," he wrote, "loom on every page you read."[31] Serious readers of Bergson, James affirmed, "can never return again to their ancient attitude of mind."[32]

It was Bergson the evolutionary thinker that had the greatest appeal in America. As A. O. Lovejoy put it in a lecture delivered in 1913, Bergson revived "radical evolutionism . . . as a serious philosophical doctrine. . . . He has presented to us . . . a world which is at bottom alive . . . in which . . . the future contains the possibility of unimaginable fresh creations, of a real and cumulative enrichment of the sum of being."[33]

In short, Bergson was received in America in the spirit of Emerson and Whitman.[34] "No philosopher had excited as much enthusiasm or controversy in America as did Bergson when he visited in 1913. Not even James himself had enjoyed such widespread and fashionable popularity."[35] A number of American artists found ways to engage the thought of Bergson with their own esthetic projects: Willa Cather, Arthur Dove, Alfred Stieglitz, William Faulkner, and Gertrude Stein, to name a few. Of course, in intellectual terms, such popularity came at quite a cost: "for the popular mind Bergsonism was nearly anything one wanted it to be."[36]

In the French context, Bergson became the philosopher of Symbolism.[37] For all those dissatisfied with the Neo-Kantian philosophy that dominated the official university curriculum, Bergson was the alternative. He was, as François Mauriac put it, "the philosopher we listened to."[38] From 1900 to 1914, his influence on French youth was said to be

31. Cited in Tom Quirk, *Bergson and American Culture: The Worlds of Willa Cather and Wallace Stevens,* 45.
32. Ibid.
33. Ibid.
34. Ibid., 79.
35. Ibid., 53.
36. Ibid., 54.
37. See my *Literary Polemics,* 159.
38. Ibid., 158.

remarkable. For some this raised considerable concern.[39] From Jacques Maritain to Georges Sorel, everyone, it seemed, had his or her own custom-made Bergsonism. As one commentator put it, "various Bergsonisms composed the very atmosphere in which almost all French realities were steeped since 1900."[40] By the early years of the First World War, Bergson had become something of a cult figure.

Not surprisingly, vicious attacks soon followed immense popular success. In a scathing critique of the celebrated philosopher, Julian Benda portrayed Bergson's thought as a "philosophy of democracy." This was not meant as a compliment. "Bergsonism," Benda adds, "was perhaps the only philosophy to have been really understood by the vulgar."[41] Bergson was vitriolically attacked not only by Benda but also by representatives of the far right (Charles Maurras and Pierre Lasserre), of the left (George Politzer and Georg Lukács) and even by the Catholic Church, which put his works on the Index in 1914. Bertrand Russell was one of the most authoritative opponents of Bergson, whom he accused of being a committed enemy of rational thought. In a remarkably condescending tone, he likened Bergson's thought to a "heaving sea of intuition."[42] He concluded that Bergson was not a philosopher at all, but merely a mediocre poet.

In the 1930s, Bergson's philosophy was displaced by a growing interest in Hegel, whose thought was magisterially presented by Kojève in lectures that became as popular as those of Bergson had once been. The importance of Marxism during this period enhanced the reception of Hegel who began to fill the space left vacant by the gradual decline of Bergson's influence. Russell's charges of anti-rationalism prevailed in the French university context, in which Bergson remained *mal vu* until quite recently. Without disciples inscribed in the official university context to rigorously offset the delirious appropriations of various Bergsonisms, the philosophy of Bergson more or less disappeared from the scene.

One episode hastened the demise of Bergson's philosophical authority and appeared to confirm Russell's judgment of him. In the 1920s Bergson

39. The Binet report, a survey conducted in 1908 concerning the teaching of philosophy in the schools, concluded that "Bergson's ideas prevailed over all others among both faculty and students" (cited in *Literary Polemics*, 195).

40. Cited in *Literary Polemics*, 195.

41. Cited in *Literary Polemics*, 197. Even Benda, however, acknowledges that Bergsonism is not merely an intellectual fashion, but a "movement . . . that embraces the whole realm of the spirit . . . religion, literature, morality, painting, music" (cited in *Literary Polemics,* 195).

42. Bertrand Russell, *The Philosophy of Bergson,* 36.

engaged in a public disagreement with Einstein over the notion of time presupposed in the theory of relativity. Einstein's prestige was at its peak. Bergson's position was so misunderstood that he subsequently tried to withdraw from circulation the book he wrote in response to Einstein, *Durée et simultanéité* (1922) [*Duration and Simultaneity*, 1965]. The issues remain in dispute to this day. Some feel Bergson simply misunderstood the theory of relativity. Others feel that Bergson's intervention was extremely subtle and, while accepting the basic premise of relativity and its critique of classical physics, did in fact diagnose a tendency of Einstein's thought to shore up the classical view of the world.[43] At the time, however, it appeared that Einstein had defeated Bergson, who was accused of rejecting the new physics of relativity because he had not understood it. To a certain extent this episode staged a public humiliation of Bergson along the gender lines that had always been invoked in criticism of his thought—it was feminine, either in contrast to the virility of (real French) Cartesian philosophy, or, in this context, in contrast to the hard truths of science. When, in 1927, Bergson was awarded the Nobel Prize in Literature, Russell's portrayal of Bergson as merely a poet appeared to be officially sanctioned. Retired from teaching, Bergson retreated from public view and devoted himself to his final work, *Les deux sources de la morale et de la religion* [*The Two Sources of Morality and Religion*].

The proliferation of Bergsonisms blurred the contours of Bergson's thought and imposed undue, and conflictual, ideological burdens on the philosopher's thinking. To this extent we could say that both too much and too little have been said about Bergson. Too much, because of the various appropriations of his thought. Too little, because the work itself has not been carefully studied in recent decades.[44] We have lost track of the discourses that inform it and forgotten how to think outside the post-Hegelian framework. In the next chapter, we will look in more detail at the cultural and intellectual world from which Bergson's thought emerged.

43. On the Bergson-Einstein controversy, see *Philosophy and the Adventure of the Virtual*, 55–65; Robin Durie, "The Strange Nature of the Instant," in *Time and the Instant: Essays in the Physics and Philosophy of Time*, ed. Robin Durie; Ilya Prigogine and Isabelle Stengers, *Entre le temps et l'éternité*; Ilya Prigogine, "Irreversibility and Space-Time Structure," in *Physics and the Ultimate Significance of Time*, ed. David Ray Griffin; Timothy S. Murphy, "Beneath Relativity: Bergson and Bohm on Absolute Time," in *The New Bergson*, ed. John Mullarkey; and Jimena Canales, "Einstein, Bergson, and the Experiment That Failed: Intellectual Cooperation at the League of Nations."

44. Until quite recently, that is. In France, Frédéric Worms has renewed Bergson scholarship. In England, Keith Ansell Pearson, John Mullarkey, and others have also engaged in careful reading of his work.

2. From the Certainties of Mechanism to the Anxieties of Indeterminism

The period in which Bergson began to write was rather like our own. In the 1890s, Bergson's contemporary, the celebrated poet and critic Paul Valéry, described it as "a period completely formed [*travaillée*] by the sciences, in perpetual technological transformation, where nothing escapes the will to innovation."[1] We now identify this period with the Second Scientific Revolution. Our own era is identified with the third.[2]

Today, space probes, the cell phone, digital images, wireless communication, laser surgery, and the kind of synthetic materials deployed by Frank Gehry in Bilbao have changed the rhythms and appearances of our daily lives. In a similar way, during the Third Republic transportation had been vastly extended and accelerated by trains, steam engines, bicycles (5 million in France alone by 1900), tramcars and, by 1902, the gasoline-powered automobile. It became possible to send a letter to many countries in the world (now linked up by an international mail system), to communicate by telegraph, and to speak by telephone. New materials of construction—iron, steel, copper, tin, and reinforced concrete—were changing the faces of cities now more populated than ever before. The Eiffel Tower caused an esthetic scandal. It was now possible to write by electric light at one's typewriter; paper had become widely available. Rolls of film made photography much easier than before; the *cinématographe* began to present moving pictures. Sewing machines and

1. Paul Valéry, *Œuvres complètes*, 1:971 (my translation). Hereafter cited in the text as OC.
2. See Thomas Kuhn, *The Structure of Scientific Revolutions*, and Paul Virilio, *L'art du moteur* and *Cybermonde: La politique du pire*.

machine guns made their appearance. Vaccinations now gave protection against tuberculosis and cholera. As one historian put it,

> By the '90s one already ate machine-made food in machine-made dishes [and] wore machine-made clothes. . . . The flow of profits from . . . mechanized industry into banking and other credit reservoirs . . . to . . . ever bigger and newer industrial plants, seemed to go on with mechanical precision and efficiency. The mechanics of capitalism had, of course, been provided with "scientific" bases and given practical application during the century prior to 1870. Afterwards it merely underwent a perfecting (and extension) like the mechanics of locomotion and mass production.[3]

In short, the "Midas touch of big business was truly golden. Profits flowed from machinery (and monopoly) as never before."[4]

If Valéry displayed his characteristic mixture of detachment and energetic fascination when he described the modern world in the 1890s, by the 1930s his tone had changed. In 1933 his account of the dizzying transformations of modern life, and what it felt like to live through them, is tinged with ambivalence and anxiety.

> Never has there been such a profound and rapid transformation . . . the whole world . . . appropriated, even the most distant events known instantly, our ideas and our powers over matter, time, and space, conceived of and utilized completely differently than they were up to our time. . . . The number and the importance of innovations introduced in so few years in the human universe has almost abolished any possibility of comparison between the way things were fifty years ago and the way they are now. We have introduced completely new powers, invented completely new means, and developed different and unforeseen habits. We have negated the values, dissociated the ideas, and ruined feelings that seemed to us unshakable. . . . And to express such a new state of affairs, we only have very old ideas [des notions immémoriales]. (OC, 1015)

3. Carleton J. H. Hayes, *A Generation of Materialism, 1871–1900,* 96–99.
4. Ibid., 101.

The tone has changed. Europe is in crisis, and not just on the economic level. It also suffers from a *crise de l'esprit*, a spiritual or intellectual crisis, that includes a crisis of values and a loss of confidence concerning our place in the world.

What has happened between the 1890s and the 1930s? A number of important political events—the Dreyfus Affair, a devastating world war, and now the coming to power of Hitler, prelude to yet another global conflict. This would be enough to account for the anxiety we hear in Valéry's voice. But the crisis is also intellectual. The poet also specifically diagnoses what he calls

> a singular crisis of the sciences, which now seem to despair of conserving their old ideal of unification, of explication of the universe. The universe is decomposing, losing all hope of a single image. The world of the infinitely small seems strangely different from the one it engenders on a larger scale. Even the identity of bodies is getting lost here, and I won't speak . . . of the crisis of determinism, that is, of causality. (*OC* 1037)

Indeed, a new physics of subatomic particles has called into question the well-established mechanistic model of the universe. During the 1890s, the universe could confidently be compared to a smoothly functioning machine, one "so orderly and compact, so simple in construction, that we may reckon its past and gauge something of its future with almost as much certitude as that of a dynamo or a water wheel. In its motion there is no uncertainty, no mystery."[5]

This machine has broken down by the 1930s. Smug certainty has given way to deep uncertainty. The paradigm of order has been undone by advances in physics, chemistry, and mathematics—entropy, statistical mechanics, and quantum mechanics—that have engendered what Valéry characterizes as a culture of disorder and chaos. If this period can be characterized as one "completely formed [*travaillée*] by the sciences," it might also be viewed as having been completely undone by the sciences. This is the message Valéry conveys in 1933. The new science has pulled the rug out from under the very certainties science had apparently guaranteed. It has dissolved the very ground of this certainty into

5. From Carl Snyder, *The World Machine*, cited in Hayes, *A Generation of Materialism*, 108.

mere statistical probability and epistemological indeterminacy. In 1927, Heisenberg demonstrated with his Uncertainty Principle that the new uncertainty confronted by microphysics was not simply the result of inadequate tools of measurement; it is inscribed in the natural world itself. Uncertainty has been demonstrated experimentally and formalized in mathematical terms. What Valéry diagnosed in 1933 as a crisis of causality has been prompted, as we shall see, by the apparent indeterminacy of the physics of quantum mechanics.

It is within this cadence that I would like to place the thinking of Bergson. On the one hand, a sense of wonder at the efficacy of science and its visible mastery over the physical world. On the other, a profound sense of crisis, not only because Europe finds itself heading for war (again) but also because science, the very foundation of that mastery which has so transformed the world, appears to have come unstuck from the world and to have left it in chaos.

Two moments, then, frame the life and work of Bergson. The first confidently assumes an orderly, mechanistic world disposed to yield still further to our mastery of it. The other imposes an experience of indeterminacy that characterizes not only a certain mathematical knowledge of the physical world but that world itself, leaving in its wake, as Valéry's essay reveals, an indeterminacy of values, of language, and of social life. Between these two moments there occurs what Bachelard will subsequently call an epistemological break.[6]

The shift from the certainties of mechanism to the anxieties of indeterminacy marks a historic dislocation. Bergson's thought comes into being on the fault line of this break. It looks backward and forward across this interval and emerges from within it. The "singular crisis of the sciences," as Valéry puts it, does not just affect what we know and what we don't know, but calls out for a new way of thinking. This is what Bergson provides, which is why his thought remains of interest to us today.

In fact, the dislocation or epistemological break cannot be so easily mapped out in a linear fashion. We need to think of it in Bergsonian terms as phases that persist and contract according to different temporal rhythms. As we shall see, the ground begins to fall out from under the

---

6. See Gaston Bachelard, *Formation of the Scientific Mind: A Contribution to a Psychoanalysis of Objective Knowledge.*

mechanistic order even as the proponents of that order celebrate its victory most loudly.

In philosophical terms, the mechanistic model of the world, and the posture of certainty before it, refer us back to Descartes, one of Bergson's principal interlocutors in the *Essai*. Descartes considered the human mind to be "constituted by God to enjoy perfect certainty about material things when conceiving them mathematically."[7] As one commentator has put it, for Descartes, "matter and mathematics were made for one another."[8] Descartes envisaged a mathematical physics according to which natural phenomena could be explained through the principles of geometry. Matter is construed in terms of distinct bodies with extension in space. Motion is measured as a change of place that occurs relative to objects at rest. It can therefore be accurately measured. The human body is compared to a machine: "I suppose that the body is nothing but a statue, or a machine," writes Descartes,[9] introducing the theme of the automatic that will haunt Bergson's work. *Essai sur les données immédiates de la conscience [Time and Free Will]* (1888), Bergson's first published work, will forcefully challenge this Cartesian view of the world, one that has not lost its grip in the late 1890s. On the contrary.

The mechanistic worldview was codified by Newton, who systemized the experimental method of Galileo and generated universal laws of nature. The title of Newton's famous work, the "Mathematical Principles of Natural Philosophy,"[10] reaffirms Galileo's confident dictum that "nature is written in mathematical symbols."[11] Newton legislates the passage from observed phenomena to universal laws of motion: the laws of inertia, of equal action and reaction, and of acceleration as proportional to force. On this basis, a mechanistic philosophy takes hold, according to which "the phenomena of the world are physically produced by the mechanical properties of the parts of matter [which] operate upon one another according to mechanical laws."[12] Bergson finds a "strange timelessness" in the Newtonian system, one that is incompatible with our

7. Tom Sorell, *Descartes,* 3–4.

8. Ibid., 4.

9. Descartes, "Traité de l'homme," in *Œuvres et lettres,* 807 (my translation).

10. Isaac Newton, *The Principia: Mathematical Principles of Natural Philosophy,* trans. Andrew Motte and Florian Cajori.

11. Cited in Isabelle Stengers, *L'invention de la mécanique: Pouvoir et raison,* vol. 2 of *Cosmopolitiques,* 83 (my translation). All translations of this work are mine.

12. Robert Boyle, "About the Excellency and Grounds of the Mechanistic Hypothesis," in *The Works of the Honourable Robert Boyle,* 4:68–69.

lived experience of time.[13] We age, we become. Time moves for us—and in only one direction.

To follow scientific developments from Bergson's perspective, we might want to pass from Newton to Lagrange, who translates physical mechanics into a formal, rational language. Through the analysis of relations between force and acceleration, Lagrange takes us a step further down the road of the formalization of physics in mathematical terms.[14] Bergson will argue that science gives us the world mediated through symbols, which deform our sense of reality to the extent that they immobilize what we experience as occurring in temporal flow. He will argue that ordinary language only reinforces the worldview established by the formal languages of mathematics, and that all of these modes of symbolic representation interfere with our ability to grasp the temporal nature of reality. They crush our sense of duration.

Lagrange introduces the abstract concept of work into physics, a principle for the measurement of the transfer of energy from one physical system to another. As Isabelle Stengers writes, with Lagrange, to know "is to construct, and Lagrangian construction does not define change in terms of movement in space in the course of time," as envisaged by Galileo and Newton; instead, change "is defined in terms of 'distances' measured by costs, by what we will henceforth call *work*, the 'price' of the passage from one state to another. . . . With Lagrange, temporal evolution itself will be subjected to this logic of equivalence."[15]

The mathematics of Lagrange transforms mechanics into a practice of mathematical calculation. This reinforces a tendency (already present in Newton) to view physical processes as reversible. In geometrical terms, if we depict a movement from left to right, we can reformulate it as passing from right to left. In algebraic terms, equations are commutable. To the extent that physical processes are conceptualized as reversible in such formalized systems, however, they are thought in a timeless manner. Against this view, Bergson will affirm a dynamic ontology of irreversible time. His philosophical position corresponds to our common sense experience: no one grows any younger—although surely people in the biotech industry are working on this.

The formalization of scientific methods into a general mode of calculation facilitated the extension of the models and methods of mechanis-

---

13. The expression is cited by David Ray Griffin in *Physics and the Ultimate Significance of Time: Bohm, Prigogine, and Process Philosophy,* 11.
14. See Stengers, *Cosmopolitiques,* vol. 2, chap. 3.
15. Ibid., 63.

tic thinking beyond the physical or natural sciences and encouraged the development of the social sciences in the second half of the nineteenth century. Indeed, the period in which Bergson receives his education and begins to write coincides with the emergence, and rapid institutionalization, of the social sciences—the *sciences humaines* as the French still optimistically call what were once known, even more optimistically, as the *sciences humanitaires*. It is during this period that a number of intellectuals start out as philosophers and end up as specialists in one of the newly established experimental social sciences.[16] During Bergson's tenure there, the Collège de France established chairs in both experimental psychology and sociology; Émile Durkheim was named professor of sociology at the Sorbonne.

It did not take long, then, for the scientific method, growing ever more authoritative as technology transformed the face of modern life, to be applied to other fields of inquiry besides mathematics and the natural sciences. The mechanistic epistemology of the physical sciences became generalized into a paradigm of rationalist thought seemingly unlimited in its range of application. Auguste Comte, known as the father of positivism, attempted to systematize these applications. His *Cours de philosophie positive* (1839) presented a hierarchy of six pure sciences (mathematics, astronomy, physics, chemistry, physiology and sociology) which he opposed to "concrete sciences" (for example, geology) said to borrow their methods from the pure sciences.[17]

Positive philosophy (or positivism) is the general label for all methods of gaining knowledge from observation, following scientific methods. Auguste Comte advances a positivism that, he claims, aims to "complete, and at the same time co-ordinate, Natural Philosophy, by establishing the general law of human development, social as well as intellectual." We can appreciate the intellectual ambition of this enterprise and the sense of satisfaction its pursuit entailed in this proud declaration by Comte that is worth citing in full:

Now that man's history has been for the first time systematically considered as a whole, and has been found to be, like all other

16. This is true of both Gustav Fechner (founder of clinical psychology) and Théodule Ribot (who will hold the chair in clinical psychology at the Collège de France).

17. Auguste Comte gives a diagram, or *tableau synoptique*, of his course that lays out the hierarchical relations between mathematics, astronomy, physics, chemistry, physiology, and what he calls "social physics [*physique sociale*]," precursor of modern sociology. See Auguste Comte, *A General View of Positivism*, trans. J. H. Bridges, 36. Subsequent references to this edition will be given in the text, marked "Comte."

phenomena, subject to invariable laws, the preparatory labours of modern Science are ended. All knowledge is now brought within the sphere of Natural Philosophy. . . . The Positive spirit, so long confined to the simpler inorganic phenomena, has now passed through its difficult course of probation. It extends to a more important and more intricate class of speculations, and disengages them forever from all theological or metaphysical influence. All our notions of truth are thus rendered homogeneous, and begin at once to converge on a central principle. A firm objective basis is laid down for that complete co-ordination of human existence towards which all sound Philosophy has ever tended.[18]

Kant's critique of dogmatic metaphysics (which aspired to knowledge of the absolute) legitimized the relative knowledge of appearances that, according to the critical philosopher, is framed transcendentally through the *a priori* conditions of space and time. Thanks to Kant, then, knowledge is guaranteed by the mechanisms of thought. Neo-Kantianism provided the epistemological basis for the distinctly modern intellectual culture of positivism. It was the dominant current of thought in the French university system when Bergson decided to become a philosopher. Bergson's first major philosophical work, the *Essai sur les données immédiates de l'expérience*, as its title already suggests, launches a powerful critique of Kant.[19]

Today we are so embedded in ideologies of positivism that we hardly recognize them. Quantification and measurement command research in the social sciences, which have become increasingly specialized. In the nineteenth-century context, however, positivism was a progressive stance. It meant the radical secularization of knowledge and held out the hope of emerging from the fog of metaphysical dogmatism, on the one hand, and of religion, on the other.

This is the view Ernest Renan presents in *L'avenir de la science* [*The Future of Science*]. Renan's conception of science is broader than that of Comte, since it includes philology and history. What all these branches of knowledge represent, for Renan, is the perspective that "reason must

18. Ibid., 35, 37–38.
19. Kant had argued precisely against immediate experience, since all experience is mediated by the *a priori* conditions of the transcendental esthetic. The very appeal to *données immédiates* [immediate data of experience] is a challenge to Kant. This is one reason the translation of this work into *Time and Free Will* is an unfortunate choice. The reversal of Kant is lost in translation.

govern the world."[20] For Renan, "only science can furnish the basis in reality [*le fond de réalité*] necessary for life." Science, in the broadest sense, embodies the modern spirit for Renan (*AS* 17).[21]

Renan's vision (shared by Comte) was to "organize humanity scientifically"—"this is the last word of modern science" (*AS* 37), he announces cheerfully. The key presupposition here is the one borrowed from the mechanistic worldview, derived from Newtonian philosophy: "nature is reason, it is the immutable" (*AS* 37). Whereas positivist rationalism, he writes, is "male and firm" (*AS* 48), spiritualism implies "weak, humble, feminine instincts" (*AS* 51). These gender positions will become attached to subsequent disputes about Bergsonism, which will be identified with spiritualism and dismissed by some detractors as "feminine."[22] Although the ideological enemy is ostensibly religion and spiritualism, Renan, in the end, appropriates the figure of religion for science, concluding majestically and authoritatively that "science is thus a religion" (*AS*, 108).

One of the fields that developed most quickly within this modern, rationalist, culture of positivism in the social sciences was experimental psychology. Huge shifts took place in this field, which brought it into line with a number of present day tendencies in the discipline. Behaviorism and associationist psychology emerge during this period, which also establishes the psychophysical model and the "dual aspect theory" for relations between mind and brain, as we now say in the language of the cognitive sciences.[23] Within the culture of positivism, subjective states

20. Ernest Renan, *L'avenir de la science: Pensées de 1848*, 26. Hereafter abbreviated to *AS* in my translation.

21. "The modern spirit [*l'esprit moderne*]," Renan writes, "is reflective intelligence [*l'intelligence réfléchie*]." See *Avenir de la science*, 6. He also refers to the culture of science as "modern culture," and opposes science to the supernatural [*surnaturel*]. See *Avenir de la science*, 47, 48. Comte refers to proponents of positivism as "the avantgarde of the human race [*du genre humain*]." See Auguste Comte, *Système de politique positive*, 149.

22. See my *Literary Polemics*, chap. 7.

23. On associationism, see Keith Ansell Pearson, *Philosophy and the Adventure of the Virtual: Bergson and the Time of Life*, 181. Thomas Nagel defines the dual aspect theory as "the view deriving from Spinoza that mental phenomena are the subjective aspects of states that can also be described physically." See Thomas Nagel, *Other Minds: Critical Essays, 1969–1994*, 105. It implies a parallel functioning between mind and body. Nagel's discussion of Searle in *Other Minds* reminds us how pertinent the issues of Bergson's *Matter and Memory: Essay on the Relation between the Body and the Mind* [*esprit*] are to us today. In the tradition of the philosophical empiricism of John Locke, which had attempted to demonstrate that all knowledge derives from sense perception, the psycho-physical model proposes that mental states can be measured on the basis of physical responses. See John Locke, *An Essay Concerning Human Understanding*. This

are accounted for by physical conditions. The work of Auguste Comte, Gustav Fechner, Hippolyte Taine, and Théodule Ribot set the path that experimental psychology and the cognitive sciences continue to follow.

In 1837, Comte published an essay entitled "Considérations générales sur l'étude positive des fonctions intellectuelles et morales ou cérébrales [General considerations concerning the positive study of intellectual and moral, or cerebral, functions]."[24] The revealing feature of this title is the equivalence implied in the expression "moral or cerebral." Indeed, psychology becomes a moral physiology [*physiologie morale*] in this context, and human psychology becomes "a mere general extension of animal physiology."[25] Comte's psychology announces the formation of "a physical theory, that consists in the combination of the anatomical point of view and the physiological point of view."[26] This, as we shall see, is the position Bergson explicitly challenges in both the *Essai* and *Matter and Memory*.

The field of experimental psychology was advancing swiftly. By 1861, Broca has demonstrated that aphasia could be linked to brain lesions in particular locations.[27] This work was promptly extended by

---

tradition (Locke, Mill, Bain, and others) oriented philosophical reflection on perception and the functions of various faculties of mind; the perspective that derives from it is subsequently informed by developments in the experimental sciences of physiology, greatly advanced in the nineteenth century by the work of Claude Bernard.

24. *Cours de philosophie positive*, 530.

25. Ibid., 534. Comte insists: "everyone who is really up to date with their century knows ... that physiologists today consider mental phenomena [*les phénomènes moraux*] in absolutely the same way as they consider other animal phenomena." *Système de politique positive*, 148.

26. Ibid., 149.

27. Freud was of course also influenced by these developments. As Frédéric Worms writes, Bergson "shares an epistemological field with Freud," *Introduction à Matière et mémoire*, 182 (my translation). Freud's "Project for a Scientific Psychology" (1895), which depicts psychical activity in terms of neuron interactions, emerges from this shared context. Freud also wrote a monograph on aphasia in which he affirms that "the psychical is a process parallel to the physiological," *Standard Edition*, 14:207. According to Thomas Nagel, Freud was a "sophisticated materialist" who "believed that even conscious mental processes were also physical events in the brain, though we know almost nothing about their physical character." He adds that "Freud's conviction that the mind, being a function of the brain, is a product of biological development, and that its structure is subject to evolutionary influences, should be evident to any reader of his writings." See *Other Minds*, 27, 37. For a study that emphasizes this perspective, in a reductive fashion, see Frank Sulloway, *Freud the Biologist of the Mind: Beyond the Psychoanalytic Legend*. Nagel acknowledges that to overemphasize this aspect of Freud's thought leads to a reductionist reading. Recent French readings of Freud refuse such reductionism. For a subtle analysis of links between Freud and Bergson, see Frédéric Worms, "Le rire et sa relation au mot d'esprit: Notes sur la lecture de Bergson et Freud," *Freud et le rire*, ed. A. W. Szafran and A. Nyseholc, 195–223.

Carl Wernicke to other types of aphasia in relation to other brain locations. Encouraged by these developments, Taine called for the methods
of scientific psychology to be applied now directly to the human soul.
He declares,

> Science approaches at last and approaches man; it has gone be-
> yond the visible and palpable world of stars, stones, and plants,
> to which it had been contemptuously confined—it now chal-
> lenges the soul, armed with exact and piercing instruments whose
> precision and whose reach have proved themselves over three
> hundred years of experience.[28]

Taine insists that "every living thing" can now be brought within the
compass of the "steel pincers of necessity."[29]

Psychology, Taine writes, has become "a science of facts; one can
speak with precision and detail of a sensation, an idea, a memory, a pre-
vision, as well as of a vibration or a physical movement."[30] Taine is alluding here to a groundbreaking book in experimental psychology published in 1860 (in German) by Gustav Fechner. Fechner is credited with
having invented the theory and techniques of psychometrics, thereby establishing the foundation for the modern neurosciences. In *The Elements of Psychophysics* (1860), Fechner compares psychic measurement
to measurement in physics and astronomy.[31] He provides a mathematical formula that states, "equal relative increments of stimuli are proportional to equal increments of sensation."[32] The important point, for
Bergson, is that Fechner proposed to measure the mental state itself (its
intensity), not merely the amount of stimulus that provoked the inner
response. This is where science tries to touch the soul.

---

28. Cited in A. E. Pilkington, *Bergson and His Influence, a Reassessment*, 219.
29. Ibid.
30. Taine, *De l'intelligence*, (Paris: Hachette, 1870), 1:4 (my translation).
31. Gustav Fechner, *Elements of Psychophysics,* trans. Helmut Adler, 55–56. Fechner also writes that "the establishment of a psychological measure is a matter for outer
psychophysics and its most immediate applications also fall into this realm. Further applications and deductions, however, necessarily impinge upon the area of inner psychophysics, and thereby bring a deeper meaning to these measures. . . . Quantitative dependence of sensation on the stimulus can then eventually be translated into dependence
on the bodily activities that directly underlie sensation—in short, the psychophysical processes. For this translation it becomes necessary to ascertain the relative dependence of
the internal motions on the stimulus. . . . It will be possible to carry out all these investigations in an exact manner, and these cannot in the long run . . . fail to achieve the success of quantitative determination."
32. Ibid., 54.

Fechner's psychometrics will become Bergson's principal target in the *Essai*. Bergson does not question the accuracy of Fechner's research, or even its effectiveness in certain limited domains. He does challenge the philosophical implications of Fechner's clinical and theoretical project and questions one of its fundamental assumptions, namely, that mental events, as such, can be measured. In other words, he challenges the implications of Fechner's work for the question of freedom or indeterminacy in the face of the strict determinism of scientific methods newly adopted by the social sciences and applied to the inner workings of the human soul. For Bergson, Fechner's psychometrics threatens to reduce the person to the body, construed mechanistically along the lines of Descartes' human machine.

The kind of research Fechner conducted in the nineteenth century is vigorously pursued today in the cognitive sciences and in research concerning artificial intelligence.[33] We begin to hear claims about the power of machines to out-think humans. A discourse of the post-human, or of machinism has emerged.[34] In Bergson's period, however, positivism was the discourse of humanism, which was the project of pushing science as far as it could go. "What is necessary," Renan wrote in *L'avenir de la Science*, "is to push science to its ultimate limits" (*AS* 31). This, for Renan, would be the ultimate humanism. "My conviction," he writes, "is that the religion of the future will be pure humanism, that is, the cult of everything human [*de tout ce qui est de l'homme*]" (*AS* 101). Humanism is the dream of complete human mastery of the world. Renan looks forward to the day when "the material world will be completely subjected to man [*parfaitement soumis à l'homme*]" (*AS* 80). Surely, we must be almost there by now!

Renan's humanism is a discourse of progress. "In the past, everything was considered as being [*étant*]," Renan writes, "now everything is con-

---

33. If you look online at http://neuro.caltech.edu/ you will find the site for the Shimojo Psychophysics Lab and see that the project Fechner launched is being pursued energetically today in relation to research into sensory thresholds, detection theory, and information processing. Concerning contemporary debates about the philosophical status of "mental events," see Vincent Descombes, *La denrée mentale*, 105–119, as well as subsequent chapters on artificial intelligence. Descombes is available in English as *The Mind's Provisions: A Critique of Cognitivism*, trans. Stephen Allan Schwartz. See also Jean-Noël Missa, who critiques Bergson from the perspective of contemporary cognitive science in *L'esprit-cerveau: La philosophie de l'esprit à la lumière des neurosciences*.

34. See, for example, Friedrich A. Kittler, *Gramophone, Film, Typewriter*, trans. G. Winthrop-Young and M. Wutz; Paul Virilio, *L'art du moteur*, and *The Politics of the Very Worst*.

sidered to be in the process of becoming [*en voie de se faire*]" (*AS*, 183). How is it that our exemplary determinist can sound so much like Bergson here? There is another element to add into the positivist mix: biology and the perspective of evolution.

Herbert Spencer took the systematic positivism of Comte one step further by applying the principles of mechanism to life processes themselves. His theory of evolution was a story of progress that pertained to life itself, and to life forms. With Spencer, evolution meets up with the new science of sociology, and, paradoxically, with mechanistic philosophy and determinism. Spencer's Synthetic Philosophy extended the biological evolutionary model to other fields of knowledge: philosophy, epistemology, psychology, and sociology. It proposed a biological theory of knowledge, according to which our concepts are formed by a process of adaptation to the environment.[35] This adaptation, Spencer announces, was completed with the advent of Newtonian physics. Newton provided Natural Science with universal laws that regulated interactions between external phenomena. By the same token, associationist psychology (Fechner and Taine) established lawful relations between mental events. Spencer's Synthetic Philosophy links these two sets of lawful relations through a concept of evolutionary adaptation. Modern science (in the sense glorified by Renan) marks the culmination of the evolution of intelligence. As Spencer put it: "mechanistic science of the last century represents the last stage of the adaptive process by which the human mind gradually adjusts itself to the structure of reality."[36] Positivist rationalism is thus anointed as the apogee of evolutionary development—the end of evolutionary history.

Life is defined from an evolutionary perspective as a process of adaptation that Spencer construes in terms of lawful development that proceeds continuously from simple to complex relations, that is, from the homogeneous to the heterogeneous. According to Spencer, all natural and social development reflects the universality of law. Just as there are laws of motion, which determine relations between things in the world, so there are laws of life that condition human existence in the social world. For Spencer, science is an "organized body of truths, ever growing, and ever being purified of errors" that yields "a veritable revelation—a continuous disclosure of the established order of the Uni-

---

35. Bergson retains this element from Spencer. It becomes a central tenet of *Creative Evolution*, a work which, however, is directed against Spencer.
36. Cited by Milič Čapek, *Bergson and Modern Physics*, 10.

verse."[37] Spencer's language is consistent with Renan's rhetoric of the religion of science.

A key feature of Spencer's evolutionary philosophy (which preceded the publication of Charles Darwin's *Origin of the Species*) was Jean-Baptiste Lamarck's subsequently discredited theory of the inheritance of acquired characteristics. This was a central feature of Spencer's evolutionary mechanism, which had implications for his evolutionary psychology. Modification, in the course of evolutionary progress, is thus explained in terms of functional adaptation to changing conditions of the physical world. With more complex beings (humans), progressive adaptation implies the adjustment of inner, mental processes (subjective relations) to the external world (objective relations). For Spencer, evolution implies the progressive correspondence between these two sets of relations.

We can see that this perspective holds major implications for both psychology and epistemology. It reinforces the view of associationist psychology that mental associations are formed by the repeated occurrences of the external events that trigger them. It also reinforces the position of psychophysics (Fechner), which holds that inner events can be reduced to physical causes, or attached to functional locations in the brain.

In other words, Spencer's Synthetic Philosophy, and his concept of evolutionary adaptation, presupposes the associationist premise of the correspondence of mental features to physical ones. Ideas become connected in our minds, he holds, when the things or events in the world that produce them repeatedly occur together. On the basis of Lamarck's theory of the inheritance of acquired characteristics, Spencer extends this associationist mechanism from the individual to the race in a discourse that has come to be known as social Darwinism: "such results of repeated occurrences accumulate in the succession of individuals; the effects of associations are supposed to be transmitted as modifications of the nervous system."[38] With Spencer, then, we find the most ambitious extension of the mechanistic model, one that applies not only to subjective experience, as Taine had envisioned, but to life itself.

Bergson was initially fascinated by Spencer, but then he began to reflect seriously on the question of time. At which point it occurred to him that Spencer had produced a theory of evolution that managed to im-

---

37. Herbert Spencer, *First Principles,* 17.
38. Ibid., 470.

mobilize time! Even the philosophy of becoming—evolution—had been subsumed by a static mechanistic analysis. From Bergson's perspective, Spencer's account of evolution considered it only retrospectively; it then reconstructed evolution mechanistically on the basis of what Bergson called the "strange timelessness of the Newtonian world."[39]

Bergson will ultimately challenge Spencer directly in his own non-mechanistic account of evolution in *Creative Evolution*. But it is the entire picture we have been painting—the picture of a mechanistic world and a system of positive sciences that yield knowledge of it—that Bergson will proceed to challenge by reinvoking, and displacing, oppositions between Metaphysics and Science that had been elaborated within the positivist tradition by Comte, Taine, Renan, and Spencer. Bergson will attempt to draw a critical line, not between phenomena and noumena, as Kant had done, but between the living and the inert. Whereas inert things are the appropriate objects of science, Bergson believed that living beings, states of consciousness, and life processes can only be known through a metaphysical method he will call intuition.

William James admired Bergson's ability "simply to *break away* from all old categories, deny old worn-out beliefs, and restate things *ab initio*, making the lines of division fall into entirely new places!"[40] But if this newness escaped attention, in some quarters, it is because it was misperceived by contemporary critics who remained attached to the positivist humanism of Renan, Taine, and Spencer. We have just heard Spencer declare that science represents the apogee of the evolution of intelligence. How could one take seriously, then, a philosopher who opposes to the edifice of science a notion of *intuition* and who appeals to metaphysics for truths that escape the methods of science!

In the context of logical positivism, Bertrand Russell accused Bergson of reasoning like the "cosmic poets"[41] and of waging a "war to the knife" with the intellect.[42] "When his philosophy will have triumphed," he writes, "it is supposed that argument will cease, and intellect will be lulled to sleep on the heaving sea of intuition."[43] If the logical positivists felt threatened by Bergson's thought, so did the Catholic Church, which

39. Cited in David Ray Griffin's *Physics and the Ultimate Significance of Time*, 11.
40. Cited in Pilkington, 21.
41. Bertrand Russell, *The Philosophy of Bergson*, 33.
42. Ibid., 13. Julian Benda was another unflinching critic of Bergson, from a perspective of rationalism. See *La trahison des clercs* and *Sur le succès du Bergsonisme*.
43. B. Russell, *Philosophy of Bergson*, 36.

put his three major works (the *Essai, Matter and Memory,* and *Creative Evolution*) on the Index in 1914, for fear that his anti-intellectualism would lead to skepticism and "to the unleashing of instincts."[44] It was feared that "the notion of duration would put into question the traditional idea of God."[45] Bergson appears to have both God and science against him. "There is something unassimilable about him," Gilles Deleuze has written of Bergson, "object of so many hatreds."[46]

"It was my mathematical studies," Bergson wrote, "that stirred my interest in duration. . . . At first this was no more than a certain puzzlement at the value given to the term t in the equations of mechanics."[47] Bergson places the notion of duration at the very center of his thinking and locates it with respect to the philosophy of science. The philosophy of physics, he wrote in 1938, "was for me something essential . . . closely related to my theory of duration . . . which lay in the direction in which physics would move sooner or later."[48] From this perspective, the charges of irrationalism and anti-intellectualism leveled against Bergson seem almost comically misplaced. Not only was the breadth of Bergson's knowledge in a wide range of disciplines quite exceptional but, even more to the point, he had received advanced training as a mathematician and took a keen interest in the most advanced developments in the hard sciences. The attunement of his thought to developments in the hard sciences is part of what makes his thought so interesting to us

44. Alexandre Papadopoulo, *Un philosophe entre deux défaites: Henri Bergson entre 1870 et 1940,* 300 (my translation).

45. Ibid.

46. Gilles Deleuze with Claire Parnet, *Dialogues,* 22 (my translation). It is available in English as *Dialogues,* trans. Hugh Tomlinson and Barbara Habberjam.

47. Cited in F. C. T. Moore, *Bergson: Thinking Backwards,* 5.

48. Cited in Milič Čapek, *Bergson and Modern Physics,* xi. As Isabelle Stengers and others have suggested, Bergson did, to a certain extent, anticipate the direction in which physics would move. See Ilya Prigogine and Isabelle Stangers, *Entre le temps et l'éternité,* 20–21, 195. See also the essay by the celebrated physicist Louis de Broglie (who affirmed the dual particle-wave structure of matter in 1924), "The Concepts of Contemporary Physics and Bergson's Ideas on Time and Motion," in *Bergson and the Evolution of Physics,* ed. P. Y. A. Gunter, 46–47. "Is there any analogy," de Broglie asks, "between Bergson's critique of the idea of motion and the conceptions of contemporary quantum physics? It seems the reply ought to be in the affirmative," *Bergson and the Evolution of Physics,* 52. He goes on to suggest that Bergson anticipated both Niels Bohr (responsible for our picture of the structure of the atom in the context of quantum physics) and Heisenberg (who formulated the Uncertainty Principle in the context of quantum physics).

today.[49] This is in large part due to the extraordinary developments that took place during his lifetime, something he was in a position to appreciate as a trained mathematician and philosopher.[50]

"The masters of modern philosophy," Bergson wrote in 1903, "have all been men who assimilated all the scientific developments of their time."[51] Bergson was one of these masters and the science of his day was remarkably dynamic. A series of moves makes possible the rupture with the model of classical physics that will find its articulation in Einstein's theory of relativity and Niels Bohr's account of the structure of the atom in terms of quantum theory. It gradually pushes the classical model of mechanics to the breaking point through investigations of motion that pertain to kinetic theory (which concerns energy transformations in relation to molecular motion of gases), thermodynamics (physical processes that concern heat), electromagnetism, and investigations of light and radioactive materials.

In Bergson's lifetime, experimental physics boasts the discovery of the X-ray, radioactivity, and the electron. Out of experimental research will emerge the laws of thermodynamics, atomic physics, quantum theory, and the laws of relativity. It is not too much to claim that the funda-

---

49. A glance at the notes to the last chapter of *Matter and Memory would* confirm Bergson's detailed knowledge of developments in physics. We find references to James Clerk Maxwell, to Michael Faraday, and to Lord Kelvin, among others. It is for this reason that we undertake to go into these developments in some detail.

50. Bergson was not only trained in mathematics, he was a successful mathematician. Still a young student, he solved a mathematical problem that Pascal had been unable to master. This, and another proof, were published when he was quite young. By the time he turned to philosophy, he had won a *prix du concours général* in mathematics for his treatment of a problem of *géométrie projective*, or topology. When he informed his mathematics teacher, Desboves, that he wanted to abandon mathematics for philosophy, Desboves reportedly responded, "You could have been a mathematician, you will be merely a philosopher." See Philippe Soulez and Frédéric Worms, *Bergson: Biographie,* 121. He characterizes the invention of infinitesimal calculus as the greatest single intellectual achievement of the modern period. He follows the work of Henri Poincaré with interest. One of his own intellectual disciples, Édouard Le Roy, was a celebrated mathematician in his own right, who worked on problems of topography and set theory. Le Roy gives an interesting exposition of Bergson's thought in *Une Philosophie nouvelle: Henri Bergson.* Bergson's competence in math has been called into question by some commentators, most notably by Gaston Bachelard. Soulez disputes Bergson's critics on this point. Given his training and interest in mathematics, he argues, it is hard to believe Bergson would not have been kept informed of the latest developments in the field by Le Roy.

51. Bergson, "Introduction à la Métaphysique," *Œuvres,* 1432. One should mention that Bergson is on record as having repeatedly supported the social sciences before the Assemblée des professeurs du Collège de France, when it was a question of deciding specific appointments to be made. See *Bergson: Biographie,* 121.

mental pieces of the puzzle necessary for the modern elaboration of these fields (nuclear physics, modern quantum physics, relativity) were in place by the end of the nineteenth century. They all concerned the questions that most interested Bergson: motion (or time) and process. It is worth the effort to try to put the pieces of this puzzle together.

Thermodynamics

During the 1850s a field called kinetic theory investigated the movement of gas molecules (based on a primitive conception of atomic theory formulated since the ancient Greeks) as well as changes of state between solids, liquids, and gases. The laws of thermodynamics emerged from studies of heat conducted in this context.[52] The first law (formulated earlier by Sadi Carnot) stated the conservation of energy in processes of energy transformation. This law shored up the closed system of classical physics, the system that grounded what I have outlined above as the mechanistic humanism of Renan, Taine, and Spencer. The second law, however, known as the law of entropy, described a degradation of energy in the passage to equilibrium. It states the law of an increase of entropy over time. The second law of thermodynamics suggests that the physical process of entropy is irreversible, that it progresses according to the one directional movement of lived time. To this extent it validates the reality of irreversible time, in opposition to the classical model, thus marking a break from earlier accounts of physical properties or natural laws. Since Lagrange, these had for the most part been expressed in a formal language that described *reversible* processes, due to a reliance on geometry in the mathematical formalization of these universal laws. That is to say (to anticipate the argument of Bergson) physical processes were considered in terms of space, not time. On a spatial model, movement is modeled as reversible: a line that goes from A to B can also go from B to A. When we shift from a theoretical account to a physical one, however, as, for example, in the second law of thermodynamics, the

---

52. In *Inward Bound: Of Matter and Forces in the Physical World,* Abraham Pais argues that the laws of thermodynamics emerged from multiple discoveries from 1830 to 1850. Some scholars credit Sadi Carnot with the discovery of both the first and second laws of thermodynamics. Some credit Helmholtz with the discovery of the first in 1847 when he publishes "On the Conservation of Force." Others credit Rudolf Clausius with the discovery of the second law, the law of entropy. My interest is simply to recall that these developments were taking place in Bergson's period.

process is observed to occur in time. The Second Law of Thermodynamics is known as the law of time's arrow.[53]

But soon enough mathematics overtakes time's arrow. In 1872 Ludwig Boltzmann provided a mathematical demonstration of the principal of entropy. He proposed a theorem (the H theorem) that characterized entropy as the measure of the degradation of energy. His mathematical demonstration transposed the observed physical process back into the mathematical terms of mechanical explanation.

A few years later (1876), Josef Loschmidt addressed the following question to Boltzmann: if entropy is an irreversible process (one does not observe a cold material becoming spontaneously warmer over time) how can you claim to derive it from a model that corresponds to reversible laws? Boltzmann responded to this challenge with a paper in 1877 that characterized entropy in terms of mathematical *probabilities* through a statistical analysis.[54] This is the beginning of what will become the field of statistical mechanics. When he translated the law of entropy into the terms of classical mechanics, and then adjusted this to statistical analysis, Boltzmann obscured the implications of the second law of thermodynamics concerning the reality of psychological time that Bergson will call Real Duration.

Electron Theory

When thermodynamics and statistical mechanics meet electromagnetism, we approach microphysics, the physics of subatomic particles. Boltzmann himself investigated questions that pertained to heat and phase change (kinetic theory and thermodynamics) and to electromagnetism. By 1872 he had identified the phenomenon of energy bundles that would subsequently be theorized as *quanta* by Max Planck. In 1892 Lorentz worked out an electron theory of electrified matter.[55] We are poised on the edge of microphysics, on our way to the discoveries of rel-

53. Isabelle Stengers, *La thermodynamique: La réalité physique en crise*, vol. 3 of *Cosmopolitiques*, 71. In the last chapter of *Matter and Memory*, Bergson contrasts physics favorably to mathematics for just this reason. It is not unlikely that he has in mind the second law of thermodynamics, which reinscribes the factor of time elided by mathematical formalism.

54. The mathematics evolved from work done on the equations for vibratory motion dating back to the 1820s.

55. This is the first theoretical framework that dispenses with the hypothesis of the ether as medium for the electron.

ativity and quantum mechanics. Bergson has not yet written *Matter and Memory*.

Another very important development that took place in 1885, just a few years before Bergson published the *Essai*, was the development of techniques for the analysis of energy line spectra. These will facilitate subsequent investigations of atomic structure. Although Newton had already explored the spectrum of light in experiments with the prism, line spectra make it possible to discern discreet energy levels. Line spectral analysis involved heating gases and then examining them through a spectroscope that revealed lines of color. These lines mark the difference between energy levels and carry the signature, or the fingerprint, of particular elements. They will subsequently be understood as traces that delineate quanta, the orbit states of electrons within the atom.

By 1852 scientists had already begun to speculate concerning the nature of atomic structure.[56] In 1885 Johann Jakob Balmer identified the line spectra of hydrogen. His work received considerable attention. It was discussed during the major international physics congress that took place in Paris in 1900 and in meetings of French learned academies.[57] The techniques of spectral analysis hastened the discovery of new chemical elements.[58] When Niels Bohr formalized his account of the structure of the hydrogen atom in 1913, he essentially picked up where Balmer left off.

Wilhelm Conrad Roentgen accidentally discovered the X-ray in 1895. The event caused a sensation. It was immediately announced in the Paris papers and was discussed at length at the January 10 meeting of the Académie des Sciences.[59] In 1896, the year Bergson published *Matter and Memory*, Henri Bequerel announced the discovery of radiation. After a discussion with Bequerel, Henri Poincaré published a semipopular article in the *Revue Générale des Sciences;*[60] in another article, he observed: "the path followed by the Bequerels [Henri Bequerel and

---

56. "Molecular vibrations by which light is produced," wrote one contemporary, "are not vibrations in which molecules move among one another, but vibrations among the constituent parts of the molecules themselves, performed by virtue of the internal forces which hold the parts of the molecules together." See Pais' quotation of Stokes in *Inward Bound*, 75. He adds that the words "molecule" and "atom" were often used interchangeably at this time and that in this context Stokes is speaking of the internal structure of the atom.

57. Ibid., 164.

58. Ibid., 169.

59. Ibid., 43.

60. *Revue Générale des Sciences* 7 (1896): 52. See also *Inward Bound*, 43.

his father, Alexander Edmond Bequerel, a physicist] . . . will open access to a new world which no one suspected."[61] Indeed.

In 1897, Lord Kelvin (William Thomson) published experiments with the cathode ray, which sends out streams of electrons. This directly engaged physics with subatomic particles and provided the technology that would facilitate further research in this area. The next year the Curies submitted a paper in which they stated that "radioactivity is an atomic property."[62] Radioactivity will soon be linked to more detailed accounts of atomic instability that will provoke further research into the inner structure of the atom. One year later, Lord Kelvin announced the discovery of the electron, affirming in a joint meeting of British and French scientists (1899) that the atom had been split: "Electrification essentially involves the splitting of the atom, a part of the mass of the atom getting free and becoming detached from the original atom."[63] This leads to the discovery of Planck's Constant (1900), to Einstein's theory of special relativity (1906), and to Niels Bohr's account of the atomic structure of the hydrogen atom in terms of quantum analysis (1913).

When Marie Curie discovered the radioactive emissions of the new elements polonium and radium, she called into question the first law of thermodynamics that states the conservation of energy. "We thus encounter," she wrote, "a source of light that functions without an energy source. There is at least an apparent contradiction here with the principle of Carnot."[64] I mention this apparently insignificant detail because Bergson, as we shall see, explicitly calls into question the principle of the conservation of energy. His gesture appears less eccentric when we realize that this bedrock principle of Newtonian mechanics was being questioned by leading scientists of Bergson's day. It will continue to be called into question, insistently, by Niels Bohr up to the 1930s. Microphysics will repeatedly detect emissions of energy that appear to be spontaneous and unexplained, in apparent challenge to the law of conservation. These phenomena will eventually be accounted for by the invention (or discovery) of new subatomic particles such as the neutron and the neutrino. In 1904, however (three years before Bergson's *Creative Evolu-*

---

61. Cited in *Inward Bound*, 49, from an article by Poincaré in *La Revue Scientifique* 7 (1897): 72.

62. Ibid., 55.

63. Cited in *Inward Bound*, 86.

64. Ibid., 111. Carnot had been credited by many with discovery of the first law, the law of conservation of energy.

tion) Poincaré presented a lecture on "the present crisis of mathematical physics" in which he raised the same question. "These principles, on which we have built everything," he wrote, speaking of the conservation of energy in particular, "are they about to crumble away in turn?"[65]

Thermodynamics, spectral analysis, radiation—all of these discoveries lead up to Max Planck's theory of energy quanta, which will open the door to theories of relativity and quantum mechanics. Inspired by Boltzmann's statistical mechanics, Max Planck begins his work in the area of thermodynamics, exploring relations between entropy and probability. Working after the discovery of radiation, and benefiting from techniques of spectral analysis, he explores entropy in relation to radiation processes. In simplest terms, he explores the color changes that occur when solid objects are heated. He undertakes to provide new and more accurate measurements of the spectra associated with energy distribution. Investigating relations between energy and the frequency of radiation, he discovered that "matter emits radiant energy [heat or light] only in discrete chunks that were integral multiples of a fundamental quantity."[66] Planck was able to determine a precise numerical value for this constant quantity, subsequently known as Planck's Constant. He demonstrated not only that energy exchange does not occur continuously but also that it occurs discontinuously in *quanta*; he also enabled the calculation of the energy contained in a quantum at various frequencies.[67] What turned out to be most important was not just the conceptual scheme of quanta (Boltzmann had already had the insight that energy can clump up in bundles), but the fact that subsequent experimental research confirmed that the constant quantity he had derived mathematically actually operated in physical processes at the subatomic level. In his reception speech for the Nobel Prize (1918), Planck put it this way:

> If the derivation of the radiation law was based on a sound physical conception, the quantum of action must play a fundamental

65. Ibid., 113. By this date the term "atomic energy" had been coined. Pais cites Rutherford and Soddy from a 1903 article to the effect that "energy latent in the atom must be enormous compared with that rendered free in ordinary chemical change . . . there is no reason to assume that this enormous store of energy is possessed by the radioactive elements alone. It seems probable that atomic energy in general is of a similar high order of magnitude." See Pais, *Inward Bound*, 116.

66. Bernard Pullman, *The Atom in the History of Human Thought*, trans. Axel Reisinger, 261.

67. Ibid.

role in physics, and here was something entirely new, never before heard of, we seemed called upon to basically revise all our physical thinking, built as this was, since the establishment of the infinitesimal calculus by Leibnitz and Newton, upon the acceptance of the continuity of all causative connections.[68]

And, as he goes on to affirm, experiment has indeed confirmed this view in the work of Einstein among others. The principle of causality is itself implicitly being called into question.

By 1905 Einstein has discovered the photon, characterizing light in terms of energy quanta. Light, in other words, can be said to function either as wave or as particle.

By 1913, Niels Bohr has worked out a theory of atomic structure that characterizes electron orbits in terms of quantum states.

By 1924, Louis de Broglie has extended the dual wave-particle hypothesis to all material particles.[69] "There were now two theories of light," he affirms, "both indispensable and . . . without any logical connection."[70]

Planck's notion of the quantum and Bohr's quantum account of the structure of the atom addressed questions of particle location. After de Broglie's dual wave-particle theory, Erwin Shrödinger invents wave mechanics, revising the account of wave propagation to dispense with the quantum structure of the atom, which had evolved in relation to a fundamentally particle view of micro-physical matter. This is a radical move to the extent that waves de-localize phenomena, since they carry energy but not mass.[71]

In 1927, Werner Heisenberg proclaims the Uncertainty Principle. Paradoxically, it was to reinforce the importance of direct observation in microphysics that he had embarked on the work that would lead to the formal account of the intrinsic limitations of direct observation when it comes to the micro-physical level. On this subatomic level, he discovered, the very act of observing or measuring matter alters the reality the scientist is trying to observe. Observation requires light. But the activity of photons interferes with particles on this microphysical scale. When the photon hits the electron, it moves it. The Uncertainty Prin-

---

68. Nobel Acceptance Speech, www.nobel-winners.com/physics/mas
69. Pullman, *Atom in the History of Human Thought*, 274.
70. Pais, *Inward Bound*, 248.
71. In the last chapter of *Matter and Memory*, Bergson appears to adumbrate these developments.

ciple that Heisenberg formulated in 1927 states that it is impossible to measure the location and the momentum of an atomic particle (such as an electron) at the same time. Because of the minutely small scale of atomic processes, all observation or measurement interferes in the processes themselves. Uncertainty has changed character. It is not just a question of what we don't yet know, there are now objective limits to what we can know. The Uncertainty Principle "introduces a fundamental indeterminism, inherent in the very nature of the universe."[72]

We have come full circle from the certainty widely shared in the 1880s, when it was confidently assumed that there were no mysteries left in the world, to a sense of overwhelming uncertainty during the 1920s and '30s. As we have seen, Valéry expressed deep perplexity when he characterized a "singular crisis" of the sciences. I would like to return to his words and examine them more closely in the light of the developments we have just traced. The sciences, he wrote,

> now seem to despair of conserving their old ideal of unification, of explication of the universe. The universe is decomposing, losing all hope of a single image. The world of the infinitely small seems strangely different from the one it engenders on a larger scale. Even the identity of bodies is getting lost here, and I won't speak . . . of the crisis of determinism, that is, of causality. (OC, 1037)

"The universe is decomposing"—the question of entropy has been rendered all the more acute by experimental evidence of the degradation of energy in radioactive decay. If "the universe is losing all hope of a unique image," this is because of the recently proposed complementarity theory, which holds not only that there are two descriptions of matter, the particle description and the wave description, but that the two are fundamentally incompatible with one another.[73] Thus, since the "world of the infinitely small seems strangely different from the one it engenders on a larger scale," there is no way to achieve a unified image of the real. There is no effective bridge between classical mechanics and quantum mechanics. "Even the identity of bodies is getting lost," because in wave

---

72. Pullman, *Atom in the History of Human Thought*, 293.
73. See Louis de Broglie, "The Concept of Contemporary Physics and Bergson's Ideas of Time and Motion," in P. A. Y. Gunter, *Bergson and the Evolution of Physics*.

mechanics matter at times appears to dissolve into energy. When we are dealing with subatomic particles, which exist in motion, it is impossible to determine their precise location. All we can determine is the *probable* location of a particle at a given time. Of course, all of this leads to a crisis of determinism—"and I won't speak . . . of the crisis of determinism, that is, of causality."

The "singular crisis of the sciences," provoked by the discoveries of quantum mechanics, forced into discussion a number of philosophical questions (concerning causality, indeterminacy, and the limits of knowledge) that Bergson had raised philosophically through the notion of duration since the late 1880s.[74] At that time, Bergson felt it necessary to affirm a sharp critical boundary between the realm of science and the realm of philosophy (or what he called metaphysics), even though he subsequently recognized that his thinking of duration "lay in the direction in which physics would move sooner or later."[75] Quantum mechanics forced these same questions to the fore within the scientific community during the 1920s and 1930s.

For Kant, scientific work implies causality. In classical physics it was assumed that the future motion of a particle could be determined, or predicted with precision, based on knowledge of its present position and momentum, plus knowledge of all the forces acting upon it.[76] According to Newton, "All things are placed in time as to order of succession; and in space as to order of situation . . . That the primary places of things should be movable, is absurd. There are therefore absolute places, and translations out of those places, are the only absolute motions."[77]

As Heisenberg demonstrated with the Uncertainty Principle, it is not possible on the level of subatomic particles to determine location and momentum at the same time. Furthermore, it is not possible with respect to atomic particles in wave motion to locate a single particle at all. Wave dy-

74. Pullman writes, "Because of the nature of the issues involved, scientists found themselves unwittingly dealing with arguments whose ramifications extended beyond a strictly scientific framework, venturing into areas that had traditionally been the province of philosophers. These scientists were forced in that direction because they were virtually the only ones with enough knowledge of the concepts and methodologies of the pertinent theories to infer with any credibility the appropriate consequences," *The Atom in the History of Human Thought*, 296.

75. Čapek, *Bergson and Modern Physics*, xi.

76. This had been formulated most explicitly by Laplace.

77. Sir Isaac Newton, 8. We also read there: "From the positions and distances of all things for any body considered as immovable we define all places; and then, with respect to such places, we estimate all motions, considering bodies as transformed from some of those places to others."

namics delocalizes matter, which under this description can no longer be said to have mass. Thus it is not possible to state the present conditions on the basis of which future effects would be predicted, according to the classical model. As one historian of science puts it: "What quantum mechanics did . . . was to assert that classical causality was irrevocably gone."[78]

Max Born is explicit on the challenge of quantum mechanics to the principle of causality when it comes to research practice. "We free forces of their classical duty of determining directly the motion of particles and allow them instead to determine the probability of states. Whereas before it was our purpose to make these two definitions of force equivalent, this problem has now no longer, strictly speaking, any sense."[79]

What is the difference, then, between Boltzmann's statistical mechanics and quantum mechanics when it comes to the principle of causality? For Boltzmann, statistical probability is a response to limitations on our techniques of knowledge, for example, our inability to count to the huge numbers that would be necessary to actually measure phenomena of entropy. For quantum mechanics, probability is inscribed in the processes of the physical world itself, which, as Heisenberg establishes, intrinsically resists precise measurement on the microphysical level. The upshot of Heisenberg's Uncertainty Principle is not "what don't I know?" but rather "what can't I know?"[80] Born is unequivocal on the question of causal determinism.

> Here the whole problem of determinism arises. From the point of view of quantum mechanics there exists no quantity which in an individual case causally determines the effect of a collision [between particles] . . . I myself tend to give up determinism in the atomic world.[81]

78. Pais, *Inward Bound*, 212.

79. From a paper read by Max Born before the British Association at Oxford in 1926, cited in *Inward Bound*, 258.

80. Ibid., 262.

81. Ibid., 257. Pais adds that "individual events do not obey the classical principle of causality." See *Inward Bound*, 329. The physical equivalent of the principle of causality would be the first principle of thermodynamics, the law of the conservation of matter. We recall that the discovery of radiation prompted Marie Curie to question the principle of the conservation of energy, given that radiation was being spontaneously emitted from radioactive materials without any force being added to them. We have heard Poincaré reiterate this concern. In 1924, Niels Bohr called the conservation of matter into question from the perspective of quantum mechanics. In relation to radiation decay, Bohr argued the case of the non-conservation of energy until 1936. The first time he took this position was in a lecture in May 1930. Here is Bohr writing to his colleague Pauli: "I am prepar-

In 1912 Poincaré affirms that "A science that is not deterministic would be no science at all."[82] But when Bergson writes that his conception of duration "lay in the direction in which physics would tend sooner or later," the tendency in which it was moving was the theory of quantum mechanics that entailed, at least for physicists like Max Born and Niels Bohr, a tendency toward indeterminism.[83] This, of course, is the thrust of Bergson's first work, the *Essai*.

The charges of irrationalism made against Bergson must be considered in the context of these developments in physics. One of the most interesting aspects of the crisis posed by quantum mechanics is what the physicist and historian Bernard Pullman calls a problem of "the shortage of words."[84]

> Quantum mechanics lacks the linguistic tools to express what it is all about. . . . Complementarity attempts to offer a possible solution to the dilemma of describing atomic phenomena while preserving the use of the ordinary language of physics.[85]

---

ing an account on statistics and conservation in quantum mechanics in which I hope to give convincing arguments for the view that the problem of beta-ray expulsion lies outside the reach of the classical conservation principles of energy and momentum." Bohr writes, "The loss of the unerring guidance which the conservation principles have hitherto offered in the development of atomic theory would of course be a very disquieting prospect." He further writes, "Just as the account of those aspects of atomic constitution essential for the explanation of the ordinary physical and chemical properties of matter imply a renunciation of the classical idea of causality, the features of atomic stability, still deeper-lying, responsible for the existence and the properties of atomic nuclei, may force us to renounce the very idea of energy balance." What is more, Bohr affirmed "energy conservation as well as causality are only valid statistically in quantum transitions." See *Inward Bound*, 311, 312, 313.

82. See Pullman, *Atom in the History of Human Thought*, 293. "Scientists," Pullman adds, "unless they were prepared to contradict themselves, really had no choice but to embrace determinism."

83. Science is an art of measurement. It requires that measurement be exact and that it apply to all properties of matter. It implies the objective method and assumes that the natural world should be knowable through observation. It implies determinism. Quantum mechanics confounds all of these criteria. The Heisenberg Uncertainty Principle and the principle of complementarity impose a view of indeterminism. Einstein insisted that this was a provisional stage in the long-term search for the truth. The debate remains open, as new versions of determinism are formulated (see, for example, Daniel Dennett). Nevertheless, Einstein's commitment to determinism should be kept in mind when evaluating the disagreement between Bergson and Einstein.

84. Pullman, *Atom in the History of Human Thought*, 298.

85. Ibid. A further point to be explored would be the impact of temporality on the conditions of uncertainty. Pullman writes of the Heisenberg Uncertainty Principle that "any observation takes place at the cost of the connection between the past and the future course of phenomena." See *Atom in the History of Human Thought*, 299.

Heisenberg himself declared that "when we get beyond this range of the classical theory we must realize that our words don't fit. They don't get a hold in the physical reality."[86] This question of the fit of words, as we shall see in more detail further on, is precisely the problem that confronted Bergson in a different key: how to write a philosophy of duration in language, when language itself crushes the experience of duration.[87] When considering the appeal Bergson makes to intuition in philosophy, we should pay close attention to Bergson's analysis of the difficulty of putting time into words, and we should remember the problem of the "shortage of words" in the context of contemporary physics.[88]

I have not tried to argue that Bergson foresaw future developments of physics.[89] What I have tried to show, more simply, are the scientific developments that would have enabled him to grasp the direction in which modern physics was heading. By 1888, the year Bergson introduced his theory of duration in the *Essai*, some are still chanting the deterministic mantra of the mastery of science even as, according to Milič Čapek, "the first rumblings under the foundation of classical physics were discernible." He adds: "hardly anyone could then guess even remotely the extent of the coming scientific revolution," a vision that "loom[ed] on a very distant horizon . . . only in a few and heretically daring minds. Bergson was one of these."[90]

Although Bergson's views evolved from the early to the later work, he never disavowed the early analyses of the *Essai* and of *Matter and Memory*, even as he followed the dizzying developments that continued up to his death in 1941.

---

86. Ibid., 291.

87. The crisis of science, which is also a crisis of its "shortage of words," suggests the flipside of the crisis of philosophy that is marked by the "turn" in the philosophy of Heidegger, the philosophical practices of deconstruction, and the narrow focus of much of analytic philosophy.

88. See, in particular, Bergson's "L'intuition philosophique," in *Œuvres*, 1345–1363. The notion of intuition is to be considered in relation to "invention," as used by Leibnitz and Poincaré. See also my " 'The Zig-Zags of a Doctrine': Bergson, Deleuze, and the Question of Experience," *Pli* 15 (2004): 34–53.

89. De Broglie suggests as much in "The Concepts of Contemporary Physics and Bergson's Ideas of Time and Motion," in *Bergson and the Evolution of Physics*, ed. Gunter, 52.

90. Čapek, x.

3. *Essai sur les données immédiates de la conscience*
[*Time and Free Will*]

Trained as a mathematician, Henri Bergson was keenly interested in the scientific developments of his day and fully appreciated the ways in which science and technology were dramatically transforming the modern world. He also saw that science posed a threat: the risk of overstepping its bounds and of trying to explain what it could never understand. We can measure things, count them and make predictions about them because they are governed by logical and natural laws—the law of causality for example and the law of the conservation of matter. If, however, we extend scientific modes of thinking to ourselves, Bergson insisted, we would become like things. If we try to measure and count our feelings, to explain and predict our motives and actions, we will be transformed into automatons—without freedom, without beauty, without passion, and without dreams. We will become mere phantoms of ourselves.

From Bergson's perspective, this threat is posed concretely by specific schools of psychology that were gaining ground in his day. The field of Photometrics, associated with the celebrated social scientist Gustav Fechner, purported to measure feelings or sensory effects. Associationist psychologists tried to explain our behavior and our motives rationally, the way events in the physical world are explained. Both shared the perspective of psychophysics, which assumes that mental, or psychological states can be explained in terms of physical ones, reducing mind to brain. From Bergson's point of view this perspective implies an encroachment of scientific thought into the recesses of the soul. It entails a determinism that threatens to objectify our subjective states of consciousness, turning human beings into things. We could say that the moral and political consequences of this perspective were to be viciously played out in the two world wars of the twentieth century.

What is at stake, then, is freedom. For Bergson this means that we are not automatons; we do not function predictably like billiard balls, subject to a set of mechanistic laws. We are active, not reactive. The English translation of the title of Bergson's study, *Time and Free Will*, is somewhat misleading, for the notion of free will might suggest something on the order of rational choice, or at least that this free will attaches to a unified, rational subject. To challenge determinism, however, it is not necessary to construe freedom in terms of the mastery of the external world by a rational subject who can bend this world to its will.

Indeed, the French title of Bergson's study, *Essai sur les données immédiates de la conscience* [Essay on the Immediate Data of Consciousness], suggests something quite different. Bergson is asking us to consider a level of experience that is immediate in that it is not mediated through language or quantitative notation, an experience of the "real," we could say, that resists symbolization. Bergson examines inner states as such; he considers feelings, sensations, passions, etc. as pure quality, or in terms of the experience of qualitative difference. His argument against determinism follows from an account of affect and sensation. Freedom is associated not with powers of reason or cognition but with the intuition of duration. We could almost say it is closer to dreaming than to knowing.

Perhaps you have already perceived the difficulty inherent in Bergson's project. How can a philosopher examine immediate experience, that is, experience that has not been mediated through the conventional symbols of language or notation, when philosophy itself proceeds discursively? Bergson's response to this problem is to try to make us aware of how we usually speak about immediate experience—about the inner experiences we have of feelings, sensations, and affects—and to reveal to us what kinds of assumptions find their way into our thinking when we do so. He proceeds, then, in a mode of critique, and begins by revealing what immediate experience is not, and what gets in the way of our awareness of it.

In the *Essai*, Bergson undertakes to teach us to think about our inner experience in a philosophically rigorous, but decidedly nonscientific, way. He invites us to respect an absolute difference between conscious, living beings on the one hand, and things, on the other, and teaches us to distinguish between the discourses that are appropriate to the one and those which can be applied to the other. This leads to reflections upon space and time, the limits of knowledge, freedom, and, ultimately, the question of being itself.

The *Essai* begins by appealing to common sense and to our own experience. The opening chapter engages us with scenes that invite us to imagine how things feel and to reflect upon how we habitually think and speak of our feelings. It is not until the conclusion of the *Essai* that Bergson explicitly addresses Kant, the philosopher who, with John Locke, is credited with founding the discourse of empiricism. At this point we become aware that the *Essay* has conducted a rigorous critique of Kant, and that every move of the argument follows a contour of Kant's thought, turning it inside out, or on its head. We must therefore not be fooled by Bergson's strategic use of metaphors and examples. His argument is rigorously philosophical; every image, every appeal to our imagination and our senses serves a philosophical purpose.

3.1. Chapter 1 of the *Essai*
"On the Intensity of Psychological States"

The first question Bergson asks is not "What are sensations?" but "How do we usually speak of sensations?" What we usually do, he observes, is speak about them as we speak of external objects. We apply the model of outer experience, experience in the realm of what Descartes called extension, when we speak of inner experience. That is why we usually refer to inner experiences as intensities and then proceed to compare or measure them. One sensation is said to be more or less intense than another, as if inner feelings could be measured or compared to one another in terms of difference of degree. Because we measure extended things—things in the world—we have gotten into the habit of measuring intensities. But these are really pure qualities and, as such, cannot be transposed into quantitative terms. When we do this, and this is what we usually do when we speak, we lose contact with our own experience. We become alienated. This is the point of departure for a critique of this way of speaking, which loses track of real experience, something Bergson will eventually portray as a specific mode of temporal unfolding. He will call it Real Duration.

Tracking Differences

We tend to speak about our sensations the same way we speak about external objects. We say, for example, that one thing feels hotter or colder than another, that one noise is louder than another, or one light brighter. What does this imply about our view of the world and of ourselves? What does it imply about our way of thinking?

When we say that one sensation is stronger, or more intense, than another, we are assuming that we can measure feelings the same way we measure things. How long is this table? And which of two tables is longer? When we speak in this way about our own sensations, we make no distinction between something we experience within our own consciousness—a subjective experience—and things we know objectively. Bergson asks us to consider that there is a fundamental difference between the physical cause of a sensation and the way it feels to us.

For example, there is a fundamental difference, Bergson proposes, between light and brightness. Light is a thing in the world. We can measure it through standardized units such as candlepower or kilowatts. We can point to the light source—the sun, a candle, or a light bulb. Brightness, however, refers to the effect the light produces on us. It refers to our feeling of the quality of that light. The same source of light can produce varying effects of brightness depending on the sensitivity of an individual's eyes at a given moment. When the eye doctor puts certain drops in our eyes, for example, they become particularly light sensitive. We leave the office wearing dark glasses to compensate for the temporary oversensitivity of our eyes, even though the afternoon light is perhaps actually weaker than it was when we went into the doctor's office an hour earlier. Brightness, then, is not the same as light. To read any further in Bergson's text we have to develop a new skill: tracking differences and remembering to keep track of them. This is how Bergson's method works.

Difference (1). *Quantity* tells us how much there is of something. *Quality* tells us how things feel to us—bright, dark, hot, cold, happy, lonesome, or beautiful. Difference (2). The difference between quantity and quality includes a distinction between two kinds of difference: *difference in degree* and *difference in kind*.

Joy

Is it possible to consider pure quality? How might we examine inner feelings in themselves, without confusing them with their external causes? Bergson proposes that we consider experiences of emotion, instead of sensation, for here what we feel cannot be referred back to any clear external cause. Take, for example, the feeling of joy, pure inner joy.

Here is Bergson speaking:

Let us try to unravel [*démêler*] what an intensity is, one that grows or intensifies, but . . . where no physical symptom intervenes. For example, let us take the experience of inner joy or sadness. Inner joy, like passion, is not an isolated psychological fact that first occupies a corner of the psyche [*âme*] and then gradually takes up more and more space. At its lowest degree, it is more like an orientation of our awareness toward the future. Our ideas and sensations flow more rapidly, as if this attraction diminished their weight. Our movements no longer require the same effort. Finally, in extreme joy, our perceptions and memories take on an ineffable quality which we might compare to a certain heat or brightness, something so novel, that at certain moments . . . we feel a sense of astonishment simply at being alive [*un étonnement d'être*]. Thus there are several characteristic forms of purely inner joy, so many successive stages [*étapes*] which correspond to the qualitative modifications of the aggregate [*masse*] of our psychological states. And even though we do not count the number of states that each of these modifications attains, we know perfectly well whether our joy has penetrated all our impressions, or if certain ones have escaped it. Thus in the interval which separates two successive forms of joy, we set up divisions, such that this gradual passage from one form to another appears to us as different intensities of one and the same feeling [*sentiment*] that changes in degree. One could easily show that the different degrees of sadness also correspond to qualitative changes. Sadness begins by being merely an orientation toward the past, an impoverishment of our sensations and ideas, as if none of them inhered completely in the little that it gives [*tenait tout entière dans le peu qu'elle donne*], as if the future were in some sense closed to us. And it ends with a sense of being crushed, which makes us yearn for nothingness. (*EDI* 7 [10–11])

The feeling of inner joy, then, does not increase or decrease quantitatively. It involves a series of qualitative changes. When we say our joy increases, what we mean is that it changes and becomes richer, the way a melody changes when it is picked up by different instruments in the orchestral treatment of a theme. It does not really become more and more intense, displaying difference in degree, it just changes, yielding difference in kind. In its successive stages, it engages with other psychic energies, qualitatively modifying or coloring the ensemble of our psyche in various ways.[1] This is what Bergson calls the richness of a feeling, which involves many elements and their changes, and which is to be distinguished from degrees of intensity that relate to a single feeling. Again, the distinction Bergson wants to emphasize is between *difference in degree* of one and the same sensation, and *difference in kind* as feelings change qualitatively and new elements enter into the event of feeling.

It is characteristic of Bergson's writing that he introduces, in what appears to be incidental detail, an element of his argument that will subsequently take on major importance and that will be elaborated at considerable length later on.[2] Here, for example, Bergson has introduced temporality and tempo into his account of the experience of an emotion. The feeling of joy, he says, involves an orientation toward the future, accompanied by a sort of *accelerando* of our psychic activity—"our ideas and feelings flow more rapidly." The feeling of sadness, however, involves an orientation toward the past and a slowing down of mental activity, which becomes sluggish.[3] The one releases movement, the other immobilizes. We are not surprised, then, when Bergson chooses to elaborate the emotion of pure inner joy through the image of the dancer.

The Dancer

Esthetic pleasure, for Bergson, yields a feeling of inner joy. In order to help us understand this emotion and to let us "see" the "rapid flow" of ideas and sensations associated with it, Bergson asks us to consider the joy we take in the graceful movements of a dancer.

> Esthetic feelings offer us even more striking examples of this progressive intervention of new elements, visible in the fundamental emotion, and which seem to increase the degree of intensity of the

---

1. This might at first appear confusing. There is, Bergson argues, an increase of sorts when an emotion appears to us to become more intense. But it involves what he will call, in the next passage we consider, "a progressive intervention of new things," instead of an increase of one and the same thing.

2. This adds rhythm to his argument, as different strands of it become anticipated, resonate, and return; in this way, Bergson produces a countercurrent, which resists the relentlessly linear structure of discourse. He prompts us to remember and to anticipate. Bergson is asking us to consider a new mode of temporality, one that is not linear, but dynamically synthetic. His writing attempts to reinforce this conceptual shift by resisting the linearity of discursive language and writing.

3. Bergson incorporates an insight any reader of Baudelaire will appreciate. Spleen immobilizes, whereas joy releases movement.

feeling even though they only modify its nature. Let us consider the simplest one of these, the feeling of graciousness/gracefulness [*grâce*]. At first it is simply a matter of the perception of a certain ease, or facility, of movement. And since these are movements which seem to flow out of each other [*se préparent les uns les autres*] we end up finding a superior grace in movements that were anticipated in present attitudes which seem to already indicate the following ones, as if they were somehow preformed. If sudden movements lack grace it is because each one is sufficient unto itself and does not announce those to come. If curved lines are more graceful than broken ones, it is because the curved line, which is always changing direction, turns in such a way that each new direction is already indicated in the preceding one. The perception of ease of motion is thus based on the pleasure we take in arresting the forward march of time and in holding the future in the present. A third element enters in when the graceful movements obey a rhythm, and when music accompanies them. This is because, by permitting us to anticipate the artist's movements even better, the rhythm and the beat lead us to believe that we are the masters of these movements. As we almost guess the pose the dancer will assume, the dancer seems to be obeying us when s/he actually strikes that pose. The regularity of the rhythm establishes a kind of communication between us, and the periodic returns of the beat are like so many invisible threads by means of which we make this imaginary marionette dance. If it stops for a moment, our impatient hand cannot help moving as if to push it, to place it back in the heart of this movement whose rhythm dominates our thinking and our will. Thus there enters into the feeling of gracefulness a kind of physical sympathy and in analyzing the charm of this sympathy you will see that it pleases you in and of itself, through its affinity with moral sympathy, which it subtly suggests. This last element, in which the others melt together, after having in a sense announced it, explains the irresistible attraction of gracefulness. We would not understand the pleasure it affords us, if we reduced it to an economy of effort, as Spencer does. . . . But the truth is that, besides the lightness, which is a sign of mobility, in everything graceful we think we discern an indication of a virtual sympathy, directed toward us, which is always on the verge of offering itself to us. This is the very essence of superior grace. Thus the growing intensities of esthetic feeling really amount here to a variety of feelings. Each, already announced by the one that precedes it, becomes visible and then definitively eclipses the previous one. It is this qualitative progress that we interpret as a quantitative change in degree of intensity. This is because we like to keep things simple and because language is poorly equipped to render the subtleties of psychological analysis.[4] (*EDI* 9–10 [11–13])

Bergson argues, then, that instead of an intensity changing in degree, what really happens is that we experience a succession of different intensities or feelings. The graceful dancing pleases us, he suggests, because the dancer's movements seem to flow effortlessly one out of the other. Each movement seems to anticipate the next, each new direction to have been indicated by the preceding one. Music and rhythm further engage us with this flow, eliciting our sympathetic participation and, in this sense, "holding the future in the present." Bergson calls this esthetic response "sympathy," appealing to the etymological sense of the term that announces a feeling [*pathos*] with [*sym*]. Art engages us to feel with it; it engages our feelings through an experience of qualities. What we might mistake for a growing intensity of esthetic pleasure is actually "an experience of a variety of feelings. Each, already announced by the one that precedes it, becomes visible and definitively eclipses the previous one." What we experience, then, is change: differences in kind, and the passage from one qualitative state to another. Bergson calls this development a *qualitative progress*. This, as we shall come to learn, is precisely what characterizes the flow of time itself.

For Bergson, esthetic feeling is paradigmatic of feeling in general. But we should pause to appreciate the artfulness of Bergson's example. The account of the dancer's art is meant to elicit esthetic feeling in us, a feeling whose dynamic nature, however, is at the same time being sketched out for us by the movement of the dancer in Bergson's example. The description of the dancer's graceful movements engages our sympathy, giving us to feel the idea Bergson wants to convey, the idea that pure inner feeling involves the progressive movement of changes of quality. The dancer is thus both the occasion of, and the figure for, inner joy, that is, for what happens *in us* when we experience it. In this fictive scene, the dancer performs for us what goes on inside us when we experience pure quality as "qualitative progress," or the dynamic unfolding of differ-

---

4. The allusion in the preceding passage is to Herbert Spencer. For more on Spencer, see chapter 2.

ences in kind. And, implicitly, since the dancer moves in time marked out by the music and rhythm said to accompany it, the example shows us that what performs the differentiation among different qualities when we experience emotion is the flow of time itself.[5] Pure quality, as we learned from the previous passage, involves the experience of a variety of feelings, but here we grasp that this variety produces itself in flow, like the movements of the dancer, which anticipate one another as they flow forth in time. The dancer figures the change or movement, characterized by multiplicity and flow, which is specific to inner, qualitative experience in general, and figures qualitative change, difference in kind as movement through time. The movement of the dancer lets us see the reality of flowing time.

"What is dance?" asked Paul Valéry, "a form of time, the creation of a sort of singular form of time."[6] Looking back, we will recognize that the dancer figures the central notion of Bergson's thinking, which he has not yet explicitly introduced: Real Duration. This is the horizon of inner experience, of consciousness, as distinct from the objective horizon of things set in space and of our knowledge of them.

Beauty and Art

If esthetic feeling becomes the paradigm of inner experience in general, this implies an esthetics somewhat different from the Kantian esthetics of beauty. In the *Critique of Judgment*, Kant holds that the subjective experience of beauty, a judgment we make on the basis of what we perceive in nature, precedes the making of art. Bergson, to the contrary, proposes an esthetics of art and process:

5. Bergson speaks of both physical sympathy, which engages us kinesthetically through the music and rhythm, and moral sympathy, by which he means perhaps, in the case of the dance, the attunement of the rhythms of our consciousness. But he also speaks of a virtual sympathy addressed to us, which suggests something like the forest of symbols which according to Baudelaire's poem "Correspondances" address us, and not the other way around. It is as if this "virtual sympathy" is performed in Bergson's writing by the complex overdetermination of the example of the dancer, which stages for us an external scene that plays out what happens in us. Because it is an esthetic experience, and esthetic response elicits sympathy, it also provokes in us the movement it depicts. For an excellent discussion of the notion of sympathy in Bergson, see David Lapoujade, "Intuition and Sympathy in Bergson," *Pli: The Warwick Journal of Philosophy* 15 (2004): 1–18.

6. Paul Valéry, "Philosophie de la danse," *Œuvres complètes*, 1:1396 (my translation).

In order to understand how the feeling of beauty can itself exist in degrees, it would be necessary to subject it to minute analysis. Perhaps the difficulty we have defining it comes above all from the fact that we consider the beauties of nature to precede those of art. Art activity becomes nothing but a means for expressing the beautiful, while the essence of the beautiful remains mysterious. But we could ask whether nature is beautiful in any other way than . . . art and whether, in a certain sense, art does not precede nature. Without even going this far, it seems more appropriate, more rigorous, to first study beauty in works where it was produced by conscious effort and to then drop by incremental transitions from art to nature, which is also something of an artist in its own way. In adopting this point of view, one will notice, I assure you, that the goal of art is to put to rest the active, or rather the resistant, forces of our personality, and to lead us to a state of perfect docility in which we actualize the idea which has been suggested to us, or sympathize with the feeling expressed. In the procedures of art we find in an attenuated form, refined, and, in a sense, spiritualized, the procedures by which a hypnotic state is ordinarily induced. Thus, in music for example, the rhythm and the beat suspend the normal flow of our sensations and ideas by making our attention oscillate between fixed points. They so overwhelm us, that even the infinitely discrete imitation of a suffering voice is enough to fill us with extreme sadness. If musical sounds act on us more powerfully than the sounds of nature, it is because nature limits itself to expressing feelings, whereas music suggests them to us. Where does the charm of poetry come from? A poet is someone in whom feelings develop into images, and images into words. . . . Seeing these images pass back and forth before our eyes [*repasser*] we in turn experience the feeling that was their emotional equivalent. But these images would not emerge before us with such force without the regular movements of the rhythm through which our soul, rocked and put to sleep, forgets itself as in a dream in order to think and to see with the poet. (*EDI* 10–11 [13–15])

Esthetic experience becomes the paradigm for inner feeling, then, because it is defined very broadly, as "any feeling that . . . has been *sug-*

gested in us, not caused in us" (emphasis added).[7] This is why the relation between the dancer and the joy we feel is quite different from the relation between the light source and the feeling of brightness we experience. The light source causes the effect of brightness. The relation of cause and effect is a necessary one. I am holding my book and if I remove my hands from it, it will drop. Necessarily. Art, however, does not operate like a physical cause. It addresses us. It invites us into a relation of sympathy. We feel with the poet, dancer, or musician by entering into the rhythms of his or her art.

Art, then, suggests feelings to us; it does not cause them. What does Bergson mean by suggestion? Suggestion influences our attention, the way music does when it invites us into its rhythms, or the way hypnotic suggestion disarms us, so to speak, and opens us up to its influence. In a similar way, art places us in a kind of dream state. It elicits a sympathetic response on our part, a virtual participation in the feeling or idea, which is imprinted in us by the artistic manipulation of qualities through rhythm, tone, or color. Before Bergson, Baudelaire had spoken of poetry as "magical evocation [*sorcellerie évocatoire*]." It is no wonder, then, that Bergson's philosophy was so well received in the Symbolist milieu, which explicitly espoused a poetics of suggestion. "To name an object," wrote Mallarmé, "is to do away with three quarters of the joy of a poem, made to be divined little by little: to suggest it, that is the dream."[8]

Sensations and Freedom: Pleasure and Pain

Bergson makes two surprising claims about the sensations of pleasure and pain. First, these sensations not only give us information about the past (about what was pleasurable or painful) they also give us information about the future. Second, they are the beginning of freedom. "Either sensation has no reason for being," Bergson claims, "or it is the beginning of freedom." (*EDI* 25 [34])

What does Bergson mean by freedom? Free or voluntary action is defined in contrast to the automatic reaction of things, which are caused to

---

7. Here Bergson's thought comes very close to Kant's notion of form in the *Critique of Judgment*. Because we are so accustomed to causal analysis (especially in the mode of stimulus-response), let me clarify that in the distinction Bergson makes here, cause implies a necessary relation and suggestion, which includes an act of address, does not.

8. Mallarmé, *Œuvres complètes*, 869 (my translation).

react in a certain ways necessarily, according to the laws of nature. Automatism implies a necessary mechanical reaction to external stimuli. For example, if one billiard ball is stationary, and it is hit by another one coming toward it from a particular angle at a particular speed, it will move in a predictable direction at a predictable speed. In a similar way, if a jellyfish is poked, it will retract into itself. Automatically. If someone pokes me, however, I don't have to respond like the jellyfish. I can do any number of things. I might recoil like the jellyfish, but I might also strike back, or make a sarcastic remark, or light up a cigarette. Voluntary or free action occurs only in higher organisms endowed with complex sensory systems. It requires a suspension or interruption of the ongoing mechanical process in order for something different to happen in lieu of the programmed reaction—a voluntary response.

Bergson argues that pleasure and pain are felt in higher organisms because they authorize resistance to a programmed automatic response. By interrupting the automatic reaction to a given stimulus, they enable us to choose a different response. They thus enable voluntary action to take the place of automatic reaction.[9] It is for this reason that what Bergson calls affective sensations—such as the feelings of pleasure and pain—are defined as being "the beginning of freedom" (*EDI* 25 [34]).[10] Bergson claims that they give information about the future because they offer a kind of preview of the nature of the automatic reaction that *would have been about to occur*, were it not interrupted by the sensation. It provides what Bergson calls a kind of "pre-formation" of the future automatic reaction that will then be resisted and replaced by a voluntary action. The affective state, therefore, corresponds not only to the experience of the stimulus, i.e., the physical phenomenon that has already taken place in the past but also, *and above all*, to those that "are preparing to happen or would like to occur." At this point Bergson de-

9. The distinction between automatic responses and free action (or the automatic and the voluntary) is crucial to the *Essai*, whose principal issue is freedom. It will also be the focus of Bergson's subsequent study, *Matter and Memory*, and will structure the essay on laughter. The work of Pierre Janet is, of course, pertinent in this context. See his *L'automatisme psychologique: Essai de psychologie expérimentale sur les formes inférieures de l'activité humaine.*

10. Note the difference between Bergson's positions here and the ideas of British empiricists such as John Locke. Affective sensations are defined as feelings that come from within the body as opposed to "representative sensations" in which the sensation is caused by a source—the heat of the boiling water, for example—and which we call representative, because we are in the habit of describing the sensory effect in a way that represents the cause.

fines the intensity of affective sensations as the "consciousness we have of incipient involuntary (or unconscious) movements, movements which begin to take place, that are sketched out in these states, and which would have followed their free course if nature had made us automatons and not conscious beings" (*EDI* 26 [35]).[11]

This formulation suggests two important points. First, consciousness is tied from the start to affective sensation and to voluntary action in opposition to the mechanistic order of automatism, which operates in the physical world in the mode of necessity. Consciousness, by definition, already means freedom, i.e., the interruption of the mechanical order of necessity and the possibility of acting otherwise. The second important point is that this consciousness is opposed to a notion of "unconsciousness" which refers to the mechanistic order of automatic response, and therefore, implicitly, to the material world.

Qualitative Multiplicity: Other Nuances of White

When we make the mistake of considering quality as if it were quantity, when we speak, for example, of something being brighter than something else, as if brightness were the same as light, the mistake we are making is to put the quantity of the cause (light) into the effect (brightness). To give us a palpable example of how this works Bergson asks us to imagine sticking ourselves with a pin in a progressively forceful manner. The force of the cause will be felt in one hand, the hand that inserts the pin, and, in our thinking, we will transfer it to what is felt in the other hand. What happens is this: "you locate in the sensation of the left hand, which is pricked, the progressive effort of the right hand which pricks the other" (*EDI* 32 [43]), identifying the effect with the cause. Unconsciously, then, we interpret quality as quantity, intensity as *grandeur*. This example invites us to feel both cause and effect, lets us imagine concretely how we might identify the one with the other, and, at the same time, lets us clearly see the difference between them. It helps us distinguish the one from the other in our minds, just as we have learned to recognize the difference between our right and left hands.

Another example is meant to help us break the habit just illustrated, the habit of taking effects for causes, and understand what is meant by

11. The allusion is to Descartes and the idea of man as machine. We also hear echoes of the counter model—the qualitative progression figured by the dance.

the richness of a sensation, an idea that will eventually be elaborated in terms of the key concept of *qualitative multiplicity* (*EDI* 39 [53]).

> Consider closely a sheet of paper illuminated by four candles, and then extinguish three out of the four candles one at a time. . . . You say that the surface remains white and that the brightness diminishes. You know, of course, that one candle has just been extinguished; or, if you don't know it, you have often noted an analogous change in the aspect of a white surface when the lighting was reduced. But suspend, for a moment, your memories and your habits of language: what you have really observed is not the reduced illumination of a white surface, it is a layer of shadow passing over this surface at the moment the candle was put out. This shadow is a reality for your consciousness, just as the light is. If you call the first surface white, in all its brightness, you will have to give another name to what you now see, since it is something else. If we could speak in this way, we might call it another nuance of white. . . . We have become habituated by our past experience, and also by physical theories, into considering black as an absence, or at least a minimum, of light sensation, and the successive nuances of gray as increasing intensities of white light. Well, black has just as much reality for our consciousness as white, and the decreasing intensities of white light illuminating a given surface would be, for a fresh consciousness [*une conscience non prévenue*] so many different nuances, analogous to the colors of the spectrum. (*EDI* 39–40 [53–54])

This example invites us to consider a new way of thinking. Instead of seeing variations in brightness as increases or decreases in the quantity of a single term, whiteness, we are asked to consider the range of nuances that exist between the two poles of black and white.

What do we experience as one candle after another is extinguished? Does the surface remain white and does the brightness of the light simply diminish? This is the way we are taught to think, since we know that candlepower is the cause of our sensation, and that this has been progressively diminished in degree. Bergson, however, asks us to redescribe the resulting visual effect with attention to nuances of qualitative difference. Since black is just as much a reality to our eyes as white, we could say that the decrease in the quantity of light lets us see different nuances on a spectrum which goes from black to white—nuances of white, nuances of gray or even perhaps, nuances of black.

The experiment points out something else as well. The qualitative changes we perceive—the nuances of white or gray—do not correspond exactly to the conditions of quantity of light. We perceive a change, another nuance of white or gray, only when the decrease in light corresponds with the creation of a new quality.

What proves this is that the change is not continuous in the sensation as it is in the external cause. The light can grow or diminish for a certain length of time without the illumination of our white surface seeming to change. It will only appear to change, in effect, when the increase or decrease of the external light source is sufficient to create a new quality. The variations of brightness of a given color . . . would thus reduce to qualitative changes, had we not formed the habit of putting the cause into the effect, and of substituting for our naïve impression what experience and science have taught us. We speak of so many degrees of saturation. In fact, if the diverse intensities of a color correspond to so many different nuances which occur between this color and black . . . then degrees of saturation are like intermediate nuances between this same color and pure white. Every color, we would say, can be considered in its dual aspect, from the point of view of black and from the point of view of white. Black would be to intensity what white is to saturation. (*EDI* 40–41 [54])

Bergson asks us to see difference *in kind*—qualitative nuances of darkness and lightness—where previously we had considered only *difference in degree* of one and the same term, whiteness. It is just this sense of qualitative nuance, this sense of a multiplicity of different qualities or states of consciousness that Bergson attributes to the inner experiences of consciousness in general. Consciousness, then, would correspond to the piece of paper, as a scene of nuances of qualitative change, that is, of *qualitative multiplicity*. Once again, then, the example plays a double role in Bergson's text. It introduces a concept—qualitative multiplicity—performed by the shifting nuances of white or gray. But it also figures the internal process of consciousness itself, giving us another anticipatory figure of what will become the concept of Real Duration.

The case of the four candles has opened up the concept of "whiteness" and replaced it with a multiplicity of nuances that display the richness of qualitative experience. It has also helped us experience the independence of quality from quantity. To this extent Bergson has successfully called into question a fundamental assumption held by the psychophysicists he opposes: the equivalence between quality and quantity which would enable the former to be reduced to the latter, such that mind can be reduced to brain and consciousness objectified like a thing. In fact, Bergson affirms, to presuppose the equivalence between quality and quantity is dead wrong: "There is no point of contact between the nonextended and the extended, between quality and quantity. One can interpret the one in terms of the other, pose the one as the equivalent of the other; but sooner or later, in the beginning or in the end, the conventional character of this assimilation must be recognized" (*EDI* 52 [70]).

What does he mean by the "conventional character" of this association? He means that the concrete experience has been covered over by a symbolic representation of it, either in language or by the tools or units of measurement. When this happens, Bergson argues, we lose track of the feeling itself.

By the end of the first chapter of the *Essai sur les données immédiates de la conscience* we realize that Bergson's argument has been specifically directed against the psychophysicists, the followers of Fechner, all along.[12] From Bergson's point of view, this school of thought exaggerates the illusions of common sense, giving them a pseudo-scientific vali-

---

12. The habitual, or commonsense, error of failing to distinguish between physical cause and psychological effect is the explicit presupposition of proponents of the psychological school of Photometrics, which purports to measure sensory effect. Bergson proceeds to critique the assumptions and methodologies of this school of thought. What enables his colleague Gustav Fechner to claim to measure not the external cause of sensation but the psychological reaction to this cause is that he divides sensation up into equal units, which he designates as minimal sensations. He defines this in terms of the minimal change necessary in order for a difference in quality to be perceived. In other words, Fechner's theory has substituted a conventional representation (i.e., a designated unit of sensation) for the direct or immediate experience of the sensation itself. What is going on here is what Bergson calls "a symbolic interpretation of quality as quantity, a more or less crude evaluation of the number of sensations that could occur between two given sensations" (*EDI* 51 [69]). As Bergson will attempt to demonstrate at some length, there is really no interval at all, only a dynamic passage from one state to another. Psychophysical theories, in Bergson's view, go round and round in a vicious circle. They "rely on a theoretical postulate that condemns them to an experimental verification, and they can only be experimentally verified if one admits their initial postulate" (*EDI* 52 [70]). And, of course, from Bergson's point of view the initial postulate, namely, that there is an equivalence between quality and quantity, is wrong.

dation, which encourages the tendency to "objectify our subjective states of consciousness" and to measure subjective states as if they were things. Illusions of common sense are one thing. Claims to scientific truth are quite another, and much more dangerous. These must be vigorously contested philosophically, Bergson implies, or we will find ourselves living in a culture of automatons. Bergson is willing to cede to science certain domains of thought previously guided by philosophy. But he insists on designating for philosophical inquiry alone areas of human experience that pertain to subjective feeling. This terrain must be protected from an intellectual imperialism of scientific methods and authority.

Bergson concludes his first chapter by returning to a distinction he made earlier between representative and affective sensations. If the former are taken to be measurable, by the transfer of measurable cause to effect (based on an imagined equivalence between the two, that is, between quantity and quality) the latter can be considered pure quality, since they cannot be attributed to any external cause. Bergson defines pure quality in the following way: "The more or less considerable multiplicity of simple psychic facts that we discern at the heart of the fundamental state" (*EDI* 54 [73]). He calls this a confused perception in contrast to the *acquired perception* of the representative sensation. But the conceptual distinction between the two is virtual because, in actual fact, the two types of sensation usually present themselves in some sort of combination. Thus "the idea of intensity is situated at the point where two currents meet. One brings us the idea of extensive quantity [*grandeurs extensives*] from the outside. The other has gone to the depths of consciousness to find the image of an internal multiplicity and to bring it to the surface. It remains to be seen just what kind of image this is, whether it can be identified with number, or whether it is something radically different" (*EDI* 54 [73]).

This will be the focus of the second chapter of Bergson's study, where we will no longer consider states of consciousness in isolation from one another, but rather in their concrete multiplicity, that is, as they unfold in pure duration. It is here that multiplicity is revealed to lie at the core of the notion of duration in its radical difference from space.

In his conclusion Bergson anticipates the line of argument he will follow in chapter two: the attack on the spatial presuppositions of Western thought. He diagnoses presuppositions concerning space at the heart of the project of quantification. In the next chapter, then, the difference quantity/quality will be rephrased in relation to the difference between space and time, time rethought in radical independence from spatial presuppositions of any kind: Real Duration. The key to thinking about flowing time in this way lies in the notion Bergson will call "confused perception" (*EDI* 54 [73]), tied to the notion of confused multiplicity. To think quality, then, without quantifying it, it will be necessary to think time without spatializing it, and to do this one must find a way to think multiplicity independently of number. This will be the task of chapter two. "Just as we asked ourselves what might be the intensity of a representative sensation if we had not projected onto it the idea of its cause," Bergson explains in the conclusion of this chapter:

> so we will have to inquire now what the multiplicity of our inner states becomes, what form duration takes [*quelle forme affecte la durée*] when one suspends the notion of the space in which it develops. This second question is important in a different way from the first. For, if the confusion of quality with quantity were limited to isolated events of consciousness it would create obscurities, as we have seen, rather than problems. But in invading the series of our psychological states, in introducing space into our conception of duration, it corrupts, at their very source, our representations of external change and internal change, of movement and of freedom. Whence the sophisms of the Eleatic school, whence the problem of free will. We will insist on the second point. But instead of seeking to resolve the question, we will reveal the illusion of those who pose it. (*EDI* 54–55 [73–74])

This is in accord with Bergson's second fundamental methodological procedure: to show the ways in which questions have been poorly posed, leading to misleading results, and wrong thinking.

In this first chapter, then, Bergson's task has been to create a discursive (or conceptual) framework for thinking interiority. The first step has been to delimit this mode of experience and to radically distinguish it from our encounters with things in the outside world. For heuristic purposes, Bergson has spoken in this chapter as if the distinction between inside and outside, or between inner experience and experience of the external world, were absolute. At the end of the chapter he acknowledges that actual experience occurs at the cusp, as it were, where inside and outside meet. Bergson will return to the hybrid nature of actual experience in his conclusion to the *Essai*. The principal task of his argument, however, is to focus our attention on the side of experience that tends to get neglected and that risks being obliterated by mechanistic psychologies: inner experience. If outer (or "objective") experience is considered in terms of quantity, then by the same logic inner experience should be considered pure quality, since it cannot be attributed to any external cause.

Up to this point, Bergson has spoken as if states of consciousness were isolated phenomena, as if they had discrete boundaries and could be delimited from one another. In the next chapter, however, he will approach states of consciousness concretely, as they flow in time in their concrete variety and multiplicity. But at this point we come across a real puzzle: how to understand the notion of multiplicity specific to inner experience? How to conceive of this multiplicity without falling back into the language of quantity and unwittingly bringing back in an assumption of equivalence between quality and quantity, inside and outside? Bergson asks if this notion of multiplicity can be identified with number or whether it is something radically different.

As we shall see in the next chapter, the examination of this puzzle of concrete multiplicity will transform our conception of time. It will lead us to understand that the concept of time we usually rely upon is only adequate to descriptions of the external world and that lived time is something quite different: Real Duration. The notion of concrete multiplicity is revealed to lie at the core of duration in its radical difference from what we usually call "time" and from our conception of space. Bergson's second chapter will launch a frontal attack on the spatial presuppositions of Western thought that underlie the culture's excessive reliance on quantification.

As we shall see, the difference between quantity and quality will be rephrased in terms of the difference between space and time. To think quality, then, without quantifying it, one has to think time without space. This challenge will yield the concept of Real Duration. To entertain this thought, one must think multiplicity independently of space. This means that we will have to find a way to think multiplicity without the concept of number! This will be the task of chapter 2 of the *Essai*.

3.2. Chapter 2 of the *Essai*
"Of the Multiplicity of States of Consciousness:
The Idea of Duration"

If, as Bergson claims, feelings or intensities cannot be identified, counted, and compared like things in the world, how are we to understand them? How, or where, do they occur, since they do not take place in space? And if this experience is characterized in terms of what Bergson calls "internal multiplicity," what might this mean? Does it have anything to do with number? Or can the concept of number even be applied to it? If not, how are we to understand this kind of multiplicity? Bergson begins his second chapter with a reflection on number. He will go on to demonstrate that counting presupposes an imagined horizon of space, and that when we measure time, we have never really left this spatial horizon.

Counting Sheep

What happens when a shepherd counts sheep? In order to count them, the shepherd ignores the specific traits of individual animals, with which s/he is perhaps quite familiar, and considers all the sheep to be identical. The animals become equivalent units that can be accumulated to form a sum, instead of being flesh and blood creatures. The shepherd situates these units in an imagined space. For to advance the count, as one passes from one animal-unit to the next, one has to hold on to the sheep already counted.

Bergson's analysis of counting yields this surprising conclusion: we count in space, not in time. The concept of number implies juxtaposition in space. In order for the numbers to grow as I advance in my counting, I have to hold onto the successive images or representations of the units I have already counted, and therefore I juxtapose them with each of the new units I evoke in my mind. The juxtaposition occurs in space (*EDI* 57–58 [77]). Even when we think we are counting in time, we are actually representing units in space.

If we obtain a sum by the successive consideration of different terms, it is necessary that each of these terms remain, as we pass on to the next one, and that it wait, so to speak, to be added to the others: how can it wait if it is only an instant of duration? And where would it wait, if we did not localize it in space? Involuntarily, we fix each of the moments we count to a point in space. For it is only on this condition that the abstract units can form a sum. Any clear idea of number implies a vision in space (EDI 59 [79]). In other words, counting requires juxtaposition, juxtaposition implies simultaneity, and simultaneity presupposes space.

Tracking Differences Again

(1) Distinct and Confused Multiplicities. Bergson distinguishes two sorts of multiplicity. One can be manipulated through number and counting and pertains to the world of things that exist in space. He calls this *distinct multiplicity*. The other, which characterizes inner affective states, will be called confused multiplicity, because its elements are fused together. *Confused multiplicity* has nothing to do with space or with number, and everything to do with the radical force of time that occurs, as we shall see, as Pure Duration.

(2) Immediate Consciousness and Reflective Consciousness. Bergson also distinguishes between two sorts of consciousness. The first, *immediate consciousness* (associated with the title of this work, *Les données immédiates de la conscience*) refers to the way something feels to us directly, before we stop and think about it, try to communicate it to someone, or represent it symbolically in any way. The second, reflective consciousness, involves thinking and implies the use of the tools that enable us to think and to know: language, logic, mathematics, and other symbols or means of representation. Reflective consciousness objectifies experiences. It treats them the same way it considers objects in space.

(3) Time and Duration. Reflective consciousness and immediate consciousness each imply a distinct notion of time. Reflective consciousness thinks time in terms of space, as we have just seen in the example of counting cited above.

> Now, let us note that when we speak of time, more often than not we think of a homogeneous milieu where the events or facts of consciousness line themselves up, juxtaposing themselves as if in space, and succeed in forming a distinct multiplicity. (*EDI 67* [90])[13]

13. If intensive quantities are, as Bergson has tried to demonstrate in chapter 1, but a conventional, symbolic treatment of inner experience (inner experience as it is repre-

Thus, what we are in the habit of calling "time" is really the equivalent of space. Immediate consciousness, however, does not think time as space; it experiences it as Real Duration. The point of the *Essai* is to introduce us to the notion of Real Duration, which we can approach only through inner states, that is through immediate, or purely qualitative, experience. Duration will involve a concept of time that is radically independent of space.

Intuition

If Bergson's thought is a philosophy of intuition, "something quite distinct from cognition or understanding, from thinking as it takes place in words and in numbers," this is not simply because, as Bertrand Russell implied, this French philosopher prefers fuzzy or poetic thinking to rigorous understanding. It is because the subject of inquiry is duration, a notion of time radically independent of space and for this reason completely inaccessible to reflective consciousness. Cognitive thinking represents things in space—this is what all forms of symbolic representation do—which is why it cannot think duration, but only time. Duration can only be lived or, perhaps, as post-structuralists used to say, "written." This is what Bergson is trying to do: to bring to philosophical awareness what has been absolutely suppressed by thought and is structurally inaccessible to it: the radical force of the time of becoming. In this sense, Bergson anticipates the deconstructive philosophers who undertake a critique of phenomenology. Since thinking implies presence, how does one think the critique of presence—except by writing it? What are Bergson's writing strategies? The same ones he has been using all along: the presentation of scenes with multiple valences that anticipate the ideas he will eventually deploy, giving us time to feel them or to live them concretely before picking them up again discursively. To this end Bergson provides thought experiments for the reader, in an effort to stimulate the reader's intuition of that which cannot be presented discursively through concepts.

---

sented, not as it is felt) then this conception of time is to real duration as intensive quantities are to the immediate experience of qualities or intensities. "Would not time understood in this way [i.e., as moments juxtaposed in space] be to the multiplicity of our inner states what intensity is to certain of them [i.e., representative sensations] a sign, a symbol, absolutely distinct from real duration [*la vraie durée*]?" (*EDI* 67 [90]).

We are thus going to ask consciousness to isolate itself from the outside world, and, by means of a vigorous effort of abstraction, to become itself once again. We will ask it these questions: does the multiplicity of our inner states bear the slightest analogy to the multiplicity of units of a number? Does real duration have the slightest relation to space? Surely, our analysis of the idea of number should, at the very least, make us doubt this analogy. For if time, as it is represented by reflective consciousness, is a medium in which our states of consciousness succeed one another distinctly in a way that would let them be counted, and if, on the other hand, our conception of number ends up scattering in space everything that can be directly counted, it is to be presumed that time, understood in the sense of a milieu in which one distinguishes things and where one counts them, is nothing but space. (EDI 67–68 [90–91])

Intuition is no sloppy matter. It involves a "vigorous effort of abstraction." Indeed, intuition, as Bergson writes it, performs an operation of critique that cuts to the bone. As Deleuze has pointed out, it implies method.[14]

Homogeneity/Heterogeneity

For reflective consciousness, time is nothing but space and space is a homogeneous milieu or medium, detached from any content. Immediate experience, however, starts from a sense of radical heterogeneity. "In fact, qualitative differences are everywhere in nature . . . heterogeneity . . . constitutes the very foundation of our experience" (EDI 72 [97]). For immediate consciousness the given is not an empty uniform scene for the representation of objects, as in Kant. It is a full, heterogeneous real. The perception of qualitative differences in immediate consciousness is singular and concrete. Our experience of qualities is unique each time. We never feel the same thing twice! Indeed, Bergson even proposes that the conception of homogenous space, or of time as space, "seems to re-

14. "Intuition is the method of Bergsonism. Intuition is neither a feeling, an aspiration, nor a disorderly sympathy, but a fully developed method, one of the most fully developed methods in philosophy. It has strict rules, constituting that which Bergson calls 'precision' in philosophy." See Gilles Deleuze, *Bergsonism*, trans. Hugh Tomlinson and Barbara Habberjam, 13.

quire a kind of reaction against this heterogeneity that constitutes the very foundation of our experience" (*EDI* 72 [97]). As if space were a defense mechanism set up against the radical force of time! Whatever we call them (and it is tempting to think in terms of consciousness and the unconscious), Bergson writes: "We know two quite different realities. One is heterogeneous, the realm of sensible qualities. The other is homogenous, which is space. This, strictly conceived by human intelligence, lets us make clear distinctions, lets us count and abstract, and perhaps even speak" (*EDI* 73 [97]).[15]

How can we say that time is space? This step of the argument is important. Bergson holds that any homogeneous milieu should be considered as space—even time. This is because it implies an absence of qualities to the extent that it is considered to be homogeneous. Thus, if one considers time as a homogenous milieu in which states of consciousness appear to unfold, one implies simultaneity and to this extent refuses duration considered as the flowing forth of time.

The conventional concept of time, Bergson suggests, is a "bastard concept" which results from an intrusion of an idea of space into the domain of pure consciousness (*EDI* 73 [98]), which reduces time to space. As soon as we begin to think and to speak, we unconsciously fall back into a spatial framework. "Time, in the form of an indefinite and homogeneous milieu, is but the phantom of that space which obsesses reflexive consciousness" (*EDI* 74 [99]). Space is the great unconscious presupposition of Western thought. This is the leitmotif of the *Essai*.

The fundamental difference, then, between external things and inner states is that external things are delimited from one another because they are implicitly juxtaposed in an ideal space. Inner states, however, have no such boundaries. They overflow into one another, interpenetrate, even as they succeed one another. Bergson arrives at the following definition of Pure or Real Duration, that is, duration that is not compromised by a surreptitious contamination by the homogeneous character of space: "Pure duration is the form taken by the succession of our inner states of consciousness when our self [*notre moi*] lets itself live, when it abstains from establishing a separation between the present state and anterior states (*EDI* 74–75 [100])." Paradoxically, then, to

---

15. Bergson's formulation suggests the Freudian distinction between conscious and unconscious processes. Freud, of course, emphasizes that there is no negation, for example, in unconscious mental life, the life of dreams. The emphasis on heterogeneity anticipates Georges Bataille.

think the temporality of duration we must first be willing to give up our conceptual separation of past and present in order to conceive of temporal synthesis *per se*.

From Dance to Music: Melody

Duration implies a mode of temporal synthesis that is different from the linear narrative development of past-present-future. It involves a temporal synthesis of memory that knits temporal dimensions together, as in a melody. Melody, which implies a certain mode of organization, is a figure for duration.[16] The identification of a melody implies an act of temporal synthesis. Melody performs this work to the extent that it binds past, present, and future together in a radically singular way.

> Could we not say that, if these notes succeed one another, we still perceive them as if they were inside one another [*les unes dans les autres*] and their ensemble were like a living being whose parts, though distinct, interpenetrate through the very effect of their solidarity? The proof is that we break the rhythm by holding one note of the melody too long. It is not its exaggerated length as such that will avert us to our mistake, but rather the qualitative change brought to the musical phrase as a whole. One could thus conceive succession without distinction as a mutual penetration, a solidarity, an intimate organization of elements of which each would be representative of the whole, indistinguishable from it, and would not isolate itself from the whole except for abstract thought.[17] (*EDI* 75 [101])

Melody is the figure of confused multiplicity, the figure of duration. We are dealing with a succession of qualities and nuances of feeling, but "a succession without distinction" (*EDI* 75 [101]). Elements overlap and

---

16. Bergson borrows a concept of organization from the biological discourse of Claude Bernard.

17. The figure of the melody suggests the experience of the character Roquentin in Sartre's novel *Nausea*. He becomes attached to the melody of "Some of These Days," which throws him into a different experience of time. The structure of the melody—or of confused multiplicity—as Bergson presents it here, also evokes Sartre's political concept of the "group in fusion" that he elaborates in the *Critique of Dialectical Reason*. See my *Literary Polemics*, chap. 3.

interpenetrate in a peculiar solidarity.[18] Bergson's point is that the very idea of an order of succession implies spatial orientation. "If one establishes an order within the successive, it means that succession becomes simultaneous and projects itself into space" (*EDI* 76 [101–102]).[19]

The metaphor of the musical phrase conveys the notion of ensemble that attaches to the experience of duration, and to the idea of heterogeneous multiplicity—a multiplicity without homogeneity, in which states or feelings overlap or interpenetrate one another, instead of being organized into a distinct succession. Ultimately this interpenetration will be explicated in terms of the temporal synthesis of duration. The art of the dance has given way to the musical phrase, because Bergson now wants to evoke the movements of a purely mental synthesis. He invites us to consider movement that does not occur in space.

The Shooting Star

What can it mean to speak about movement that does not occur in space? This is what Bergson will call "real movement" or "mobility" (*EDI* 83 [111]), something quite distinct from the space that is moved through. Think of what we experience when we suddenly see a shooting star:

> In this extremely rapid movement, the dissociation operates by itself between a space, which has been traversed, which appears to us as a line of fire, and the absolutely indivisible sensation of movement or mobility. . . . In short, there are two elements to be distinguished in movement, the space traversed and the action by means of which one has crossed this space, the successive positions and the synthesis of these positions. The first of these elements is a homogeneous quantity. The second only has reality in our consciousness. It is . . . a quality or intensity. (*EDI* 83 [111–112])

The example of the shooting star registers the distinction that Bergson is drawing out. Here the space traveled is vast but the speed is so rapid that our sense of the actual movement of the star is almost instan-

18. This implies the kind of temporal synthesis that is performed by memory. This is precisely the point Bergson will pick up in his second major work, *Matter and Memory*.
19. See pages 77–78 in the original and pages 103–104 in the Pogson translation concerning melody.

taneous. Whereas the distance traveled can be measured in space—we can map out the successive positions of the trajectory—the mobility itself is felt as intensity. It performs the synthesis of the positions moved through. Mobility is not a thing, it is an action. As such, it is indivisible. It cannot be divided up into units, counted, or mapped onto space. The shooting star is another figure for duration, understood as an act of temporal synthesis performed by, or as, consciousness. This synthesis requires memory. But the point Bergson wants to stress here is that memory does not act like a slide projector, which displays past moments in distinct isolation from one another. It is cinematic. It performs an operation of temporal synthesis.[20] The problem with scientific discourse is that it slices up time and movement into isolated positions, the way a slide projector does.[21] Science eliminates qualitative features of experience. It ignores duration, the qualitative element of time, and mobility, the qualitative element of movement.[22]

The Problem of Language

To return to the differences we are tracking, then, distinct multiplicity pertains to things in space, things we can count. Confused multiplicity—which pertains to interiority and duration—is a temporal multiplicity, associated with operations of temporal synthesis. It has nothing to do with number. Why is it so hard for us to keep this distinction straight? Bergson explains that it is because language constantly confuses the two.[23] Thus the problem is not so much space per se, but our symbolic representation of space and the way this contaminates all our

20. The cinematic images for memory appear in *Matter and Memory*. Deleuze picks this up and discusses them in his *Cinema 1: The Movement Image*, trans. Hugh Tomlinson and Barbara Habberjam, and *Cinema 2: The Time-Image*, trans. Hugh Tomlinson and Barbara Habberjam.

21. Bergson goes on to discuss the paradox of Zeno in detail, attempting to show that it is not a real paradox but a function of a badly posed problem and a misconception of movement which involves a confusion between quantity (the interval crossed) and quality (the act of crossing). Scientific discourse often makes the same mistake, he adds, judging by the ways astronomy and mechanics treat questions of time, movement, and speed (*EDI* 86 [115]).

22. "When science operates on time and movement it does so only on condition that it first eliminate the essential, qualitative, element, duration when it comes to time, and mobility when it comes to movement" (*EDI* 86 [115]).

23. Bergson's critique of language, which we return to at greater length further on, provides the philosophical basis for what Jean Paulhan terms the "terrorist" literary position in *Les fleurs de Tarbes*.

concepts of thought by imposing an implied framework of homogeneity upon them.

The difference between time and duration is thus not exactly a difference between two concepts. It is more exact to say that time is the *concept* of what we experience directly as Pure Duration. *Time is the symbolic image of Pure Duration*. It stands in for it in reflective consciousness; it is what duration becomes when we think and speak it. In actuality, we are almost always caught up in modes of symbolic representation.[24] This is what prevents us from having intuitive knowledge of real duration and a richer experience of the heterogeneous world of singular qualities. And this is so because:

> Our external, and, so to speak, social life has more practical importance for us than our individual, inner experience. We instinctively tend to solidify our impressions in order to express them in language. It is for this reason that we confuse the feeling itself, which is in a perpetual mode of becoming, with its external object, which is permanent. Above all we confuse it with the word that expresses this object. Just as the fleeting duration of our inner self fixes itself by projecting itself into homogeneous space, so our impressions are constantly changing, wrapping themselves around the external object, which is its cause, adopting its precise contours and its immobility. (EDI 97 [130])

It is above all language that alienates us from direct experience.[25] Language imposes the horizon of *distinct multiplicity* on what we would experience directly as *confused multiplicity*. It carves up our experiences into objects designated by words. Words exist because of their iterability; this means that they stabilize, or fix, our experience when they attach names to it. Bergson will go on to show that language simplifies and reduces experience, evacuating mobility of impressions, nuance, complexity, and qualitative richness. In this sense, Bergson's critique of

24. This progressive encroachment of symbolic thought over immediate experience is one way to understand Proust's statement, toward the end of *Combray*, that real experience only happens in childhood, and that the Hawthorne flowers Marcel saw later in life were not real Hawthorne flowers: "The flowers I am shown today for the first time do not seem to me to be real flowers," in *Swann's Way*, trans. Lydia Davis, 188.

25. See Mark Poster, *Existential Marxism in Postwar France: From Sartre to Althusser*, 49, concerning the importance of Bergson's concept of alienation for Lukács's concept of reification, as well as for Sartre in *Being and Nothingness*.

language parallels the critique of number already given. It is the very fact of iteration, a structural feature of language in general, that is problematic. For this is fundamentally at odds with the radical concrete singularity of qualitative experience.

The Divided Self: Phantoms and Dreams

Thus the two types of multiplicity, the two notions of duration (what Bergson elsewhere calls time and Pure Duration) correspond to two modes of subjective experience, and, ultimately, to two instances of the self: a superficial self that conforms to social conventions and the pressures of language, and a passionate self, in touch with the heterogeneous real. In this context, dream experience becomes a figure for immediate experience. It withdraws us from the world of reflective consciousness and gives us access to duration, just as art, earlier, was said to disarm us of our usual defenses and to open us to the influence of suggestion.

In short, the self only touches the external world by its surface. . . . That is why our superficial psychological life unfolds in a homogeneous milieu, without this mode of representation costing us much effort. . . . What clearly proves that our ordinary conception of duration [i.e., what Bergson elsewhere calls "time"] results from a gradual invasion of space into the domain of pure consciousness, is that, in order to remove from the self the faculty of perceiving homogeneous time, it is enough to detach this superficial layer from the psychic events that it uses to regulate itself. Dream places us precisely in these conditions. For sleep, by slowing down the play of our organic functions, mainly modifies the surface of communication between the self and external things. We no longer measure duration, we feel it. From quantity it returns to the state of quality. Mathematical determinations of elapsed time no longer occur, giving way to a confused instinct, capable, as with all instincts, of committing enormous errors [grosses méprises] and also sometimes of proceeding with amazing assuredness. (EDI 93–94 [125–127])

It is thus not only a question of two conceptions of multiplicity, and two conceptions of time, but of two distinct selves.

Beneath homogeneous duration [i.e., "time"],[26] extensive symbol of real duration, an attentive psychology discerns a duration whose heterogeneous moments interpenetrate; beneath the numerical multiplicity of conscious states, there is a qualitative multiplicity; beneath the self of well defined states, there is a self where succession implies fusion and organization.[27] But we usually content ourselves with the former, that is, with the shadow of the self, projected into homogeneous space. Consciousness . . . substitutes the symbol for the reality, or only perceives the reality through the symbol. As the self, refracted and subdivided in this manner, lends itself much better to the demands of social life in general and of language in particular, it is preferred, and little by little one loses sight of the fundamental self. (*EDI* 95–96 [128])

The Task of Philosophy

How might one reconnect with the passionate self? Through a "vigorous effort of analysis." The task is to isolate living psychological facts from their symbolic representations by means of analysis, and then to approach this real, or immediate, experience through an effort of intuition. This is the task of philosophy as Bergson sees it, and we recognize in this account exactly the process Bergson has been putting us through. Analysis entails a critique of concepts, which identifies them, precisely, as symbolic representations. Intuition, in turn, is enabled through the examples, or thought experiments, Bergson addresses directly to us. These function rhetorically to figure living psychological facts, such as qualitative multiplicity, duration, mobility, etc. Bergson does not conceive of intuition as an easy return to naïve experience. To make contact with immediate, or pre-reflexive, experience is a philosophical task that requires effort. It involves something like swimming upstream against a very strong current—the obsession with space that haunts Western thought, and the structure of language, which infuses space into concepts and immobilizes thought.[28]

26. When Bergson writes "homogeneous duration," he means what he elsewhere refers to as "time," as distinct from what he calls "Pure Duration" or "Real Duration." "Time" and "homogeneous duration" amount to the projection of time onto space.

27. Again, Bergson uses the term "organization" in the sense of organic solidarity (in the sense of Claude Bernard) not in the sense of rational structure.

28. Bergson writes, "space . . . obsesses reflexive consciousness" (*EDI* 74 [99]).

Our perceptions, sensations, emotions, and ideas present themselves in a double aspect: one is clear, precise, but impersonal. The other is confused, infinitely mobile, and inexpressible, because language would not know how to grasp it and fix its mobility, nor how to adapt it to its banal form without making it fall into the common domain. If we end up distinguishing two forms of multiplicity, two forms of duration, it is clear that each of the facts of consciousness, taken independently, will have to display a different aspect according to whether one considers it in relation to a distinct multiplicity or of a confused multiplicity, qualitative time, where it produces itself, or in quantitative time, where it projects itself.[29] (*EDI 96* [129])

Passion and Terror (and Language Again)

The problem with language is not just the instrumental use to which it is so often put in what Mallarmé called the "crude [*brut*]" state of language.[30] It is the fact that language imposes a repetition of the same just by the act of naming. This is at odds with the radically concrete singularity of qualitative experience.

A particular taste, a particular scent, pleased me when I was a child and repels me today. Nevertheless, I give the same name to the sensation, and I speak as if the scent and the taste had remained identical, and as if it were just my tastes that had

29. This adds yet another important precision. A mental phenomenon can be considered from two points of view. One is a horizon of representation (we might think of Kant and his notion of phenomenon) and the other is something more like an ontological horizon (something closer to the late thinking of Heidegger) because it is the horizon through which things or events come into being, produce or engender themselves. To return to the Kantian dichotomy, we see that Bergson places what Kant might call the "noumenal" in an ontological register of autoproduction, which is dynamic and mobile. The noumenal would not be considered a sort of fixed essence, and to this extent there could not be any ultimate phenomenology (in the sense of Husserl) of immediate experience because there is no fixed or stable essence to be known. Moreover, what Kant would call the noumenal (i.e., that which is not constructed through representation) is not beyond knowledge or experience; it is in a sense before it (in French we could say *en deça*). It belongs to the dual aspect of the fact of consciousness and attaches to a particular point of view. Bergson returns to just this perspective, i.e., the relation of his thinking to Kant's distinction between the phenomenal and the noumenal, in his Conclusion.

30. In "Crise de vers," Mallarmé speaks of the "double state of speech, crude or immediate here, essential there [*le double état de la parole, brut ou immédiat ici, là essentiel*]." See *Œuvres complètes*, 368.

changed. . . . I solidify this sensation . . . but in reality there are neither identical sensations nor a multiplicity of tastes. For sensations and tastes appear to me as things as soon as I isolate them and name them. For in the human soul [*âme*] there is hardly anything but progressions [*des progrès*]. What needs to be said is that all sensations are modified through repetition [*en se répétant*] and if it does not appear to me to change from one day to the next, it is because I now perceive it through the object that was its cause, or through the word that translates it. This influence of language on sensation is more profound than is generally believed. . . . The brutal word, which stores up what is stable, common, and therefore impersonal in human impressions, crushes, or at least covers over, the delicate and fleeting impressions of our individual consciousness. To fight back equally well armed, these would have to express themselves by very precise words. But these words, as soon as they are formed, would turn on the sensation that engendered them. Invented in order to bear witness to the instability of the sensation, they would impose their own stability. (EDI 97–98 [131–132])

It is in the context of this critique of language that Bergson makes his strongest claim yet concerning the intimate relationship between intensities and time: one never experiences the same sensation twice. All sensations are modified through repetition for the very fact of recurrence alters the nature of the sensation. It is only the influence of language on sensation that makes us think otherwise. Language makes us believe in the invariability of our sensations because invariably, it provides the same name. The only way to fight back against the conventionality of language would be to seek a very precise language. This, of course, was the solution of Mallarmé who sought to counteract the ordinary state of language [*l'état brut*] with a pure state of poetic language, which operates through suggestion, not naming.[31]

---

31. Proust also aspired to retrieve fleeting impressions in all their singular richness through recourse to very precise language, deployed in very long sentences that made his language seem all the more singular. And yet one can't help feeling that Marcel is closer to the spirit of the passage just cited when, still unable to find any words to express the powerful emotion he feels at the beauty of the scene before him, he is only able to utter "Wow! Wow! Wow!" poking his umbrella into the air for emphasis. See *Swann's Way*, 159.

Bergson's critique of language had repercussions in the literary world, as we might imagine. In an important essay, *Les Fleurs de Tarbes*, Jean Paulhan identified two competing literary positions, which he called Terror (roughly aligned with romanticism) and Rhetoric (roughly aligned with classicism). As Paulhan indicates, Bergson's critique of language gives authority to the position of Terror, characterized as the writer's desire to escape from the conventions of language and the aspiration toward direct or original expression. In an analysis which influenced the subsequent literary theory of Maurice Blanchot, Paulhan revealed the paradox in which these two positions are caught up. "No writer is more preoccupied with words than the one who is determined at every turn to get rid of them."[32] As we have seen, Bergson had already announced this insight when he spoke of the need to fight back against the brutal effects of language on sensation by using "very precise words." While Paulhan notes that even the most precise words, when repeated, risk becoming cliché, this too is adumbrated by Bergson who indicates above that even newly invented expressions, chosen for their extreme precision, impose their own stability when repeated. Thus, if Bergson starts by articulating the terrorist position here—accusing "the brutal word" which renders experience banal or cliché—he goes on, according to the logic that Paulhan will make explicit, to suggest that the only way to fight back is to give even closer attention to language.

What suffers most at the hands of the conventions of language, and the dull constraints of reflective consciousness, are the passions. Nowhere is the crushing of immediate consciousness more striking, Bergson continues, than in the field of love:

> A violent love, a deep melancholy invades our soul, provoking a thousand diverse elements that melt together, interpenetrate, without definite contours, without the least tendency to separate themselves one from another. Their originality is at this cost. A moment ago each one of them borrowed an indefinable coloration from the milieu where it was placed. Now it is bleached out [*décoloré*] and ready to receive a name. . . . Feeling is a living being, which develops, and is therefore always changing . . . when we separate those moments out, unfurling time into space,

---

32. Jean Paulhan, *Les fleurs de Tarbes*, cited in Michael Syrotinski, *Defying Gravity*, 85. See also Maurice Blanchot, "How Is Literature Possible?" in *A Blanchot Reader*, ed. Michael Holland, trans. Michael Syrotinski.

the feeling loses its animation and its color. Then we are left with only the shadow of ourselves. (*EDI* 98–99 [132–133])

Bergson's impassioned protest will be seconded by André Breton in his first *Manifesto of Surrealism*.[33]

Dead Leaves on the Pond (Ideology and Social Life)

Whereas the cell occupies a determined point of the organism, an idea really fills our whole self. It is necessary that all our ideas become incorporated in this way into the mass of our states of consciousness. Many float on the surface, like dead leaves on the water of a pond. By this we mean that when our mind [*esprit*] thinks it always finds them again in a state of immobility, as if they were outside it. These are ideas we receive ready made and that inhabit us without ever becoming assimilated into our substance, or ideas that we have neglected to take up, and that have been dried out, abandoned. If, to the extent that we distance ourselves from the deeper layers of the self, our states of consciousness tend more and more to take the form of a numerical multiplicity and to deploy themselves in a homogeneous space, it is precisely because, increasingly, these states of consciousness take on an inert mode of being, a more and more impersonal form. . . . But if, digging beneath the surface through which the self makes contact with external things, we penetrate into the depths of living and organized intelligence, we will observe the superimposition, or even the intimate fusion of many of these ideas which, once dissociated, seem to mutually exclude one another according to logical contradictions. The most bizarre dreams, where two images overlap, and present us with two different people at the same time, that have become one, would give us a feeble idea of the interpenetration of our concepts dur-

---

33. In the *First Manifesto*, Breton makes a similar point. Speaking of modern man, he writes: "If, later, he tries to regain his identity [*se reprendre*], having felt that he was lacking all reason to live, since he has grown incapable of rising to the occasion of a situation as exceptional as love, he will not be able to do so. This is because he now belongs, body and soul, to an imperious pragmatic necessity. . . . He will only recognize [*se représentera*] in what happens to him and might happen to him, what links this event to any number of similar events, events he did not take part in, events he missed [*événements manqués*]." See André Breton, *Œuvres complètes*, 1:312 (my translation).

ing the waking state. The imagination of the dreamer, isolated from the external world, reproduces with simple images, and parodies in its own way, the work that is ongoing on ideas, in the deepest regions of intellectual life.[34] (*EDI* 101–102 [135–136])

Ultimately, it is Bergson's view that to speak of deep states of consciousness at all is to deform them. We seem to be better off dreaming.

Language is of course necessary for social life, and to this extent it is required for self-preservation. Indeed, the very act of projecting a common spatial world, the world implied by language, is itself a step toward social life. And yet in Rousseauistic fashion, Bergson speaks as if social life were radically alienating. He suggests that the pressure of social life requires the doubling of the subject, the engendering of a second self that covers over the first, like a second skin made up of dead leaves, or dead cells.[35]

Bergson concedes that in practical terms it is in one's interest to avoid the chaos and disorder of immediate experience. The collective obsession with space that characterizes Western culture may even involve a kind of defense, in the psychoanalytic sense, on the part of the superficial self, against the fluidity of psychic operations in what Bergson calls their natural, or nonalienated state. However, with real effort of attention, it is possible to disarm this defense. One can reverse the orientation of the spatial framework and fuse back together the states of thought and feeling that have been isolated from one another because of it. This is the challenging work of philosophical intuition.

Bergson ends this chapter by addressing his colleagues in the world of experimental psychology. Associationist psychologists think they can explain mental operations mechanically, treating the mind as if it were a machine and determining the laws of its operation just as natural scien-

34. Bergson's account of dream activity here suggests Freud's analysis of the dream work in *The Interpretation of Dreams*.
35. Here again we hear distant echoes of Kant for whom the world of nature as representation is called a "second nature," which covers over, as a phenomenal reality, a noumenal reality inaccessible to us. In this sense one could say, perhaps, that Bergson is doing for the subject something like what Kant did for nature. He is distinguishing between a phenomenal self and a noumenal, or in this case, real self, which would be the subject of immediate experience. He must make this distinction, because he will subsequently be able, in the next chapter, to deflect all of the arguments against subjective freedom toward this (merely) phenomenal self and go on to locate freedom in the real self and its horizon of real duration. Again, his analysis of alienation was influential for thinkers such as Georg Lukács, Lucien Goldman, and Antonio Gramsci.

tists, since Newton, have sought to establish laws of nature that apply to the entire physical world. These psychologists can succeed, Bergson writes, but only at the level of dead leaves, only at the level of the superficial self, the one constructed, we might say (to borrow an expression from Louis Althusser) by all the interpellations of conventional social life. However, these psychologists cannot touch the passionate self where feelings and ideas are not distinct from one another and associations can therefore not be mapped out.

Bergson's strategy is to challenge the validity of the methods of associationist psychology on the basis of their fundamental misprision: the suppression of the dynamic force of time, or Real Duration. This requires an enormous effort, since the habits of reflective consciousness are deeply entrenched in our culture. We are used to thinking in terms of product, not process. This is the habit of mind that Bergson is going to try to induce his readers to change. And this is why we read him. In any case, when reading Bergson, we must learn to think in terms of process, not product or we will simply miss the rigor of his argument.

3.3. Chapter 3 of the *Essai*
"Of the Organization of States of Consciousness: Freedom"

Bergson begins this chapter by directly posing the main question of his study: freedom vs. determinism. To treat the inner world of living beings—the world of consciousness—on the model of the physical world, he affirms, is to eliminate the possibility of freedom. The stakes are high, and, in response, Bergson makes a radical move. He will claim that time is a form of energy, one that does not obey the principle of conservation. It is on this basis that he will proceed to make a strict delineation between the realms of the animate and the inanimate, of consciousness and matter, and that he will argue for the existence of what he calls "free will."

Bergson opens his attack on the deterministic psychologists, then, from a surprising angle. He attacks the scientific premise of the conservation of energy. Or, more precisely, he attacks the universal application of this scientific principle, a tendency reinforced by the recent discovery of the laws of thermodynamics, which demonstrated that the principle of the conservation of energy could be applied to the totality of physico-chemical phenomena (*EDI* 114 [151]). The problem, from Bergson's point of view, is the failure to distinguish between two quite different realms: the inanimate and the animate. Against the tendency to hold the conservation of energy to be a universal law, Bergson will propose a new type of energy to which it does not apply: time (*EDI* 114 [151]).[36] Where the law of the conservation of energy holds, Bergson argues, time has no impact: "The vague and instinctive belief in the conservation of one identical quantity of matter, and of force, depends on the fact that inert matter does not seem to exist in time [*durer*] or at least does not conserve any trace of past time [*temps écoulé*]. But this is not the case in the realm of life. Here duration in time seems to act as a cause, and the idea of putting things back in their place after a certain period of time is absurd, since this kind of regression in time [*retour en arrière*] has never occurred in a living being" (*EDI* 115 [152–153]).

If, for living beings, duration in time acts as a cause, then time is a form of energy! This is the radical novelty of Bergson's thought. Time is a form of energy that does not obey the principle of conservation. Nothing remains the same for us in time.

Retracing the Differences

The pertinent difference in this discussion, then, is between matter and consciousness, two terms that the psychophysicists insist on placing in equivalence and that Bergson is determined to distinguish.[37] Two basic facts underlie Bergson's insistence on the radical difference in kind between these two domains. First, the irreversibility of lived time. When we consider things moving through space, we assume that their movements are reversible, that it is possible for them to return to their original positions. We move things to the right, and then back again to the left. But movement is not reversible for beings that live in time because

36. Here is the most ambitious, not to say audacious, formulation of this issue: "Let us note that the most radical mechanism is the one that considers consciousness an epiphenomenon, capable of being added, under certain circumstances, to certain molecular movements. But if the molecular movement can create sensation without any consciousness [*un néant de conscience*] then why couldn't consciousness, in turn, create movement either with zero kinetic or potential energy, or by using this energy in its own way?" (*EDI* 115 [152]). This is a standard move for Bergson, i.e., to take a position to the extreme limit and then to imagine its reversal or inversion. See my chapter 2, above, concerning the laws of thermodynamics, clearly invoked here when Bergson speaks of "the mechanical theory of heat" (*EDI* 114 [151]), and subsequent scientific challenges to the law of conservation of energy.

37. This, of course, will be the point of departure for his next work, *Matter and Memory*, that will displace, as the title suggests, this fundamental metaphysical opposition.

time moves in only one direction. Alas, I can only grow older, not younger! Second, the phenomenon of memory. Time becomes energy by passing, by the mere act of becoming. It acts as a force in conscious beings because it accumulates in them. Just as a solar panel collects and holds the energy of the sun, so our living body and memory hold the energy of time.

The Force of Time

What does it mean to say that time is a force? It means, as Bergson puts it, that "the same does not remain the same here" (*EDI* 115 [153]). He uses the sensation of pain as an example. "By the very fact that it lasts," he argues, "a sensation changes to the point of being unbearable" (*EDI* 115 [153]). Thus, "whereas past time constitutes neither a gain nor a loss for a supposed system of conservation, it is a gain . . . for a conscious [being]" (*EDI* 116 [153]). To the extent that it is a gain, and acts as a cause, it is a force. Time is a force, like the other forces of nature, but it does not obey the laws of nature, which pertain only to the physical world.

> One will agree, at least, that the hypothesis of . . . moving back in time becomes unintelligible in the realm of consciousness. By the very fact that it lasts, a sensation changes to the point of becoming unbearable. Here the same does not remain the same, but reinforces itself and seems to fill and enlarge itself with its whole past [*se grossit de tout son passé*]. In short, if the material point, as the mechanists understand it, remains in an eternal present, the past is a reality for conscious beings . . . whereas past time constitutes neither a gain nor a loss for a supposed system of conservation, it is a gain . . . for a conscious [being]. Under these conditions, might one not propose the hypothesis of a conscious force or free will, which, subject to the action of time and storing up duration, would, by this very fact, escape the law of the conservation of energy? (*EDI* 115–116 [152–153])

Bergson has opened an abyss between matter and consciousness through this claim that time acts as a force. Time is a force that affects quality, feeling, or sensation—what Bergson has called "intensities" in chapter 1. But this analysis depends upon the distinction Bergson made in the previous chapter between a spatialized conception of "time" and Real Duration.

> As we are not accustomed to observing ourselves directly but instead perceive ourselves through forms borrowed from the external world, we end up thinking that real duration, the duration lived by consciousness, is the same as the duration that slips past inert atoms without changing anything. For this reason we do not see the absurdity of putting things back in their place once time has passed, or of believing that the same motivations repeatedly act on the same people, and concluding that these causes will always produce the same effect [this, of course, is the hypothesis of the associationist psychologists]. We will show further on that this hypothesis is unintelligible. For the moment, let us just affirm that once embarked on this path, one inevitably ends up erecting the principle of the conservation of energy into a universal law. And this is because one has abstracted out the fundamental difference that a careful examination reveals to us between the external world and the internal one: one has identified real duration with apparent duration. (*EDI* 116 [154])

"Apparent duration," then, implies presence, whereas "real duration" depends upon the passage (or becoming) of time. For Bergson, time is always flowing and consciousness is always just working through this flow. Paradoxically, time becomes energy by passing, by losing itself in the very act of becoming, and by being stored through memory. There is a sense in which we are always already in the past.[38] This is why Bergson constantly reminds us to consider lived experience in all its concrete specificity, instead of through abstract ideas. It is very simple. Abstraction evacuates the force of time. We cannot know flowing time cognitively. We can only know it concretely through the way different qualities feel to us at different times. That is why the appeal to the concrete—to lived experience—is fundamental. And, once again, this is why language is a problem, for, as we have seen, it is inadequate to the task of conveying quality in all its singularity.

---

38. In *Matter and Memory*, as we shall see, Bergson will claim that memory does not involve a movement from the present back into the past but rather a movement from the past toward the future.

Hypothesis: Free Will

It is the force of time that makes free will possible. We could even say that free will *is* the force of lived time. "[There is] a conscious force or free will, which, subject to the action of time and storing up duration, would, by this very fact, escape the law of the conservation of energy" (*EDI* 116 [154]). It is because consciousness implies memory, and memory is a force, that we have free will. This is precisely what always escapes the grasp of mechanistic explanation and the laws of nature that pertain to matter. This escape, for Bergson, is the essence of what free will means: the possibility of voluntary action as opposed to automatic reaction.

The force of time as duration is the horizon of inner life, that is, of the experience of qualities, feeling, and sensation. Free will emerges from this ground. It is not a humanistic notion, and does not imply a stable subject position. There is no necessary reason why it should even be limited to human beings. It has little to do with intelligence and everything to do with memory, and even with sensation. The notion of free will divides the world of consciousness from the world of matter. It depends on operations of memory.

Bergson refutes determinism within the psychological realm by affirming the creative force of time, that is, by affirming that time itself is a force. This conception of time as energy is the radical idea that will serve as the point of departure for all of Bergson's major works. It leads into the discussion of memory in *Matter and Memory*. It also provides the point of departure for the radical shift Bergson introduces in *Creative Evolution*. In that work, Bergson will consider the energy of time to be not just a feature of consciousness, but an ontological principle in itself—a fact of being. The creative force of time, the *élan vital*, will become a principle of the external real.[39]

Automatons and Robots

To follow the development of Bergson's argument in this chapter closely is to pursue an extended argument with associationist psychology. The thrust of Bergson's argument is perhaps more pertinent than ever. Today

39. In this sense we could say it meets up with Heidegger's notion of the *es gibt*. See *On Time and Being*.

we are faced with new disciplines that share some of the fundamental assumptions Bergson challenges—computer science, for example, and the field of artificial intelligence. These are not only subjecting behavior to mechanistic analysis, but also designing robotic agents accordingly, with the most sophisticated tools of statistical analysis and mathematical formalization.

The thrust of Bergson's critique is that mechanistic psychologies divide mental states into discrete units, as if they could tag or identify them; then they analyze their operation as if they were things. This may be appropriate, Bergson argues, to the activities of automatons or robots, or even to those of the most superficial modes of human behavior that are oriented toward the external world and rely upon the symbolic representations of language and mathematics. But this approach is completely unable to account for the energies of inner life—the energies of free will.

Associationist accounts of mental behavior become the dupe of language, Bergson argues. They speak as if people experienced the same feelings over and over again, when in fact feelings are entirely singular each time they occur to the extent that they are tied to a particular moment of time and engage the whole psychic life—the whole personality—of the person. Associationist psychology construes inner experience on the model of the external world, confusing quality with quantity, as well as all the other distinctions Bergson has carefully laid out in the preceding chapters, especially the one between time and duration. As we have seen in the last chapter, language has been said to crush the experience of duration by imposing fixed, abstract terms on concrete lived experience that never repeats itself in the same way. It imposes a repetitive grid on what is each time singular, since, as quoted earlier, "the same is never the same" in time. What escapes these psychologies is precisely the concrete singularity of experience lived in Real Duration.

Earlier, Bergson spoke of two selves. There is the superficial self, which is programmed by language and social constraint. We could say it is ideologically produced. It is made up of fixed names and conventional images that cover over, and by implication suffocate, living feelings. Then there is what Bergson has called the "deeper, passionate self," associated with the notions of inner life and qualitative experience. This is what Bergson associates with free will or free action. Free will involves experience in the mode of duration, uncontaminated by the "bastard concept" of time as space and by the dulling repetitions of language. The psychologists want to try to reconstruct the person by analyzing the associations of various psychic states. From Bergson's point of view, when people act freely, "the person is completely there in each one of [these actions] . . . and the manifestation of this internal state will be precisely what one calls a free action" (*EDI* 124–125 [165]). When feelings are considered concretely, in their real depth of feeling, they can be said to freely express the whole person; they are fused with all one's other feelings in what Bergson calls a confused multiplicity. "Confusion" literally means *with fusion* here, since feelings are fused together; they overlap such that each lends a particular coloration to the other. "It is from the whole soul that the free decision emanates" (*EDI* 125 [167]). Bergson describes the superficial layer of consciousness as a kind of crust of language and symbols that covers over living feelings. At moments of strong passion, our energies break through this crust. "The self rises up again to the surface. The outer crust bursts" (*EDI* 127 [169]). It is at these moments that we act freely. Our actions tumble from us the way a ripe fruit drops from a tree. They cannot be rationally explained.

A Logic of Freedom?

To act freely is not to choose between two alternative actions, as a certain logic of freedom maintains against the determinists who deny freedom altogether. Bergson represents this logic of freedom with the diagram on the next page (page 84).

The diagram, Bergson argues, misrepresents what really happens. It gives a retrospective analysis of a situation after it has already happened, after we already know what action has been taken. This kind of explanation only works when we read backwards and construct a kind of narrative that moves inexorably toward one action as opposed to another, and then reconstructs motives for this choice. The problem is that the choice never really happens, because the alternatives are never really given as such in advance. They are fictions, invented after the fact, in order to tell a story that has a beginning, a middle, and an end.

What really happens occurs in a time of becoming where there are no clear alternatives, only a "multitude of different and successive states" and "a self that lives and develops through the effect of . . . hesitations, until the free action separates from them like a fruit, which has become too ripe" (*EDI* 132 [175–176]). Bergson locates freedom, then, in hesi-

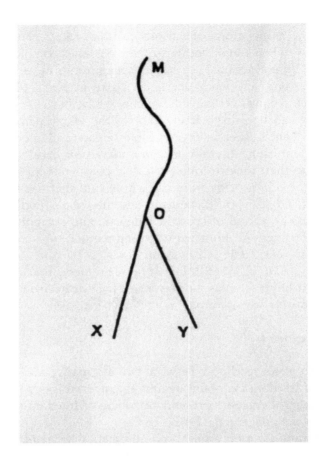

tation, not in choice.[40] Freedom happens as it happens, not as it is reconstructed after the fact.

Paradoxically, Bergson argues, the diagram of a free choice situation
falls back into determinism. The figure implies that we can follow the
process of psychic activity the way we track the movements of "an advancing army on a map" (*EDI* 135 [180]). Such a figure, Bergson argues, represents a thing, not an event. It replaces succession with simultaneity. We have projected time (or real duration) into space. We have
replaced an event or progression—the actual happening of something—

40. See chapter 1 of the *Essai*, where Bergson provides an account of affect as the
locus of freedom.

with a thing, represented by a static geometrical figure. We are back to the familiar problem: the fundamentally alienating gesture of projecting time onto space. Again, time cannot be translated into space because it only moves in one direction. It is irreversible. "If I glance at a route traced out on a map, nothing prevents me from turning around and looking to see if it divides at certain places. But you can't go in reverse on the line of time" (*EDI* 136 [181]).

Of course, after the fact, once the action has been performed, we can think about it abstractly as if there had been distinct moments, one external to another, and we can depict this abstractly as a line in space. But we have to be aware that this line no longer symbolizes flowing time; it symbolizes time that has already passed [*écoulé*]. It is an abstraction. As we have already seen, there can be no freedom in abstraction since abstraction necessarily eradicates time from its representations. Freedom requires our concrete engagement with the flow of time.

[One] must look for freedom in a certain nuance or quality of the action itself, the action as it happens, and not in a relation of this act with what it is not, or what it might have been. The whole obscurity which surrounds this question comes from the fact that both sides [proponents of freedom, who explain it rationally, and determinists] represent the deliberation as an oscillation in space, when it consists of a dynamic progress where the self and the motivations themselves are in a continual state of becoming, like real living beings. (*EDI* 136–137 [182–183])

After the fact, we can reconstruct an event as if it involved a fork in the road; while the event is happening, there is no road and no fork.

Bergson concludes that the question of freedom has been badly posed in conventional debates between determinists and those who believe they are upholding free will. The act performed has taken the place of the act of performing it. Symbolic representation of the event has taken the place of the event itself. And ultimately, once again, time has been confused with space. Bergson's position is radical. Freedom is something we can't talk about at all! We certainly cannot explain it through concepts. The moment we try to explain freedom—we eradicate it. This is because an absolute difference exists between immediate experience, which just happens, and experiences reconstructed in thought (reflective experience). The latter is represented through a spatial figure where direction is reversible; the former occurs in real duration, where time flows in only one direction.

A Logic of Determinism (Same Thing)

Having demystified a certain logic of freedom, Bergson next considers the logic of determinism to show us that, in fact, the two amount to the same. He examines the kind of predictive claim that has been so successful in scientific research. Prediction, he reveals, really acts just like retrospection, only it pretends to look ahead into the future. Astronomers can predict a future solar eclipse by projecting past information forward. But this logic does not work when it comes to people.

Imagine, for example, that there is a philosopher named Paul, endowed with complete knowledge of all the conditions that will impact the future action of someone named Peter. Would Paul be able to predict Peter's action the way astronomers predict an eclipse? We soon see that when Paul tries to predict Peter's action, he tries to do just what we did in the previous example when we diagrammed the decision making process retrospectively as a fork in the road. Just as retrospection misrepresents the event of freedom, so prediction is impossible when it comes to free action. Bergson concludes that Paul could never predict Peter's action because he could never have the knowledge of Peter's experience unless he had lived it himself. What is missing when one person tries to grasp the experience of another is the factor of intensity, of how things actually feel as one experiences them.

Bergson's radical claim is that the way things feel in experience depends upon the particular moment in which they occur. We never have exactly the same feeling twice, because the very fact of having felt something before changes the nature of the experience the second time around. It becomes something else. Ultimately, for Paul to grasp the experience of Peter it would not be enough to relive it, as an actor might play a role. He would have to live it in the same temporal flow that Peter lived it. He would have to share the same concrete duration, and to do this—Paul would have to be Peter! "But if Peter and Paul have experienced the same sentiments in the same order, if their two souls have the same history, how do you distinguish the one from the other?" (*EDI* 141 [188]). In other words, the only way to have all the information necessary to predict an action would be to have lived that experience *and its history*.[41] There is no other way to know all the conditions that

41. "You do not have the right to abridge—even by a second—the various states of consciousness through which Paul is going to pass before Peter, for the effects of the same sentiment, for example, add to one another and reinforce one another at each moment of duration, and the total of these effects could not be felt all of a sudden if one did not

enter into action, for the force of time is itself a factor in its most concrete, fleeting, and singular occurrence.

Influence

What are we to conclude from Bergson's deconstruction (*avant la lettre*)
of the opposition between determinists and self-proclaimed proponents
of free will? Inner knowledge cannot be translated into objective information.[42] Living creatures are not analogous to inert matter. When science predicts a future natural event, an eclipse, for example, it envisages
the future in present time. It does so because it calculates time. Time becomes number, and to this extent, as Bergson has demonstrated in the
previous chapter, it is implicitly translated into space (*EDI* 126 [167–
168]). Inner states, however, are in perpetual flux (*EDI* 147 [198]).
They are, as Bergson puts it, in progress:

> We forget that states of consciousness are progressions, and not
> things, that if we call each of them by only one name, it is for the
> convenience of language. We forget that they are living, and that,
> as such, they are continually changing and that, therefore, one
> cannot reduce them by a single moment without losing some of
> their impressions, and thereby modifying the quality. I under-
> stand full well that one observes the orbit of a planet all at once,
> or in very little time, because the successive positions, or results
> of its movement, are the only things that matter, and not the du-

---

know the importance of a feeling, taken as a whole [*pris dans son ensemble*] in relation
to the final action, which precisely remains in obscurity. But if Peter and Paul have experienced the same sentiments in the same order, if their two souls have the same history,
how do you distinguish the one from the other. By their bodies? They would be continually changing in one way or another [*par quelque endroit*], since they would not represent
the same body at any particular moment of their history. Would it be by the place they
occupy in duration? They would not, then, participate in the same events. Now, by our
hypothesis they have the same past and the same present, having the same experience.
Now you have to reach your conclusion: Peter and Paul are one and the same person."
(*EDI* 140–141 [188]).

42. "In pursuing the implications of this example," Bergson says, "we come upon the
two fundamental illusions of reflexive consciousness. The first consists in considering intensity as if it were a mathematical property of psychological states and not, as we said at
the beginning of this essay, the special quality, the nuance specific to these diverse states.
The second consists in replacing concrete reality, the dynamic progress that consciousness perceives, by the material symbol of this progress arrived at its term." This would be
"to wrongly suppose that the symbolic image by means of which one represented the performed operation had been drawn [*dessiné*] by this operation itself in the course of its
progress, as if registered by some recording device" (*EDI* 142–143 [189–190]).

ration of the equal intervals that separate them. *But when it is a question of a sentiment, it has no precise result, except to have been felt.* And to adequately appreciate this result, it would have been necessary to have passed through all the phases of the sentiment itself, and occupied the same duration. Even if this sentiment finally culminates in certain actions or events [*démarches*] of a determined nature, comparable to the position of a planet in space, the knowledge of this act will hardly help me appreciate the influence of the sentiment on the ensemble of a history, and it is a question of understanding precisely this influence. . . . Thus when one asks if a future action could be foreseen, one unconsciously identifies the time of the exact sciences, which reduces to a number, with real duration, where what appears to be quantity is really quality which one could not reduce by a single instant without changing the nature of the facts or events that fill it.[43] (*EDI* 147–148 [196–197], emphasis added)

The very foundation of mechanistic psychology is attacked here. Whereas the psychophysiologists and the associationist psychologists want to apply models taken from the natural sciences to psychological events, Bergson demonstrates that this cannot legitimately be done. The world of the natural sciences and the world of psychology or consciousness are two different universes. In the former, matter and energy are conserved, movement is reversible (because we position things in the homogeneous medium of space) the laws of cause and effect prevail, and we obtain knowledge by measuring things and discussing them in terms of laws of logic. In the latter, a form of energy that is not conserved prevails: time as duration. Movement occurs in only one direction. Quality is irreducible to quantity. States of consciousness, or feeling, cannot be separated from one another, identified, named, and counted. Instead of cause and effect we have a force of influence. *The influence of a feeling is simply the fact of its having been felt.* And this fact influences not an isolated element or event but the ensemble of a history. The impact of a state of feeling is influence in the literal or etymological sense of the word. It is a question of the way the fact of having been lived flows into the whole of a person's personality and the ensemble of his or her history. Here the word *ensemble* carries the musical overtones introduced earlier when Bergson proposed the musical phrase as a figure for dura-

---

43. See discussion of chaos theory, chapter 6.

tion and the symphony as a figure for confused multiplicity of states of consciousness in real duration.

The determinist claims that all phenomena, including psychological ones, are subject to law. Bergson argues that this is impossible. When it comes to inner experiences, *the same cause never presents itself twice*. So it is impossible to claim that the same causes produce the same effects. Inner experience consists of qualities, and the identity of a quality includes the quality of the moment in which it occurs.

> Now, our conception of duration tends toward nothing less than the affirmation of radical heterogeneity of deep psychological events [*faits*] and the impossibility for any two to completely resemble one another, because they constitute two different moments of a history. Whereas an external object does not carry the mark of past time [*du temps écoulé*], and, therefore ... the physicist will be able to identify identical elementary conditions, duration is a real thing for the consciousness that conserves a trace of it and one cannot speak here of identical conditions because the same moment never presents itself twice ... psychological elements, even the simplest ones, have their own personality and a life of their own. They are continually in the process of becoming, and the same sentiment, simply by virtue of the fact that it repeats itself, is a new sentiment. We even have no reason to keep its old name. ... In short, if the causal relation still exists in the world of inner phenomena, it can in no way resemble what we call causality in nature. For the physicist, the same cause produces the same effects. For a psychologist ... a deep internal cause only yields its effect one time, and will never produce it again.[44] (*EDI* 150–151 [199–201])

If this passage is difficult to understand, it may be because our imaginations remain obsessed with space, even as we try to follow Bergson's argument. We tend to see time on the model of space, i.e., as a homogeneous field in which things happen. We expect to be able to abstract these contents from the temporal horizon and to be able to consider

---

44. In relation to Bergson's critique of causality, see chapter two concerning the challenges to the principle of causality in relation to the physical world from within quantum physics.

them independently—as so many things that happen. Bergson is asking us to think in a completely different way. Duration and its contents are one and the same, and because the feelings or sensations that occur in time carry the mark of their temporal moment, and because time moves in only one direction, no temporal moment can ever return again. One never feels exactly the same feeling twice.

Concrete experience is radically singular because it attaches to the unique moment in which it occurs. Whereas we imagine space as an empty homogeneous medium, to be filled up with things we can juxtapose and count, duration is not an abstract framework for something else. Bergson asks us to think duration as fullness instead of emptiness. Duration *is* the qualitative lived experience that occurs in and through it, in its irreducible concreteness and singularity. It cannot be known because it is always changing. It can only be lived in the very specific time of its unfolding. The most important point to emerge from this discussion, then, is that duration does not contain intensity;[45] it *is* intensity, or the unfolding of intensities through, or as, the irreversible time of becoming.

A feeling, therefore, is not held within time as a particular content within a form, or as a thing is held within the uniform field of space. When we give it a name—"joy" or "brightness," for example—we act as if it were such a thing, and as if it could return again and again. But there is no separation between form and content in duration. Time itself, as real duration, enters into the identity of inner experiences. These involve not only *what* is felt but also, quite specifically, *how it feels*. And how it feels depends on everything else that is happening at that particular moment, a moment that "never presents itself twice." It even depends on one's whole history.

Identity

What, then, becomes of the principle of identity? It radically changes. It is no longer a function of repetition, or of a return of the same. It is no longer determined by a lawful relation between present and future (as in the logic of causality where the same cause will always produce the same effect). It attaches what happens to the moment in which it occurs.

45. By "intensity" I mean everything Bergson has called "qualitative experience," sentiment, feeling, sensation, etc. See my discussion in Section 3.1. of this chapter.

The principle of identity is the absolute law of our consciousness. It affirms that what is thought is thought at the moment that one thinks it. And what makes for the absolute necessity of this principle is that it does not link the future to the present [as in the law of causality] but sensibly links the present to the present: it expresses the unshakeable confidence that consciousness feels in itself, to the extent that, faithful to its role, it limits itself to affirming the actual apparent state of the soul. (*EDI* 156 [207–208])

Paradoxically, the only way to appreciate the power of temporal flow—the force of duration—is to be here now, as they used to say in the sixties, to engage completely with the feelings of the present moment in all their contingency. Here Bergson redefines inner identity in terms of the radically singular quality of each lived moment. By redefining it in this way, he separates identity from causality.

What is at stake here is what Bergson has alluded to earlier as the radical heterogeneity of real time. Each moment is internally heterogeneous. It is made up of what Bergson calls a dynamic qualitative multiplicity or "confused multiplicity." This means that we cannot separate out the various states of feeling that overlap, or interpenetrate, at any given moment. But it also means that we are dealing with a multiplicity of states of feeling because these are in a mode of becoming in which each state succeeds another, develops into another, or overlaps with another in a temporal way. Finally, what contributes to this heterogeneity of inner experience is that each moment is radically discontinuous from the next, even though it flows out of one and into another. Duration involves a production of radical difference.[46]

Unthinkable Time, Radical Difference

This notion of real, or pure, duration is almost unthinkable. Bergson is asking us to stop thinking in terms of sameness and to start thinking in terms of radical difference, which occurs in an irreversible way. Perhaps

---

46. We note the affinity with "l'expérience intérieure [inner experience]" of Georges Bataille, and, of course, the importance of these notions of multiplicity and heterogeneity for Deleuze. We also note, in passing, the misunderstanding on the part of Bachelard who, in his critique of Bergson, did not appreciate the internal discontinuity within duration. See Pearson, *Philosophy and the Adventure of the Virtual*, 70–74; 87–88.

all we can do, to think duration, is to unthink the way we usually think—to unthink sameness, repetition, etc. because duration itself is not something that can be thought. It is incompatible, at least, with conceptual thought, which succeeds because it spatializes.[47]

Duration involves, as Bergson puts it, a relation that binds the present to the present. Paradoxically, this relation of the present to the present gives us not a continuous temporality but a discontinuous time. No blueprint of the future is given in the present, no pre-formation of it.[48] And for this very reason it is incompatible with the empiricist laws of identity and causality through which we attempt to master time by drawing the future into the present. One can anticipate the future mathematically, but this reduces time to number and crushes our experience of the real time of duration, which differentiates as it becomes.

Bergson has effectively challenged the methods of his colleagues by disabling the concept of causal explanation in the domain of psychic life. He has performed a critical gesture by radically separating the dynamics of inner life from the world of things governed by natural law. Is his job done? Not quite. He has critiqued a false logic of freedom, and shown that it effectively reduces to another form of determinism, but he has not yet really said how he understands free action.

The Fact of Freedom

In the *Critique of Practical Reason*, Kant boldly asserts that the moral law is a fact. It is, in other words, something we know through experience. It cannot be demonstrated or deduced theoretically. In the same way, Bergson affirms that freedom is a fact. It is something that can be known only through immediate experience, not through reflective consciousness. Bergson characterizes freedom as quite simply "the relation of the concrete self to the act it performs" (*EDI* 165 [220]). If it cannot be further defined, he adds, with a certain irony, it is precisely because

47. Duration would be closer to what Lacan calls the Real—that is, something that cannot be symbolized.

48. Time is discontinuous because there is no given relation between one moment and the next. It is important to consider that although Bergson uses vitalist images—he speaks of living, for example, as a way of expressing radical change—this does not mean he is thinking time on the model of a smooth progression or of something like organic growth. The point that will be made explicitly further on is that what is specific about a living being is the way it holds time, unlike things that do not absorb time. In this sense living is inner experience, which is the experience of time lived as radical difference and discontinuity. This is an attempt to think radical singularity.

we are free. To define something is to analyze it. To analyze it is to break it down into component parts. But when we do this, we project into space, and the force of time is immediately evacuated. Since it is the force of time that is the force of free action, this cannot be analyzed. As soon as we start to reason about freedom we turn time into space and that is why "any definition of freedom will end up justifying determinism" (*EDI* 165–166 [220]), as Bergson has just shown in his discussion of the logic of free choice.

> In summary, when it comes to freedom, any demand for clarification inevitably returns to the question: "Can time adequately be represented by space?" To which the reply is: yes, if it is a question of time already past. No, if you want to speak of the time that passes. Free action occurs in the time that passes and not the time already past. Freedom is thus a fact and among the facts that one affirms, none is clearer. The whole difficulty of the problem, and the very problem itself, derive from the fact that one wants to attribute the same attributes to duration that one attributes to extension, that one wants to interpret succession by simultaneity and express the idea of freedom in a language into which it obviously cannot be translated. (*EDI* 166 [221])

Bergson has demonstrated, or performed, the very problem he diagnosed in the beginning of this study: the fact that language crushes [*écrase*] duration (*EDI* 98 [132]). In this chapter, he has analyzed the various discourses and arguments traditionally invoked in the debate concerning freedom vs. determinism. He has shown that in each instance—even when thinkers attempt to defend freedom—it is impossible to logically, or intellectually, grasp freedom. Freedom cannot be explained in language, or grasped by reflexive consciousness. It is an immediate experience.

3.4. Conclusion of the *Essai*

It was Kant, Bergson recalls, who taught us to consider the empirical world objectively. He taught us that we perceive things according to certain structures of the mind, and can therefore only know things as the mind lets us represent them to thought, that is, as *phenomena* and not as *noumena*, or things in themselves. Since in order to think at all we imagine that things occur in space and in time, this is how we necessarily represent them to ourselves. We construct our sense of reality accordingly, regardless of whether things *really* exist in space and in time, in some absolute sense, independently of us.

Since only a divine being could have knowledge of things in themselves, our knowledge is limited to phenomena, to things as they appear to us. Within these limits (the limits of the empirical world) we can have rigorous knowledge. Scientists do not tend to feel constrained by these limits. Unlike philosophers, they are not particularly concerned with the question of the thing in itself, or perhaps they consider such questions to be personal matters of faith. They are quite satisfied to take the world of phenomena as the domain of empirical truth and to claim to establish true knowledge of it. To this extent the empirical investigations of science follow from Kant's Copernican Revolution, which structures the truth of the external world according to the given forms of mental activity. Bergson turns the Kantian perspective inside out. He asks whether we do not unconsciously tend to construct our understanding of the inner world according to forms borrowed from the way we view the external world. This, of course, is the charge he has made from the start against the deterministic psychologists. It is the charge he makes against all those who would attempt to acquire scientific knowledge of the actual workings of inner life.[49]

When we consider the world objectively, or scientifically, we try to edit out subjective elements. Bergson is asking us to make a comparable gesture in reverse when we consider ourselves subjectively. When we want to understand ourselves, we need to edit out objective modes of thought: "Just as when we try to determine the true relations of physical phenomena amongst themselves we abstract out what, in our way of perceiving and thinking, goes manifestly contrary to them, so, to contemplate the self in its original purity, psychology should eliminate or correct certain forms that carry the visible mark of the external world" (*EDI* 168 [223–224]).

---

49. "For, if we suppose that the forms we are speaking of, and to which we adapt matter, come entirely from the mind, it seems hard to apply them constantly to objects without these [the objects] soon rubbing off on them [the forms of the mind]. When we then use these forms to obtain knowledge of our own person, we risk taking for the coloration of the self a reflection of the frame in which we place it, in the final analysis the external world. . . . Thus, when we try to return to ourselves and to understand ourselves after an excursion into the external world, we no longer have our hands free" (*EDI* 168 [223]).

Chief among these is visibility itself, since to see something is to see it presented in space. It is in this spirit that Bergson has, throughout the *Essai*, undertaken a critique of concepts and a reconfiguration of them, fitting them to subjective experience. He has focused on three concepts: intensity, duration, and voluntary determination, and attempted to purify them all of features that are appropriate to scientific investigation of the external world, but inappropriate to inner experience. "Intensity, duration, voluntary determination, here are the three ideas that must be purified, by ridding them of all that they owe to the intrusion of the sensible world and, in a word . . . to the obsession with the idea of space" (*EDI* 168 [224]).

These are the three ideas that Bergson has discussed in each of the three chapters of this essay: intensity in chapter one, duration in chapter two, and freedom, or voluntary determination, in chapter three. He now summarizes the argument he has made in each case, although here he frames his critique of concepts with explicit reference to the Kantian conceptual framework.

Intensity. When we consider sensation, there are two sides to experience. When we feel a sensation of bright light, for example, we feel it both outside us and within us. We feel it outside us when we refer to the external cause of the sensation. We can identify a cause—a bright light bulb, for example—and we can even quantitatively measure the force of this cause, for we can measure the wattage of the light source. This way of considering sensation approaches it in the terms we use to explain the external world. But if we face inward and consider the sensation— brightness, for example—in itself, independently of any external cause or light source, there is just the way brightness feels, a succession of qualitative states that overlap with one another and merge together. Inner consciousness only experiences the quality of brightness, not how bright something is.[50]

The concept of intensity, then, has two faces. It is quality for inner consciousness and quantity when we attach it to its external cause and

50. Bergson is essentially deconstructing the Kantian concept of intensive quantity [*grandeurs intensives*]: "When you study external things . . . you leave aside the forces themselves, supposing that they exist, to consider only the measurable and extended effects of these forces. Why should you retain this bastard concept when you analyze the phenomenon of consciousness in its turn? If quantity, outside you, is never intensive, intensity, within you, is never quantity" (*EDI* 169 [225]). Bergson goes on to argue that there are not two types of quantity, extensive quantity of things in space and intensive quantity of non-extended things. There is rather quantity, on the one hand, and quality, on the other.

describe it as we describe external things that present themselves in space. It is either quality or quantity, then, depending how we look at it.

Multiplicity. This is also a double notion, or what Bergson calls a "bastard concept" (*EDI* 169 [225]). On the one hand, we associate multiplicity with quantity, with numbers that presuppose a homogeneous space in which units can be juxtaposed and lined up to be counted.[51] Bergson explains this, as we remember, in chapter two of the *Essai*. But then there is the multiplicity of consciousness in which states of mind overlap, merge with one another and add together dynamically, forming a qualitative, or "confused," multiplicity.

When we consider things in the world we intentionally neglect this second, qualitative, side (the way different qualities color one another) and consider objects to be clear and distinct from one another. We rely on the notion of distinct multiplicity, associated with number. But conversely, this would mean that when we consider inner experience, we should forget about the objective side of experience and be careful *not* to consider inner states as distinct and separate from one another, that is, as things that can be measured, or which have causes that can be explained. For here there is no sameness, only difference.

Duration. What is duration? Bergson starts by reminding us what it is not: "What is duration within us? A qualitative multiplicity, which bears no relation to number; an organic development which is nevertheless not a growing quantity; a pure heterogeneity in the heart of which there are no distinct qualities. In short, the moments of internal duration are not exterior to one another" (*EDI* 170 [226]).

But is duration also two-sided? Is there an external face of duration? On the outside, Bergson answers, it appears as the present, that is, as simultaneity. Here Bergson reaches a sort of limit. Unlike the concepts previously mentioned, it is not possible to "put duration into space." This would involve a "veritable contradiction," namely, putting succession in the heart of simultaneity. "One must therefore not say that external things endure [*durent*] but rather that there is some inexplicable reason why we cannot consider them at successive moments of our duration without affirming that they have changed" (*EDI* 171 [227]).

The difference between duration and space functions as a kind of *a priori* in Bergson's thinking at this point (although it may be only a

51. Number is a unit of multiplicity that we can organize mathematically with other units of multiplicity.

strategic one).[52] It corresponds with the divide between internal and external, or between consciousness and matter. Here Bergson articulates the fundamental opposition which has directed the entire argument of the *Essai*: "In consciousness, we find states that succeed one another without distinguishing themselves from one another, and in space, simultaneities that, without succeeding one another, distinguish themselves from one another, in the sense that the one no longer is when the other appears. . . . Outside us, reciprocal exteriority without succession, within us, succession without reciprocal exteriority" (*EDI* 171 [227]).

If we cannot put duration into space, we have already, unwittingly, put space into our concept of time. When we speak of time as something that can be measured and cut up into distinct units like space, it becomes a hybrid concept: "The hybrid idea [*idée mixte*] of a measurable time, which is space in that it is homogeneity and duration to the extent that it is succession, that is, at bottom the contradictory idea of succession in simultaneity" (*EDI* 171–172 [228]).

The conventional concept of time carries just this contradiction, and the hybrid nature of the concept works to the advantage of science. For when science considers things in the world, it dissociates the two elements of extension and duration and considers only the former: "Science dissociates these two elements, extension and duration, when it undertakes the in-depth study of external things. We believe we have proved that from duration it only retains simultaneity, and from movement itself it only retains the position of the moving thing [*le mobile*]. Which is to say immobility. The dissociation operates very clearly to the advantage of space" (*EDI* 172 [228–229]).

Bergson calls for the same kind of dissociation to be made to the advantage of duration:

> We need then to perform the dissociation again, this time to the advantage of duration, when we study inner phenomena. Not inner phenomena in a completed state . . . nor after discursive intelligence has separated them and spread them out in a homogeneous milieu in order to account for them, but the inner phenomena as they occur [*en voie de formation*] and as they constitute,

<hr>

52. This issue is a subject of some debate. See Deleuze, *Bergsonism*, Mullarkey, *Bergson and Philosophy*, chap. 2, and my "The 'Zig-Zags of a Doctrine': Bergson, Deleuze, and the Question of Experience."

through their mutual interpenetration, the continuous development of a free person. Duration, thus returned to its original purity, will appear as an entirely qualitative multiplicity, an absolute heterogeneity of elements, which come to melt into [*se fondre*] one another. (*EDI* 172 [229])

What is at stake in this purification of concepts, this sharp delineation of inner experience from experience of the physical world? In a word: freedom. "Now it is for having neglected to perform this necessary dissociation that some have been lead to deny freedom, and others to define it, and, by doing so, involuntarily to deny it further" (*EDI* 172 [229]). Thus the purifying of concepts aims to prevent space from seeping into our conception of duration so that it cannot disable a conception of freedom. "In a word, however one envisages freedom, one only denies it on the condition of identifying time with space. One only defines it on the condition of demanding of space the adequate representation of time. One only discusses it, in one sense or in another, on the condition of initially confusing succession with simultaneity. All determinism will thus be refuted by experience, but any definition of freedom will justify determinism" (*EDI* 173 [230]). To speak is to unconsciously transpose succession into simultaneity. Even attempts to define freedom discursively only end up confirming determinism. The only rigorous refutation of determinism is experience—immediate experience.

Bergson's strategy, then, is to diagnose what happens in empirical thought and to invite us to turn this inside out in the consideration of inner experience. Once we see what we do when we think objectively, we know just what not to do when we want to consider feeling, to intuit real duration, and to encounter the possibility of free action. To grasp the fundamental nature of inner experience we must do just the opposite of what we do when we think objectively about the external world.

But if it is as simple as this, why are we so reluctant to do it? The answer is simple: the intuition of duration disrupts our habits of speaking and thinking. It is at odds with the imperatives of social life, which require us to objectify ourselves just as we objectify things in the world in order to know and master them.

Inquiring why this dissociation of duration and extension, that science performs so naturally in the external world, requires such an effort and excites such repugnance when it is a question of inner states, we have not taken long to find the answer. . . . But when it is a question of our states of consciousness, we have every interest in maintaining the illusion that they participate in the reciprocal exteriority of external things, because this distinction, and at the same time this solidification, also enable us to give them stable names. . . . They enable us to objectify them, in a sense, to make them enter into the current of social life. (*EDI* 173 [230–231])

As experience faces both outward, toward the external world of cause and effect, and inward, toward qualitative change in duration, the subject of experience must also be double, as Bergson has suggested in the first chapter of the *Essai*.[53] "There would thus be two different selves, of which one would be the external projection of the other, its spatial and, so to speak social representation" (*EDI* 173 [231]).

Although we have met the metaphor of the "phantom self" before, Bergson defines it here as a projection in space of the free self. This projection in space also presents the social representation of the free self, the conscious automaton. Whereas the free self can be approached only through intuition, the social representation of this self is known scientifically. These two selves (or the self and its social representation, the sign of itself) let themselves be known in two distinct ways, the one by intuition and the other by scientific knowledge.

We reach the first [the inner self] by a deep reflection, which lets us grasp our inner states as living beings, continually in the process of being formed, as states that resist measurement, that penetrate one another and whose succession in duration has nothing to do with juxtaposition in homogeneous space. But the moments where we tune into ourselves [*nous nous ressaisissons*] in this way are extremely rare and this is why we are rarely free. Most of the time, we live outside ourselves; we only perceive the colorless phantom of ourselves, the shadow that pure duration projects into homogeneous space. Our existence unfolds then in space rather than in time. We live for the external world rather

53. We might consider this on analogy with Kant for whom there is the phenomenal self of cognitive understanding and the moral self which is something quite distinct, and which operates in the theoretical domain of practical knowledge.

than for ourselves. We speak rather than think; we are acted upon rather than acting ourselves. To act freely is to retake possession of oneself [*le soi*]; it is to place oneself back in pure duration. (*EDI* 174 [231–232])

In an ingenious reversal of Plato's metaphor of the cave, Bergson suggests that we are in the cave of illusion, when we "live outside ourselves" as a phantom projection of our real selves (*EDI* 174 [231]). We enter into a semiotic realm of illusion when we become reduced to merely the social sign or representation of ourselves, turning our back, as it were, on the possibility of free action. We become "acted upon instead of acting ourselves" (*EDI* 174 [231]) when we let ourselves be written into discourses of causal explanation instead of acting freely and passionately.

At this point in his conclusion, Bergson returns to Kant and explicitly situates himself in relation to the thought of the German philosopher. Kant was right to pose time as the form of inner apperception and space as the form of external apperception, Bergson affirms. His mistake was to let space surreptitiously contaminate his conception of time. Had he understood duration in its radical difference from space, that is, in its utter heterogeneity, Bergson would have no quarrel with Kant. Since Kant did not grasp the radical alterity between time (as duration) and space, a critique of the critical philosopher becomes necessary: "Kant's mistake was to consider time as a homogeneous milieu. Apparently he did not notice that real duration is composed of moments that are interior to one another, and that when it takes on the form of a homogeneous whole, it is because it is expressing itself as space. Thus even the distinction he establishes between space and time fundamentally amounts to a confusion of time with space, and of the symbolic representation of the self with the self itself" (*EDI* 174 [232]). Because he confused time with a homogeneous milieu, like space, Kant attributed causality to inner mental operations as he attributed causality to objects in the external world. "In this way he was lead to believe that the same states are capable of reproducing themselves in the depths of consciousness, just as phenomena do in space. At least this is what he admits implicitly when he attributes the same meaning and role to the relation of causality in the internal world as he does to the external world. From this point on freedom becomes an incomprehensible fact" (*EDI* 174–175 [232]). For Bergson, *this* is the decisive gesture in Kant, the one that precludes freedom, and enables the invasion of empiricist methods and approaches into the study of psychology.

But this is a bit too simple, because Kant does not exclude freedom altogether. He simply excludes it from the world of phenomena, banishing it to the realm of things in themselves. We cannot know these theoretically; we can only experience the absolute as moral obligation in the realm of ethics. Here, in the domain of what Kant calls practical reason, it is a question of the absolutely autonomous subject, the subject of freedom who is no longer affected by the determinations of space and time. Bergson will call this the "noumenal" self. "Nevertheless, through an unlimited, though unconscious confidence, in this internal apperception whose reach he tried to limit, he believed unshakably in freedom. So he raised it to noumenal heights. And just as he had confused duration with space, he made of this real and free self, who is in effect a stranger to space, a self equally outside duration, inaccessible, therefore to our faculty of knowledge" (*EDI* 175 [232–233]). Bergson is describing the Kantian moral subject whose autonomy separates it completely from the determinations of natural law (specifically the law of causality) and enables it to relate directly to what Kant calls the transcendental, or absolute, fact of the moral law.

Kant was correct, Bergson affirms, to separate this autonomous or free subject from space. But he was mistaken when he separated it also from time, and relegated it to the unknowable domain of the thing in itself. Bergson's solution is to transpose time into duration and to locate the free subject there, within duration. In this way it becomes knowable, precisely through immediate experience.

Bergson stands Kant on his head, then, because he displaces this self of freedom from what he calls the "noumenal heights" of Kant's moral philosophy to the depths of immediate sensual experience (*EDI* 175 [232]). It is a gesture not unlike the one Baudelaire made for poetry in *The Flowers of Evil*.

> But the truth is that we perceive this self every time that, by a vigorous effort of reflection, we detach our eyes from the shadow that follows us in order to return to ourselves. The truth is that, if we live and act, most of the time, outside our own bodies [*extérieurement à notre propre personne*], in space instead of in duration, and if, by doing so, we submit to the law of causality, which chains the same effects to the same causes, we are nevertheless always capable of placing ourselves in pure duration,

whose moments are interior and heterogeneous to each other, and where a cause never reproduces its effect, because it never repeats itself twice. (*EDI* 175 [233])

Thus, if Kant placed freedom completely beyond our reach, Bergson places it in our most immediate experience. Freedom is possible for us if we reclaim ourselves from the horizon of space and place ourselves back in duration.

Bergson summarizes the essentials of Kant's position in the following terms:

Kant imagined the thing in itself, on the one hand, and, on the other hand, a homogeneous Time and Space through which the thing in itself is refracted. Whence, on the one hand, the phenomenal self, the one consciousness perceives, and, on the other hand, external objects. Time and space would thus be no more in us than outside us. But the very distinction between the outside and the inside would be the work of time and space. This doctrine has the advantage of furnishing our empirical thought with a solid foundation and of assuring us that the phenomena, as phenomena, are adequately knowable. We could even erect these phenomena into absolutes and dispense with recourse to the incomprehensible things in themselves, if practical reason, which reveals obligation [the moral law], did not intervene like a platonic reminiscence to warn us that the thing in itself exists, invisible and present. (*EDI* 175–176 [233–234])

In Kant, it is thus practical reason, the realm of ethics, that reminds scientists that the empirical domain is not the absolute truth of the matter, that it is merely a realm of appearance, and that "the thing in itself exists, invisible and present" (*EDI* 176 [234]). "Instead of concluding that real duration is heterogeneous . . . Kant preferred to place freedom beyond time, and to erect an absolute barrier between the world of phenomena, which he yields entirely to our knowledge, and the world of things in themselves, to which we are denied access" (*EDI* 17 [235]). Again, Bergson stands Kant on his head. For whereas Kant places freedom in the moral realm, beyond time and space, Bergson places it within time understood as heterogeneous duration. Instead of erecting a barrier between time and freedom, Bergson situates freedom within time (reconceived as duration) and in closest proximity to us—at the heart of our immediate experience. "But perhaps this distinction is too sharp," Bergson continues, still speaking of Kant,

> and this barrier easier to cross than one might imagine. For if, by chance, the moments of real duration, perceived by an attentive consciousness, interpenetrate instead of being juxtaposed, and if these moments form a heterogeneity in relation to one another at the heart of which the idea of a necessary determination loses all meaning, then the self grasped by consciousness would be a free cause. We would know ourselves absolutely, and furthermore, precisely because this absolute mixes itself continually with phenomena, impregnates itself with them, and penetrates them; these phenomena would not be as accessible to mathematical reasoning as they are assumed to be [*ne seraient pas aussi accessibles qu'on le prétend au raisonnement mathématique*]. (EDI 176–177 [235])

That is to say, inner phenomena are not as accessible to reason and analysis as science claims that they are, since duration cannot be grasped cognitively, and freedom cannot be conveyed discursively.

For Bergson, the absolute is not separate from the world of experience; it runs through it. Kant's critical project was to delimit the domain of reason, to separate what can be known from what cannot—the unknowable absolute. To this end, he imposes the distinction between phenomenon and noumenon. The two are separated by a transcendental divide, which delimits the world of nature, where objects are represented in time and space, from the realm of the thing in itself. For Bergson, the dividing line must be redrawn to separate space absolutely from time. It is to this end that he invites us to consider duration.[54]

To understand Bergson's position as a response to Kant (and the discourse of empiricism generally) is to realize that Bergson is not speaking as a mystic when he invokes the absolute here. He is speaking as a philosopher. The difference Kant depicted as a transcendental limit does not separate appearance from some ineffable thing in itself, in Bergson's thought. It carves out a radical difference between space and time, reconceived as duration. It cuts out a difference between experience of

---

54. For an important reading of Bergson in relation to Kant, see Alexis Philonenko, *Bergson ou De la philosophie comme science rigoureuse.*

the outside world and inner experience, and, structurally, it delimits a fundamental alterity between homogeneity and heterogeneity. The absolute—understood as freedom itself—runs through experience, unless we cover it over, of course, by allowing forms of objective consciousness to dominate and to objectify us. Then we lose our freedom. We become automatons.

"We have thus presupposed a homogeneous Space and, with Kant, distinguished this space from the matter that fills it. With him we have admitted that homogeneous space is a form of our sensibility" (*EDI* 177 [236]). Bergson follows Kant concerning space as an *a priori* form of sensibility that, in Bergson's words, "reveals the objectivity of things to us" (*EDI* 177 [236]). Moreover, space as form of sensibility "announces and prepares" social life and "facilitates language" (*EDI* 177 [236]). Because all human beings situate things in space, and ultimately situate themselves in the same space, it is easier for them to establish communities. Space provides a common scene for social life.[55] The Kantians, however, allow automatism to gradually "cover over" freedom to the extent that they substitute homogenous time for the heterogeneous multiplicity of duration. For Bergson, this is precisely what the scientific psychologists do.

From Bergson's point of view, then, the fundamental mistake is to place freedom—the absolute—outside time when it rightfully belongs *in time*, considered in its radical difference from space, that is, as duration. How do we correct this view? How do we learn to know freedom, if we cannot know it cognitively, the way we know things in the world? We must listen to our own experience. For we do act freely when we act passionately and decisively. We learn to know freedom when we acknowledge these moments. When we remember them, we sense clearly that they cannot be explained rationally, or even expressed in words. We sense clearly that we cannot say what caused them, and that such experiences are unique and will never happen again in quite the same way.[56] The problem, and Bergson concludes on this note, is not that we

55. "Through this double operation, therefore, it facilitates language on the one hand, and on the other, announces and prepares social life by presenting us with an external world quite distinct from ourselves in the perception of which all minds can concur" (*EDI* 177 [236]).

56. It is necessary "to bring ourselves back, through thought, to those moments of our existence where we had a serious decision to make, unique moments of their kind, and that will never reproduce themselves any more than for a people the disparate phases of their history. We would see that if these past states cannot be adequately expressed in

are not free. It is that we do not want to be free: "[i]f we are free each time that we want to return to ourselves, it rarely happens that we want to do so" (*EDI* 180 [240]).

Ultimately, Bergson concludes: "The problem of freedom is . . . born of a misunderstanding. It has been for the moderns what the sophisms of the Eleatic school were for the ancients, the illusion by means of which one confuses succession with simultaneity, duration with extension and quality with quantity" (*EDI* 180 [240]). These are the concepts Bergson has attempted to "purify" in this study through the notion of duration, which reinvents an idea of time purified of all elements that belong to the way we think space. Bergson hopes to have cured us of our obsession with space by inviting us to think inside out. But the problem of freedom is not, strictly speaking, an exclusively philosophical problem. It is also a question of desire; it is a problem that concerns social life. It might even be considered a political problem. These are the kinds of questions Bergson will return to in his very last book, *The Two Sources of Morality and Religion.*

---

words, nor reconstituted artificially through the juxtaposition of simple states, it is because they represent, in their dynamic unity and their completely qualitative multiplicity, phases of our real and concrete duration, of our heterogeneous duration, of living duration" (*EDI* 179 [239]).

4. Matter and Memory: Essay on the Relation between Body and Mind

The *Essai*, as we have seen, set out to prove that subjective experience cannot be objectified, that quality (how something feels to us) has nothing in common with quantity (how much there is of it). To this end Bergson cut out a rigid boundary between inside and outside, or between consciousness and things. This enabled the specification of duration, an inner mode of time that has nothing to do with space.

Matter and Memory: Essay on the Relation between Body and Mind circles back to reexamine the difference between inside and outside presupposed in the *Essai*. It explores the relation between consciousness and things—or the mind/body dualism—from the entirely new angle opened up by the *Essai*: duration. "Questions relative to the subject and the object should be posed as a function of time, rather than space" (*MM* 74 [71]). What does Bergson mean? He means that the difference between past and present will be more important than the difference between inside and outside. This is implied in the title of the book, which rephrases the traditional metaphysical opposition between matter and mind in terms of the difference between matter and *memory*. This work takes as its point of departure not the traditional dualism, mind vs. matter, but precisely the question of *relations between* the body and the mind. Bergson is reputed to have studied neurophysiology during the five-year interval between the *Essai* and *Matter and Memory*.

In *Matter and Memory*, then, the book that first established his reputation, Bergson begins by taking up the traditional philosophical formulation of the mind/body dualism, that is the difference between inner and outer construed as a difference between mind and matter, or idealism and realism. Idealism will say that the world is all in our heads, or at least amounts to our representation of it. Kant, we remember, proposed that all we can know of the external world is representation, i.e., the image we give to it in accordance with the structure of our minds. This is the definition of "phenomenon." Realists will say that our perception occurs as a function of our brains and of the body's neuro-chemical circuitry, which responds to elements of the empirical world. They will say that representations in our minds can be explained in terms of physical causes.

Bergson will displace both positions in light of the experience of duration explored in the *Essai*. He is not committed to the mind/body dualism *per se*; that is, he is not interested in choosing one term to dominate the other. He is interested in exploring the *relation* between the two terms, as the subtitle to his book indicates: "Essay on the Relation of Body to Mind." From his point of view, the question involves a three-term problem: one of mind, matter, *and the relation between the two*. This is where the question of memory will come in.

Bergson's first step is to deconstruct the opposition between idealism and realism. As different as these two positions may appear to be, Bergson points out that both share a fundamental assumption: that perception occurs in the service of truth or knowledge about the empirical world. Bergson refuses this premise. Perception, he maintains, serves action, not knowledge. It functions so that we might protect ourselves, or satisfy our needs. Action, driven by need, occurs as movement.

How does Bergson arrive at this shift in fundamental assumptions? He introduces an evolutionary perspective into his philosophical analysis. Even primitive creatures, he reasons, have a form of perception. If a jellyfish is poked, it reacts. It does so automatically, by reflex. People also react when they are poked. But they can usually choose how they will respond. This is because the stimulus passes through the detour of more complex brain circuitry, which delays the reflex response and enables a considered response to occur in its stead.

Bergson maintains that the basic model of perception in the service of action is analogous for primitive and for higher organisms. There is a physical stimulus, which can be described in terms of movement, and a response, which is also a movement, one that returns what has been received and passes it on through the total system of the material world. This is the basic model of action. There is only a difference in degree—in degree of complexity and speed of response—between the primitive organism and the body endowed with a brain. This difference in degree in turn engenders a difference in the kind of action that is possible. Only higher organisms are capable of voluntary action, that is, of choosing the response made to a stimulus. Thus Bergson defines the brain as "an instrument of analysis with respect to received movement" (external stimulus or excitations) (*MM* 26–27 [30]), and "an instrument of selection with respect to the performed movement" (*MM* 27 [30]), i.e., the action taken. The nervous system proposes possible actions and the organism chooses one.

What is the significance of this emphasis on action as opposed to knowledge? It means that Bergson radically separates perception from representation, which will be reserved for memory. Thus the difference between what Bergson calls "presence" and what he calls "representation" will be a fundamentally *temporal* one. Again, "Questions relative to the subject and the object . . . should be posed as a function of time, not space" (*MM* 74 [70–71]). This is something quite different from the Hegelian recognition scene in which relations between subject and object pass through the spatial distance inscribed by the gaze.

Matter and Memory introduces the fundamental difference between automatic and voluntary action. This difference is a function of complexity. The more complex the sensory system of an organism, the greater the zone of indeterminacy that surrounds the incipient action. This results in an interruption of the reflex of stimulus response. It functions like static on the telephone line that prevents the message commanding the reflex response from getting through. This indeterminacy delays the automatic response, thereby opening up a horizon of choice. The further into the distance we can perceive (through sensory systems like vision and hearing) the greater the zone of indeterminacy, and the longer the potential response time—or time of choice—for action.

"It is the indeterminacy that implies perception," Bergson writes, "i.e., a variable relation between the living being and the influences (more or less distant) of the objects that interest it" (*MM* 29 [33]). Thus, if one wants to maintain a distinction between the reflex response of a primitive being and the perception of higher organisms, one would have to say that it is the indeterminacy engendered by the complexity of the sensory system, or configuration of systems, that yields perception. This would be defined specifically as a "variable relation" between inside and outside. The body is embedded in the material world of which it is a part. But as an animate being (and therefore an agent) it is variable, since it is capable of changing its relation to that within which it is embedded. Unlike inanimate material bodies, living bodies are "center[s] of action" (*MM* 14 [20]).

Bergson's conception of matter involves a dynamic energy system in which each point is always acting on all the others. It implies embeddedness. An element of matter necessarily acts on all the others, "transmits the totality of what it receives, opposes an equal and contrary reaction to every action, is finally nothing but a path along which all the modifications which propagate themselves in the immensity of the universe pass in every direction" (*MM* 29 [36]). This is what Bergson understands by presence, as opposed to representation. Representation requires the isolation and immobilizing of a particular feature of this totality: "I would convert it to representation," he writes, "if I could isolate it" (*MM* 33 [36]).[1]

Bergson's strategy is not only to establish a radical difference in kind between perception and representation, but also between perception and memory. To this end he introduces a completely hypothetical notion of Pure Perception, which gives us an idea of what perception would be like if it occurred outside time. Pure Perception would enable an immediate and instantaneous vision of matter. It thus implies a radical impersonality, a total transparency, and a total interactivity. In Bergson's view of the material world, everything acts on everything else.[2] Perception, for Bergson, not only serves action; it is modeled on action, since the basic model of action is given as a mode of contact. Pure Perception, then, involves direct contact, contact as it operates in the material world. Pure Perception thus implies a virtual total perception.

When we shift from the hypothetical model of Pure Perception to actual perception, then, what we need to consider is not how perception arises, but how it limits itself. For, "in principle, it would be the image of everything and, in fact, it is reduced to what pertains to your interest" (MM 36 [40]). Whereas the model for activity in the material world is mechanical—automatic action ordered by the laws of nature—perception (at least in higher organisms) occurs through a body that is defined as a center of action. This is because it is the source of voluntary action.

---

1. In this difference between representation and presence—or materiality—we recognize a version of the difference Bergson introduced in the *Essai* between *confused multiplicity*, which he located in consciousness, and *distinct multiplicity*, which he associated with the external world. He seems to have transferred the "inner" onto the "outer" as a material, real prelude to the displacement of duration out from consciousness into the being of the real that will occur in *Creative Evolution*.

2. This is a view compatible with chaos theory, discussed later in chap. 6.

We remember that it is a center of voluntary action because of the complexity of the sensory systems that requires coordination of its various component systems, and that is capable of perceiving at a distance. This complexity, we remember, introduces a "zone of indeterminacy" into the system. In higher organisms, then, actual perception will be limited by the purview and interests of this moving and variable center of action that is the body.

If perception, analyzed in the extreme hypothetical or pure case of Pure Perception, has nothing to do with representation, actual perception does include representations: "The reality of matter consists in the totality of its elements and of their actions of every kind. Our representation of matter is the measure of our possible action on the [material] bodies; it results from the elimination of what does not interest our needs and, more generally, our functions" (*MM* 35 [37–38]).

Actual perception is thus converted into representation through a process of reduction, or elimination, of what does not pertain to our own actions, which occur in the service of our interests and needs. "What you have to explain, then, is not how perception occurs [*naît*] but how it limits itself, because, in principle [*en droit*], it is the image of everything [*du tout*] whereas in fact it is reduced to what pertains to your interest . . . Indefinite, in principle, it limits itself, in fact, to depicting [*dessiner*] the degree of indeterminacy left to the activity [*démarches*] of this special image that you call your body. And, therefore, the indeterminacy of the movements of the body" (*MM* 38 [40–41]).

Bergson suggests the following opposition: that between what he calls a "material unconscious" (*MM* 29 [38]), in which every element of matter is in contact with all the others and every point "receives and transmits the actions from every point of the material world" (*MM* 29 [38]) (in other words Pure Perception) and consciousness, which only connects with certain parts of the material world from certain angles. "When it comes to external perception, consciousness consists precisely in this choice" (*MM* 35 [38]).[3]

Here is how Bergson characterizes perception:

> The truth is that my nervous system, interposed between the objects that affect my body [*ébranlent mon corps*] and those that I influence, plays the role of a simple conductor that transmits,

---

3. Once again, the proximity to Sigmund Freud is significant, as are the differences from Freud's topography of mental operations.

distributes or inhibits movements. This conductor is made up of an enormous multitude of threads [*fils*] that go from the periphery to the center and from the center to the periphery. There are as many points in space capable of . . . posing a basic question to my motor activity, as there are threads going from the periphery to [*the center*]. (*MM* 43 [44–45])

Each question posed is what we call a perception (*MM* 43 [44–45]). Perception, then, is a question posed to the body that responds to it.

4.1. Chapter 1 of *Matter and Memory*
"On the Selection of Images for Representation: The Role of the Body"

Action: Not Knowledge

Idealism says that the world is all in our heads. It says that we can never get past our perceptions to know what really is. As Kant put it, we can only know our representations of things, phenomena, not things in themselves, noumena. Realists, to the contrary, say that our perception merely translates what is happening in our bodies, that representations in our minds can be explained in terms of physical causes, and therefore that mind can be reduced to brain. Both positions mistakenly assume that perception is an epistemological function.

Bergson argues that perception enables us to act on the real, not to know it. It enables us to protect ourselves and to satisfy our biological needs. Living beings are obliged to act. This is a law of life, and perception follows from this law. Action, "the faculty that we have to effect changes in things . . . and towards which all the powers of the organized body seem to converge" (*MM* 65 [63]), is driven by need and occurs as movement. A physical stimulus, perceived as movement, will be followed by another movement, one that returns the movement it has received and passes it through the total system again.

Bergson succeeds in rephrasing a major philosophical issue because he approaches it from an interdisciplinary perspective, bringing biology and evolution to bear on the problem. Perception serves action, not knowledge. To think about perception in terms of action and movement changes the way we consider the brain. The brain is no longer a knowledge center, a machine that produces representations of the world. It becomes a center of action. "The brain is nothing but a kind of central telephone switchboard. Its role is to connect communications or put them on hold. It adds nothing to what it receives. . . . In other words the brain appears to us to be an instrument of analysis with respect to incoming movements and an instrument of selection in relation to movements . . . performed. But in the one case as in the other, its role is limited to that of transmitting and dividing movement" (*MM* 26–27 [30]). The brain either puts communication through immediately, in which case the result is an automatic action, or it puts the communication on hold, in which case a voluntary action can follow.

Images

The shift in perspective from knowledge to action also changes the language we use to speak about perception. Words such as "things" or "appearances" belong to an epistemological discourse and carry implications of truth, on the one hand, and illusion, on the other. Bergson will not use either term. He will speak instead of images.

This is the opening line of *Matter and Memory*: "Here I am in the presence of images, in the vaguest possible sense of the term, images that are perceived when I open my senses and not perceived [*inaperçues*] when I close them" (*MM* 11 [17]). With this first sentence, then, we enter a new horizon of thought, one of images. In philosophical terms, it is as if we had landed on another planet. Images are not things, although they are real. They are not merely appearances either, since they persist even when I shut down my senses and no longer perceive them. They are also constantly in motion, "acting and reacting the ones with the others in all their elementary parts" (*MM* 11 [17]) according to the laws of nature.

What is given, then, are images. Images are matter and at the same time they are perceptions. How can they be both? It will take the entire book to answer this question, and we shall follow the development step by step. But one thing is clear at this point. Bergson has taken as his point of departure a term that is neither a materialist element (a thing) nor an idealist one (a representation). The term is meant to interrupt our usual habits of thought so that we might think differently, that is, in terms of action, not knowledge.

The Body

Here I am, then, in the presence of images. But what is the status of this "I"?[4] To begin with, it is a body, and therefore an image like any other. It is acted upon by the other images in the universe and acts upon them in turn. But there is something special about this particular image. It stands out from the others for a couple of reasons. First, I know it from the inside through affect, as well as from the outside. My body feels pain. It carries with it a "mobile limit" (*MM* 83 [78]) between an external and an internal world. Second, my body's sensory apparatus is complex. When a jellyfish is poked, it reacts by reflex, immediately. Its perception *is* an action. As we advance on the evolutionary scale, however, the perceptual apparatus becomes more and more complex. Several senses operate together and contribute different registers of information, which occur in different rhythms and have to be coordinated by the brain. Some, such as the senses of sight and hearing, can perceive at a distance, and distance introduces a time factor in the form of a delay between the perception of the stimulus and its actual movement. We see and hear the approaching car before it hits us, for example. This gives us time to decide which way to jump to get out of the way. The time required to coordinate the various registers of sense data—touch, smell, hearing, and sight—together with the time introduced by perception at a distance, produce what Bergson calls a "zone of indeterminacy" (*MM* 29 [39]) around our action. This interferes with the mechanism of immediate automatic response to a stimulus. It interrupts it, and, in so doing, makes voluntary action possible: "I see clearly how the external images influence the image I call my body. They transmit movement to it. And I see how this body influences the other images: it returns this movement to them. In the . . . material world, then, my body is thus an image that acts like all the other images, with this small difference, perhaps, that my body is able to choose, to a certain extent, the way in which it returns the energy or motion it has received" (*MM* 14 [19]).

Whereas most of the other images in the universe act and react according to the laws of classical physics, my body can act voluntarily. It can decide how and when to respond to outside stimulus. It can affect

---

4. "My body is what emerges [*se dessine*] at the center of my perceptions; my personhood/body [*ma personne*] is the being to which these actions are referred" (*MM* 46 [47]).

changes in the world around it, introducing novelty into the system of actions and reactions that constitutes the universe as a whole.

Bergson defines the body as a "center of action" (*MM* 14 [20]). This means it has an impact on the images around it. To this extent, however, it also has an impact on perception. Since my body moves, acts, and changes its environment, perception cannot correspond exactly to the universe of images that make up the exterior world independently of us. Perception is individualized by the body whose voluntary action cuts through the surrounding world of images according to the specific agenda of its own biological needs. Does this mean that our perception is subjective? Not at all. It just means that we do not get the whole picture, but only part of it. But I am speaking only metaphorically here. Because, for Bergson, there is in a sense no "picture" to get. The brain is not a center of knowledge that gives us a true picture of the world when it functions well, and a distorted picture when it malfunctions, or is chemically altered. The brain does not give us a picture at all, because it does not produce representations.[5] It merely transmits movements and causes delay. And then the body interacts with the world.

Framing Perception

Our bodies' actions and needs *filter* the images that make up the external world, setting up the particular configuration of images we perceive. Think of a kaleidoscope, Bergson suggests, or a frame (*MM* 20 [19]). Our actions frame what we consciously perceive, such that perception will always be *less than* the totality of images. Our perception gives a kind of transcript, or reflection, of our interactions with the external world. It provides a record of the ways in which our body, as an image that is also a center of action, imprints the images which surround it and is imprinted from this particular angle in return. It records these images in their dynamic relation to the possible actions of my body. It is selective. The images that do not concern our needs and actions pass right through us without leaving a trace, like X-rays. Does this mean that the colors and configurations we see through the kaleidoscope of perception are our own mental constructions? Not at all, says Bergson. "My body,

5. We are not in the world of Heidegger's notion of the "worldview," for example. From Bergson's perspective, perception does not take a picture of the world. If there is a picture at all, it has already been taken out there in exteriority itself. The brain merely provides a kind of screen for its viewing or paper for its printing.

an object destined to move other objects, is . . . a center of action; it cannot engender a representation" (*MM* 14 [20]). If perception does not correspond to what is given, this is not because it misrepresents the real. Perception is neither illusory nor subjective. It is simply *less than* the real. Perception is to the real as part is to whole.[6]

The images that make up what we call objective reality "transmit the totality of what [they] receive [and] oppose to each action a reaction, equal and contrary . . . [T]hey are nothing, finally, but . . . path[s] through which the modifications that are propagated in the immensity of the universe pass in every direction" (*MM* 33 [36]).

In the world of images, each image transmits all the movements of all the other images that make up the material world. However, not all of these modifications are pertinent to our interests. Just as people do not perceive X-rays, or certain colors of the spectrum, they "let themselves be traversed, so to speak, by those among the external actions that are indifferent to them" (*MM* 33 [36]). On Bergson's account, then, perception involves a kind of limitation or framing of the real according to pragmatic criteria. It converts images into something like a code, which accords with the scale, reach, and interests of our action.[7] The rest is edited out.

Pure Perception

The hypothesis of Pure Perception is what Kant would call a "regulatory idea," an idea that, by proposing a virtual limit case, helps us grasp the edges of a concept. It shows what the idea is in principle. In this case Bergson's hypothesis of Pure Perception gives the idea of what perception would mean "for a being placed where I am, living as I live, but absorbed in the present, and capable, through elimination of all forms of memory, of obtaining an immediate and instantaneous vision of mat-

---

6. Perception involves a "variable relation between the living being and the influences of more or less distant objects that interest it" (*MM* 29 [33]). This occurs because the body is a center of action and its actions are surrounded by the "zone of indeterminacy" alluded to earlier. "It is because there is such a thing as voluntary action that perception is conscious, and that we identify it with consciousness *per se*" (*MM* 29 [33]).

7. External perception is a reflection: "the living body [is] like a kind of center from which are reflected, on surrounding objects, the action that these objects exert on it: external perception consists in this reflection" (*MM* 57 [56]). So the objects act on the body, which reflects action back onto the objects as perception. But not all of the action received by external things is reflected or deflected. Some is absorbed—this is affection.

ter" (*MM* 31 [34]). We might call Pure Perception a theoretical fiction because in actuality, as Bergson will go on to show, perception always includes memory; there is no such thing as instantaneous vision. Bergson's point, however, is that it will be easier for us to grasp the difference between perception and memory if we first consider perception without memory. He calls this Pure Perception.

In principle, perception is impersonal, objective. As a "system of nascent actions that dives into the real [*qui plonge dans le réel*]" (*MM* 71 [69]), it places us outside ourselves, directly in the universe of images where it encounters the real.[8] In principle, then, "to perceive all the influences of all the points of all the bodies would be to descend to the state of a material object" (*MM* 48 [49]). There would be no fundamental difference between the objective reality of images and the perception of them, except that even Pure Perception will be split or shattered [*scindée*] by our needs: "Pure Perception of matter is thus no longer relative or subjective, at least not in principle, and abstracts out, as we shall see momentarily, affection and above all memory; it is simply split [*scindée*] by the multiplicity of our needs" (*MM* 49 [50]).

It would even be possible to speak of a material, or unconscious, perception *of* matter itself: "One could say that the perception of any unconscious material point, in its instantaneity, is infinitely more vast and more complete than our perception, because this point receives [*recueille*] and transmits the actions of all the points of the material world, whereas our consciousness only attains certain parts of it, from certain perspectives" (*MM* 35 [38]).[9]

8. The difference between perception and affect or sensation is a difference in kind. Perception occurs outside my body in the external world of images; affection occurs in my body. "Just as external objects are perceived by me where they are, in themselves and not in me, so my affective states are experienced there where they produce themselves, that is, at a particular point of my body" (*MM* 58 [57]). So, "when we say that the image exists outside us, we mean that it is external to our body. When we speak of sensation as an inner state, we mean that it rises up in our body. And this is why we affirm that the totality of perceived images subsists, even if our body disappears, whereas we cannot do away with our body without making our sensations disappear" (*MM* 59 [58]). In Pure Perception we would "touch the reality of the object in an immediate intuition" (*MM* 79 [75]). It is thus only according to Pure Perception that Bergson could be said to be truly a phenomenologist. But the thrust of his work is to show that actuality never coincides with Pure Perception. In the first place, perception always includes affect (*MM* 59 [58]). Affect is defined as the absorption of action by the body (*MM* 57 [56]). What interests Bergson is memory, which disrupts or complicates what would be the phenomenological relation.

9. Perception occurs as a relation of part to whole with respect to matter, because, being conscious (with discernment) involves the separating out of what interests our var-

Bergson is evoking the kind of direct contact that each image finds itself in with respect to all other ones.[10] It is thus the hypothesis of Pure Perception that accounts for the fact that, as already noted, the term "image" is used to signify both reality and perception. For according to the hypothesis of Pure Perception, the two coincide. And it is according to the hypothesis of Pure Perception that perception is to reality as part is to whole: "To perceive all the influences of all the points of all the bodies would be to descend to the state of a material object" (*MM* 48 [49]). Ultimately, then *in principle*, Pure Perception would coincide with matter itself. Through it we would "place ourselves from the start in the totality of extended images."

What would the role of consciousness be, then, in perception? According to the hypothesis of Pure Perception, both affect and memory have been abstracted out of consideration. The sole function of consciousness would be to perform a temporal synthesis. Its role would be simply to "gather together an uninterrupted series of instantaneous visions" (*MM* 67 [65]). These visions, however, would "be part of things, not part of us" (*MM* 67 [65]). They are not our visions, produced by us; they would be the visions *of* things. The role of consciousness would be to link these visions together like beads on a string, or on the thread [*fil*] of memory.

What we learn from the hypothesis of Pure Perception is that perception, in principle, has very little to do with consciousness. It therefore has very little to do with the kind of inner life Bergson discussed in the *Essai*. Pure Perception is embedded in the real, in the outside world, because it is glued to the present.[11]

---

ious needs. So: "there is in matter something more, but not something different, than what is actually given." This formulates the notion of unconscious materialism (*MM* 35,74 [35,71]).

10. The only difference between the Pure Perception of matter that is objective reality and the Pure Perception of living beings who are centers of action is that in conscious beings, beings who have bodies that are centers of action, Pure Perception would involve a direct intuition of images selected according to the criteria of our needs and actions. It would thus be less than the totality of the real.

11. Bergson identifies the limit idea of Pure Perception with the notion of exteriority. "An impersonal foundation [*fond*] remains, where perception coincides with the perceived object . . . this foundation [*fond*] is exteriority itself" (*MM* 69 [66]). We also see from this quote that instantaneity pertains to matter, not to conscious beings.

Concrete Perception

All of this may be true of perception *in principle*. But, in actuality, perception never really occurs in this pure state.[12] "In actuality, there is no instantaneity for us" (*MM* 72 [69]). Memory mixes in with perception all the time for the simple reason that it takes time for perception to occur. We remember the previous discussion of the way sight and hearing perceive at a distance and therefore involve a temporal delay and introduce a zone of indeterminacy that enables voluntary action. This showed that in concrete perception we are not dealing with instantaneous visions at all. The delay, introduced because of the detour of sensory information through the brain yields a temporal difference between past, present, and future. Consequently, there has to be a way to hold on to perceived images over time. "The indetermination of acts to be accomplished requires . . . the conservation of perceived images" (*MM* 67 [65]). Voluntary action involves anticipation. We have no hold on the future, Bergson argues, without a corresponding hold on the past. "The pressure forward of our activity opens up a void behind it into which memories flow" (*MM* 67 [65]).[13]

What this involves is not the kind of impersonal memory alluded to above in connection with Pure Perception—the memory thread onto which external instantaneous visions would be strung like beads. In relation to concrete perception, memory is defined as the survival of past images. It is therefore a personal memory because, as we have seen, my perception has been individualized according to my needs and actions. The images that subsist from my perception, and serve my voluntary action, are decidedly mine. This memory is subjective and overlaps with consciousness, just as Pure Perception corresponds to matter. And here we link up again to the fundamental argument of the *Essai*. Consciousness implies duration, and for this reason, memory is a necessary supplement to perception. "These two acts," Bergson writes, "perception and remembering [souvenir] always interpenetrate, exchanging some-

12. "What we call by that name [perception] already includes a work of memory, and therefore of our consciousness, which prolongs numerous moments of an indefinitely divisible time, the ones in the others, so that they might be grasped in a relatively simple intuition" (*MM* 72 [69–70]).

13. "Memory is thus the repercussion, in the realm of knowledge, of the indetermination of our will" (*MM* 67 [65]). The term "knowledge" is introduced here because it is a question of consciousness and memory and thus of representation. Bergson restricts representation to the past and to the operation of memory, which, as we shall see, has little to do with the brain.

thing of their substances by a process of endosmosis" (*MM* 69 [67]). They always interpenetrate because in consciousness (i.e., in duration) past, present, and future interpenetrate in the mode of heterogeneous multiplicity that Bergson elaborated in the *Essai*.

Perception: A Pretext for Memory

There is also a pragmatic reason why, in actuality, memory is yoked to perception. Past images are useful in determining a choice of action. Bergson even claims that memory images are more useful to us than perceived images because they carry knowledge of the consequences that attached to past actions. Even more radically, Bergson suggests that the principal function of perception is to activate memory. He arrives at the startling conclusion that perception is, in actuality, merely an "occasion for remembering [*une occasion de se souvenir*]" (*MM* 68 [66]). Perception alone, he maintains, without memory, would give us little more than "signs of the real [*signes du réel*]" (*MM* 68 [66]) to which our memories attach. Pure Perception therefore is impersonal and coincides with exteriority itself—and the rest is memory!

> First of all. Let us say that if we pose memory, that is, the survival [*survivance*] of past images, these images are constantly mixed in with our perception of the present and can even substitute for it. For they are only conserved in order to be useful. At every instant they complete the present experience by enriching it with acquired experience. And as this is always increasing [*va en grossissant*], it ends up by covering over and submerging the other. It is undeniable that the background [*fond*] of real, and so to speak instantaneous, intuition, against which our perception of the external world emerges [*s'épanouit*] is slight [*peu de choses*] in comparison with everything our memory adds to it. Precisely because the memory of anterior intuitions is more useful that the intuition itself, being linked in our memory to the whole series of subsequent events and therefore being able to better enlighten [*éclairer*] our decision, it displaces the real intuition, whose role becomes reduced to that of soliciting memory [*appeler le souvenir*], embodying it [*lui donner un corps*], activating it, and thereby actualizing it. We therefore were right to say that the coincidence of perception with the perceived object exists in principle, rather than in fact. We must take into account the fact

that perception ends up being nothing but an occasion for re-membering [*de se souvenir*], that, practically speaking, we mea-sure the degree of reality of something by the degree of its utility, that we therefore have every interest in erecting as simple signs of the real [*signes du réel*] these immediate intuitions that coincide, at bottom, with reality itself. (*MM* 68 [65–66])

Time Factor

One of the reasons for abstracting out a notion of Pure Perception is to underscore the radical difference (a difference in kind, not merely in de-gree) between perception and memory. People tend to confuse the two because memory and perception operate together. They tend to believe memory is just a weaker form of perception, a kind of "perception to a lesser degree."[14] Or, conversely, they consider perception to be a more intense mode of memory. But this presupposes that both perceptions and memories are representations, and assumes memories to be just fainter copies of perceptions. From Bergson's point of view, of course, perception is not representation at all. It involves contact. And relations between subject and object (or inside and outside) must be thought from the perspective of time, not space. From this point of view, there is a radical difference between perception and memory. The former is at-tached firmly in the present, whereas the latter is anchored just as firmly in the past. The role of the psychologist, Bergson claims, is to dissociate the two.

Why is the present absolutely different (different in kind) from the past? Because we can only act in the present. Bergson defines the present as that which acts [*l'agissant*] and the past as "that which no longer acts [*ce qui n'agit plus*]" (*MM* 71 [68]). Our bodies, as centers of action, come into contact with matter (or images) in the present. They have an impact on the world in the present. Action in the past is impossible—*hélas*! The past is merely representation.[15] "The past is nothing but idea, the present is ideo-motor" (*MM* 71 [68]).[16] Since the present is ab-

---

14. This is the view of H. Taine who considers memory to be an "absent sensation" [*sensation nonprésente*]" in *De l'intelligence*, 1:462.

15. We recall that perception was distinguished from representation and defined in terms of action. As his argument proceeds, Bergson redistributes the distinction action/representation over the temporal domains of present and past. The past, i.e., mem-ory, becomes the realm of representation, whereas perception binds us to the present in the mode of action.

16. We now realize that the title "Matter and Memory" includes the distinction be-tween action and representation, on the one hand, as well as the opposition between

solutely different from the past, perception is absolutely different from memory. Excluded from perception by the hypothesis of Pure Perception, representation returns here as memory.

Pure Perception is not contemplative or speculative. It occurs in the service of action and establishes ties to the real in the present. The nervous system, which itself consists of "images," only functions to "receive, inhibit or transmit movement" (*MM* 75 [72]). Whereas Pure Perception is objective, "the subjectivity of our [concrete] perception consists above all in what memory brings to it" (*MM* 72 [69]). Memory is subjective. It mixes in with perception because, in actuality, perception takes time. Because perception occurs in time, "our successive perceptions are never the real moments of things, but rather moments of our consciousness" (*MM* 72 [69]). In other words, they are thick with duration.

> The qualitative heterogeneity of our successive perceptions of the universe occurs because [*tient à ce que*] each of these perceptions extends itself [*s'étend elle-même*] through a certain thickness of duration, because memory condenses here an enormous multiplicity of shocks [*ébranlements*] that appear to us all at once [*tous ensemble*], although they are successive. In order to pass from perception to matter, from subject to object, one would ideally only have to divide this undivided thickness of time, to distinguish here the desired multiplicity of movements, in a word, to eliminate all memory.... It is ... in an extended perception [*perception extensive*] that the subject and the object would first unite the subjective aspect of perception consisting in the contraction that memory operates, the objective reality of matter merging with [*se confondant avec*] the multiple and successive shocks [*ébranlements*] in which this perception breaks down internally. (*MM* 73–74 [70–71])

Memory

Bergson has characterized Pure Perception as if consciousness had almost nothing to do with it, as if it involved simply a mode of direct encounter with the real. Its only job, we remember, was to link instantaneous visions of the real to one another like beads on a string. On closer

---

present and past, on the other, consistent with the injunction that questions of subject and object be treated in terms of time not space.

analysis, Bergson reveals, there is no such thing as an instantaneous vision. "What we call by that name," he explains, "already includes a work of memory, and therefore of our consciousness, that prolongs numerous moments of an indefinitely divisible time, the ones in the others, so that they might be grasped in a relatively simple intuition" (*MM* 72 [69–70]).

In concrete perception, memory functions in two important ways. First, it interweaves [*intercale*] the past into the present, such that memory is practically inseparable from perception. Second, it gathers together multiple moments of duration and contracts them into a single intuition.[17]

What have we learned from this first chapter? Let's start with the body. The body is a center of action that acts in the present. The nervous system of the living body is nothing but "passageways [*lieux de passage*] for . . . movements that are received in the form of excitations [and] are transmitted in the form of reflex actions or voluntary actions" (*MM* 77 [73]). The body is capable of voluntary action because of the complexity of the sensory system, which introduces a time factor into the act of perception, surrounding action by what Bergson has called a "zone of indeterminacy." The brain functions only to conduct movement. As it coordinates the disparate registers and rhythms of sensory information it receives as excitations or movements, it delays automatic response. This, together with the survival of past images in memory, is what makes voluntary action possible.

Consciousness helps the body cope with time. Time is always on the move. Consciousness serves the body as center of action by synthesizing the heterogeneous rhythms of duration into temporal horizons of past, present, and future. Consciousness is more or less equated with memory and therefore with the past. The present is defined in terms of action. Everything else is already past—even as it heads into the future! There is no present moment except the moment of action, the event of contact with the real. All the rest, essentially, is memory.

The logic of Bergson's argument goes something like this: the body acts in the present through perception that encounters matter. Memory refers us to the past, which no longer acts, and is therefore purely idea. The present is radically different from the past. Therefore memory must

---

17. "It is because of this dual function of memory that we perceive matter in us (in consciousness), whereas in principle we perceive in it [i.e., in matter]" (*MM* 76 [72–73]).

be a force that is completely independent from matter. To this extent, memory demonstrates an independence of mind from matter. This is essentially an argument for the reality of mind [*esprit*] as something that cannot be reduced to material causes: "Since Pure Perception gives the totality, or at least the basic essentials [*l'essentiel*] of matter, since the rest comes from memory and adds itself to matter, then memory must be, in principle, a force absolutely independent from matter. If, therefore, *esprit* is a reality, it is here, in the phenomenon of memory, that we should be able to examine it experimentally [*le toucher expérimentalement*]" (MM 76 [73]).

As we shall see, what distinguishes Bergson's approach to the mind/body problem is the interdisciplinary character of his analysis. Instead of talking about consciousness in metaphysical terms, he examines experimental studies that pertain to memory function and dysfunction. Not only does he take advantage of the extensive clinical studies on aphasia performed by his contemporaries, but, after writing the *Essai*, he spends five years studying neuro-physiology in order to introduce a scientific, as well as a social-scientific, perspective into his analysis of relations between mind and body.

Bergson announces at the end of this chapter that it is through the phenomena of memory that we can examine consciousness experimentally and "are able to grasp the *esprit* in its most palpable form" (MM 77 [74]). Through memory we can examine the workings of the mind [*le travail même de l'esprit*] concretely and explore its interactions with, and independence from, the body. In the following chapters, Bergson will appeal to psychology in the elaboration of his theory concerning the interaction of perception and memory. In metaphysical terms, however, this interaction provides Bergson's answer to the philosophical problem of the mind/body dualism. There *is* a dualism, since mind cannot be reduced to matter and matter cannot be reduced to mind. But functionally, mind and body interact all the time in concrete perception. In terms of the metaphysical argument, then, memory becomes, for Bergson, "the point of contact between consciousness and matter" (MM 77 [74]).

In retrospect, we can appreciate the strategy of Bergson's argument. In this first chapter he has set things up so that perception corresponds with matter (this was the point of the hypothesis of Pure Perception) and memory corresponds with consciousness or mind (*esprit*). Since perception and memory are intertwined in concrete perception, body and mind are already implicitly in a relation of interaction with one another in a way that complicates any strict dualism.

In the meantime, however, a number of tricky questions remain. Most notably, what is the relation between memory and the body? Why is it attached to the body, and how? What is the influence of the body on memory? Where does memory begin and where does it end? These are the questions Bergson will take up in the following chapter.

4.2. Chapter 2 of *Matter and Memory*
"Of the Recognition of Images: Memory and the Brain"

As Bergson will explain in his conclusion, "The theory of memory, which forms the center of our study, should be at one and the same time the theoretical consequence and the experimental verification of our theory of Pure Perception."[18] Bergson's strategy is to challenge theories of cerebral localization that would explain memory functions in terms of physiological causes, reducing mind to brain.

Bergson's second chapter opens with a few reminders concerning the body as theorized earlier in connection with the notion of Pure Perception. "We said that the body, interposed between the objects that act on it and those it influences, is nothing but a conductor, charged with receiving movements and with transmitting them . . . to certain motor mechanisms, determined, in a reflex action, chosen, if the action is voluntary" (*MM* 81 [77]).

Given this account, it follows that the body can only hold onto the past through motor mechanisms [*dispositifs moteurs*] and that what we call memory images must be conserved in some other way. On this basis, Bergson proposes the following three guiding hypotheses.

A. "The past survives in two distinct ways: (1) in motor mechanisms; (2) in independent memories [*souvenirs indépendents*]" (*MM* 82 [78]).

B. "The recognition of a present object occurs through movements when it proceeds from the object, by representations when it proceeds from the subject" (*MM* 82 [78]).

C. "One passes, by minute degrees, from memories arranged temporally [*selon le long du temps*] to movement that in-

18. Ibid., 91. For connections between Bergson's theory of memory and that of his contemporary, the psychologist Théodule Ribot, see Worms, *Introduction à Matière et mémoire,* 106.

scribes its incipient or possible action in space. Brain lesions can affect these movements, but not the memories" (*MM* 83 [79]).

Two Forms of Memory

The question of memory concerns how the past survives in the present. Bergson argues that it does so in two different ways. One involves the body and occurs through movements; the other involves images and occurs through representations.

As usual, Bergson begins with an example. Think about what happens when we learn a text (a poem, for example) by heart. This kind of rote learning, which occurs through repetition, will be associated with habit and with a memory of the body. But overlapping with this learning by repetition we also remember the various acts of reading that went into the task of memorization. When we think of these distinct readings, we realize that each one is unique and can be placed in time or precisely contextualized. Bergson will call this the memory of imagination, or spontaneous memory. "How is it possible," he writes, "not to admit that there is a radical difference between what is achieved [*se constitue*] by repetition and what, by its very essence, cannot be repeated?" (*MM* 88 [83]). He adds, "Spontaneous memory is immediately perfect; time can add nothing to its image without denaturing it; it will conserve its place and its date for memory. On the contrary, a memory which has been learned [*souvenir appris*] will escape time [*sortira du temps*] as soon as the lesson is learned; it will become more and more impersonal, more and more a stranger to our past life" (*MM* 88 [83]).[19] He concludes, "Of the two memories that we have just distinguished, the first appears to be memory par excellence. The second, the one psychologists usually study, is *habit informed by memory* rather

19. Here the link to Proust is important. Although Bergson does not call the two types of memory voluntary memory and involuntary memory, as Proust will do, he does identify the one with habit and utility and the other with images and with the specific concreteness of lived experience. Bergson writes "the first [the memory of habit and repetition] is achieved by effort and remains dependent upon our will [*volonté*]; the second, completely spontaneous, shows as much capriciousness in its reappearance [*met autant de caprice à reproduire*] as faithfulness in its conservation [*que de fidélité à conserver*]" (*MM* 94 [88]). The relation to Proust warrants further rigorous investigation, especially in light of Bataille's discussion of Proust and the image in *Inner Experience* [*L'expérience intérieure*].

than memory itself" (*MM* 89 [84], original emphasis). Bergson's theory of memory will follow from this first example of learning a text by heart.

Automatic Memory

Thus far we have considered the body as a conductor of motion in a static framework. To speak of memory, however, is to speak of time—flowing time. From this perspective, my body is always situated at the precise point where my past has just expired into an action (*MM* 83 [78]). The body, in this context, is redefined as a moving limit between past and future. It is "like a moving point that our past pushes into our future. Thus we have considered the body as a conductor of motion or energy, but this is from a static perspective. When we consider the body from a temporal perspective—i.e., in relation to flowing time—it is always situated at the precise point where my past has just expired into an action" (*MM* 83 [78]). The past registers itself as motor habit.

When I get into my car, for example, I put the key in the ignition automatically; I don't even think about it. It is as if my body remembers what to do all by itself. This is what Bergson calls motor memory, or the memory of the body. It is automatic. It is produced through repetition and occurs as repetition. Bergson says that it performs [*joue*] (*MM* 87 [82]) the past in the present when it repeats a gesture or action by habit. To the extent that perception is linked to action, on Bergson's account, it is accompanied by movements that are repeated and, over time, form reflexes or habits. "Afferent nerves carry an excitation to the brain, which, after having intelligently chosen its response [*sa voie*] transmits the excitation to motor mechanisms, created by repetition. In this way the appropriate reaction is produced. . . . The adaptation, in a word, which is the end of life" (*MM* 89 [84]). As we see, this kind of memory is to be understood in biological (or evolutionary) terms, that is, as a mechanism of adaptation to the external world. It is built right into the nervous system.[20]

20. Worms notes a link to the work of Félix Ravaisson, *De l'habitude: Métaphysique et morale,* which placed habit as "the lowest form and the first sign, of the activity of *esprit,*" *Introduction à Matière et mémoire,* 102. All translations from this work are mine.

Image Memory (La mémoire qui revoit)

There is also another kind of memory, however, one that spontaneously retains the past in the form of images, images that carry the mark of the unique moment in which they were lived. Bergson calls this is a memory of imagination. This is a memory that sees [revoit] the past events of one's experience in all their concreteness, with "their contour, their color and their place in time" (MM 94 [88]). This memory, Bergson announces, operates by "natural necessity" (MM 86 [80]). In principle, this spontaneous memory registers every aspect of the concrete real in all its detail. Nothing escapes it. It registers "all the events of our daily lives as they occur" (MM 86 [81]). Bergson calls it a "regressive memory" because it does not engage with the present. This is what gives us dream images. "To evoke the past in the form of image, it is necessary to be able to detach oneself from action in the present, to attach value to what is useless, to want to dream" (MM 87 [82–83]). During waking hours, the motor memory of habit inhibits the image memory because of the imperatives of action. The memory of imagination has nothing to do with action. And since it is pure representation or idea, it has nothing to do with the brain. For, as we learned in the last chapter, the brain cannot produce representations (MM 96 [73]). The radical feature of Bergson's analysis is that memory has nothing to do with the brain. This is the notion Bergson will proceed to elaborate as Pure Memory, on analogy with the Pure Perception we encountered in the last chapter.

Pure Memory is entirely virtual. It operates spontaneously, and its memory image "is necessarily imprinted right away in my memory." As Frédéric Worms writes, "It is as if a perception automatically became a memory [souvenir] by virtue of being placed in time, that is, in the unfolding [déroulement] of a personal history, by becoming not only the consciousness or perception of something, but of someone." As Worms further explains: "Once past, that is, once it has become my past, the image changes in meaning: the memory of a perception or of an object is no longer a perception or an object, it only exists for a memory or a subject. Each instant of time, each perception, thus takes on a double meaning, or takes on the sense of an intersection between the spectacle of an object which initially defines it, and the memory of a subject that it becomes right away. . . . All the rest of Bergson's demonstration and of his psychology depends on this initial doubling."[21]

21. Ibid., 102, 103.

The rest of Bergson's chapter, however, will be devoted to the investigation of *actual* memory, which, as we shall see, involves the practical collaboration of the two types of memory that have just been distinguished *in principle*. The two types of memory work "side by side and lend each other mutual support" (*MM* 91 [86]). This, of course, only reinforces Bergson's broader argument, which concerns the intimate functional interaction of mind and body.

What has Bergson accomplished with this double theory of memory? First, he has interrupted the tendency to take memory as one term of a dualism in opposition to the body. For it is as if he had cut the ideal/real opposition right through the term memory, doubling memory as a memory of the body and a memory of the imagination. In the second place, he has established a difference in kind between these two types of memory, to the extent that he has identified one with the body as center of action. This precludes any interpretation of the memory of images as just a version of the memory lodged in the body. It thus establishes the radical independence of Pure Memory that Bergson will go on to elaborate.

Pure Memory exists in principle (if not in fact) in symmetry with the notion of Pure Perception introduced in the last chapter. We remember that Bergson posed the virtual term Pure Perception (impersonal and outside time) and then elaborated his account of actual perception (individualized and suffused with memory). Here, in the same way, he poses a term he will subsequently call Pure Memory, the spontaneous memory of images (the memory of a *re-voir*). He then goes on to show how this memory only actually operates in relation to perception. In both cases, it is a question of linking the present—defined in terms of action, and therefore in relation to both the body as center of action and the brain as incipient action [*action naissante*]—to the past, which is defined in terms of inaction or powerlessness [*impuissance*]. The past is by definition incapable of action.

Memory images, however, serve a useful function in relation to action. Indeed, there would be no voluntary action without them. If memory and perception usually work in tandem, what is the point of going to such lengths to distinguish them? It is because psychologists who study memory tend to lump the two together and then analyze the composite in terms of automatic memory alone. This is what leads to theories that neglect the specificity of the memory of imagination, theories that want to explain all memory function in terms of brain location or brain lesion—theories that reduce mind to body.

Recognition

The image memory, then, is staged as a kind of Pure Memory that only actually operates in relation to perception, which includes a certain memory of the body. The mechanism of interaction between perception and memory (and, it is a two-way street, between memory and perception) is recognition, "the concrete act by which we grasp the past again [*resaississons*] in the present." Recognition articulates past and present, memory and perception, and also the two types of memory. It provides that "mixed state" that actually occurs, where the spontaneous memory can assist in the voluntary direction, or redirection, of motor memory.

The second part of the second chapter of *Matter and Memory* is thus titled: "Of Recognition in General: Memory Images and Movements" (*MM* 96 [90]). Here Bergson takes up, critiques, and reworks a simple notion of recognition derived from the familiar but nevertheless disconcerting experience known as *déjà vu*. According to this view, widely accepted by psychologists of Bergson's day, recognition is merely the association we make between a perception and a memory. Bergson criticizes this theory, held by associationist psychologists, through painstaking analyses of specific clinical cases of memory pathology. I will not recount them here.

He then proposes his own theory of recognition (*MM* 100 [92]). He starts from the experience of the body alone: "There is first of all, as a limit case [*à la limite*], a recognition in the instant [*dans l'instantané*], a recognition of which the body is capable all by itself, without the intervention of any explicit memory image. It consists in an action and not in a representation" (*MM* 100 [92–93]). He offers the following example:

> I go for a walk in a city for the first time. With each turn in the street I hesitate, not knowing where I am going. I am uncertain, and I mean by that that the alternatives pose themselves to my body, that my movement is discontinuous . . . that there is nothing, in one of the attitudes, that announces and prepares for the attitudes that follow. Later, after a long stay in this city, I will circulate mechanically, without having the distinct perception of the objects before which I pass. . . . I started in a state where I could only distinguish my perception; I ended up in a state where I was hardly aware of my automatism any more: in between was a

mixed state, in which a perception was underscored [*souligné*] by a nascent automatism. (*MM* 101 [93])

Bergson analyzes the feeling of familiarity that comes from the body and its own mode of recognition. On the basis of this example, he draws the following conclusion: recognition, in its simplest form, depends upon motor activity.

Perception, as we have seen, occurs in the service of action, not knowledge. According to the hypothesis of Pure Perception introduced in the last chapter, it is already a mode of action. It therefore implies an organized motor response. To this extent recognition occurs physically. According to an opposition Bergson invokes repeatedly (and which will play a major role in his analysis of the comic in *Le rire*) he says that ordinarily "we perform our recognition [*le jouer*] before we think it" (*MM* 101 [95]). Take the problem of learning how to use a tool. Incipient movements in the body, which follow perception like a reflex, help us recognize how to use a hammer, for example (*MM* 101 [94]). We learn how to use a tool or a machine through the development of "motor impulses [*impulsions motrices*]" (*MM* 101 [94]).[22] Recognition (or what Bergson will call the "primordial condition of recognition") occurs physically—we perform or enact it [*jouer*] rather than thinking it.

This sense of familiarity, developed as motor response, organizes itself into habit. "Motor tendencies," Bergson writes, "would thus be sufficient to give us the feeling of recognition, but . . . usually something else is added" (*MM* 103 [95]).

Attentive Recognition

To this automatic recognition, which Bergson will also call "recognition by distraction," it is time to add "attentive recognition" (*MM* 107 [98]) the other mode of recognition that involves memory images.[23]

---

22. As Worms points out, Bergson's theory of the memory of the body can usefully be thought in relation to the schematism of Kant that relates intuition to concept (114).

23. Bergson's discussion of distraction and attention is particularly interesting in relation to the theories of Walter Benjamin concerning the passage from the structure of experience he refers to as *Erfahrung* to the one he calls *Erlebnis* and identifies with modernity and with distraction. See Walter Benjamin, "On Some Motifs in Baudelaire" and "The Storyteller," in *Illuminations*, trans. Harry Zohn.

Whereas . . . motor mechanisms are activated [*se montent*] under
the influence of perceptions that are better and better analyzed by
the body, our previous psychological life is there: it survives . . .
with all the detail of its events localized in time. Always inhibited
by practical and useful consciousness of the present moment, that
is, by the sensori-motor balance of the nervous system held in
tension [*tendu*] between perception and action, this memory simply waits for a break to announce itself between the actual impression and the concomitant movement into which it projects its
images [*y faire passer ses images*]. Usually an effort is required to
go back over the course of our past [*pour remonter le cours de
notre passé*] and discover the memory image known, localized,
personal, which would pertain [*se rapporterait*] to the present. By
means of this effort we disengage from the action to which our
perception inclines us. This would push us towards the future; we
have to move backwards [*reculons*] into the past. Although the
totality [*ensemble*] of our past images remains present to us, it is
still necessary that the representation that is analogous to the actual perception be chosen among all the possible representations. . . . Movements, either performed or incipient, prepare this
selection, or at least delimit the field where we will go to pick
them [*où nous irons les cueillir*]. By virtue of the very constitution of our nervous system, we are creatures whose present impressions prolong themselves in appropriate movements. If old
images also see fit to prolong themselves in these movements,
they seize the occasion to slip into the actual perception and become adopted by it. . . . We could therefore say that the movements that provoke mechanical recognition inhibit the recognition by images, on the one hand, and enable it [*favorisent*], on
the other. In principle the present displaces the past. But, on the
other hand, precisely because the suppression of the old images
has to do with their inhibition by the present attitude, those
whose form can fit into the frame of this attitude encounter a
lesser obstacle than the others. . . . It is the image that resembles
the present perception that will overcome the obstacle. (*MM* 103
[95–96])

What Bergson is trying to demonstrate, in this long and very
nuanced passage, is both how memory images can insert themselves

into brain movements and how they cannot be reduced to such movements.[24]

Recognition is said to be attentive when "memory images regularly rejoin present perceptions" (*MM* 107 [99]). There is one rather surprising difference between motor (or automatic) recognition and attentive recognition: "Whereas, in automatic recognition, our movements extend our perception in order to produce useful effects, and to this extent remove us [*nous éloignent*] from the perceived object, here, on the contrary, they bring us back to the object to underscore its contours. Whence the preponderant role the memory images play here" (*MM* 107 [98]).

Bergson is alluding to the essential role memory images play in the constitution of the act of *cognitive* perception. We have already seen that in his view perception serves action. This is what Bergson has in mind when he says that motor recognition "removes [us] from the object." We are already on our way toward the future action we will take in response to our perception. Our body has already, so to speak, set us in motion. The epistemological moment only comes in, then, thanks to the supplement of attentive recognition. This brings us closer to the object as we imaginatively underscore, or resketch, its contours. By this gesture, we actually facilitate its emergence as an object of perception that can be known; it can now be consciously recognized.[25]

The third part of this chapter is entitled "Gradual Passage from Memories to Movements" (*MM* 107 [99]). Here, Bergson writes, "we arrive at the essential point of the debate" (*MM* 107 [99]), which is linked to the following question: in attentive recognition, do present perceptions determine the recall of specific memory images? Or do memory images spontaneously project themselves in the act of perception? Bergson declares that the answer given to this question will deter-

---

24. The point is made by Worms, *Introduction*, 112.

25. Worms writes, "the complete memory [*la mémoire complète*] claims priority as a form of knowledge of the object: paradoxically, by going beyond the immediate utility to which the body is limited, it does not lose itself [*ne s'enfonce pas*] in the depths of a subjective consciousness. On the contrary, whereas the knowledge of the body is completely *interested* and pragmatic, a supplementary knowledge or recognition [*connaissance ou reconnaissance*], characterized by its disinterestedness, would explore precisely the depths of the object, not in order to make use of them but to know them, that is, for themselves," *Introduction*, 116.

mine the nature of relations between memory and the brain (*MM* 108 [100]).

In order to answer this question, Bergson will have to go more deeply into issues of experimental psychology. He will have to explore "general relations between perception, attention, and memory" (*MM* 109 [100]) in greater detail. In this section he will focus on the question of attention and invoke the more general psychology of levels of consciousness that he will elaborate more fully in chapter three of *Matter and Memory*.

Attention

"What is attention? On the one hand, attention . . . renders perception more intense and brings out its details; considered materially [*dans sa matière*] it would amount to a certain enlargement [*grossissement*] of the intellectual state [*état intellectuel*]. But, on the other hand, consciousness affirms an irreducible formal difference between this increase in intensity and one that results from a higher level of external excitation. It seems to come from within, and to bear witness to a certain *attitude* adopted by the intelligence" (*MM* 109 [100], original emphasis). Here, Bergson admits, we run into a problem, since we can't say just what an intellectual attitude might mean.

Bergson settles on a different kind of explanation. "Let's suppose," he writes, "that attention implies a turning back of the mind [*esprit*] which gives up pursuing any useful end of the present perception: there will be at first an inhibition of movement, a pause [*une action d'arrêt*]. But rapidly, other, more subtle, movements will graft themselves onto this attitude . . . whose role it is to go over the contours of the perceived object. With these movements the positive work of attention begins, and not just the negative work. It is continued by memories" (*MM* 110 [101]). What is attention, then? It is not something measurable, like an increase in intensity or mental action that could be reduced to a physical event. Bergson proposes that it is a kind of turning back on the part of consciousness or the mind [*l'esprit*] that refuses to pursue the utilitarian end of the present perception (*MM* 110 [101]).[26]

Here is how it works. Perception, as we have already seen, affects us physically. It provokes movements in us that inscribe the contours of

26. Note the similarity to Kant's depiction of esthetic judgment as a "purposiveness without purpose" and to this extent distinct from cognitive judgment.

the object. It is as if the object were imprinting us physically, on a motor level, as we prepare ourselves to respond to it. Memory then directs onto the received perceptual input (still considered on a physical level) old images from the past that resemble it. Our movements have already sketched out the lines of the object. We then project the memory images into this frame, as if to fill in, or supplement, the provisional sketches.

This gesture can be understood in two ways. First, it means that our memory recreates the initial perception. This would be necessary because of the passage of time that requires an act of temporal synthesis on our part. This was the first function given to memory. Secondly, however, it means that the memory can substitute a similar memory image for the perceptual data received [*quelque image souvenir du même genre*] (*MM* 111 [101]). If this memory image does not correspond exactly, in every detail, "an appeal is made [*un appel est lancé*] to the farthest reaches of memory, until other known details [*détails connus*] come to project themselves onto those we are not aware of [*ceux qu'on ignore*]" (*MM* 111 [101]). This operation can go on forever, with memory "fortifying and enriching perception, which, in turn, becom[es] more and more developed, attracting a growing number of complementary memories" (*MM* 111 [101]).

According to the model Bergson rejects, attention would function like a beam of light, "that can either be allowed to diffuse or be concentrated onto a point" (*MM* 111 [102]). For Bergson, attention operates more like a telegraph operator, "who, upon receiving a message, spells it back word for word to the sender in order to verify its accuracy" (*MM* 111 [102]). To pursue this figure, then, in perception we receive an image, and in order to verify this message, we have to be able to reproduce the image, to reconstruct it through an effort of synthesis (*MM* 111 [102]). It is the first level of recognition (the automatic recognition of the body) that generates the "hypotheses" (*MM* 112 [102]) that enable this reconstruction, that is, that gives us the particular frame, as a motor schema, into which the memory image must fit.[27]

---

27. "What suggests the hypotheses, what presides from afar over their selection [i.e., of images], are the movements of imitation by means of which the perception continues [*se continue*], and which will serve as the common frame, shared by the perception and the remembered images" (*MM* 112 [102]). This analysis is based on psychological data. Bergson relies principally on clinical studies that concerned cases of aphasia or other memory pathologies. The starting point is the phenomenon of the "after image" which, Bergson argues, actually comes before, or belongs to, the related perception.

Attention, then, involves an active appeal to memory. Memory, in attentive recognition, "melts into the present perception."[28] As Worms puts it, "Attention is therefore not a reactive force of the body, or an empty power of the mind, that would be aimed at an indifferent point in space: it reveals a contact between the objects of Pure Perception and the memories of Pure Memory, thanks to the double filter of a structure at once motor and cerebral."[29] Bergson argues that the articulation of perception and memory performed by attentive recognition happens through an act of reflection, "an external projection of an image actively created" (*MM* 112 [102]). This image is crucial for a number of reasons. Memory acts like a mirror. But, because of the dynamic flow of time, we would have to consider it more like a magic mirror that has accumulated a multiplicity of past images. It can therefore activate a certain number of past images, as well as give back the echo (or reflection) of the image it has just received through sense perception. There is no real limit to this multiplicity.

Bergson's analysis of perception is based principally on clinical studies that concerned the act of reading. In this sense he returns, in clinical justification of his theory of memory, to the image presented earlier in the chapter to suggest the two types of memory: reading a text one is learning by heart. Contrary to what was previously believed, Bergson affirms, we do not read letter by letter. Instead, the mind picks out certain characteristic traits and fills in the rest with memory images it projects onto the paper. These memory images substitute for the words really printed on the page (*MM*, 113 [103]). Thus, to a linear model of reading (and of perception) Bergson opposes a circular one: "Our distinct perception is really comparable to a closed circle, in which the perception image, directed toward the mind and the memory image, projected into space, run after one another" (*MM* 193 [103]).

Thus, for Bergson, perception does not occur according to the kind of linear model advanced by Locke, among others, according to which an object engenders sensations that in turn engender ideas. This would imply that the memory image was caused by perception and that the brain determined all of memory. Instead, Bergson proposes that recognition (or memory) operates more like an electrical circuit: "Any excitation which leaves from the object cannot stop *en route* in the depths of

28. Worms, *Introduction*, 121.
29. Ibid.

the mind. It must always return to the object itself" (*MM* 114 [104]). (Here Bergson adumbrates the general psychological theory of levels of consciousness and memory that he will elaborate in chapter three of *Matter and Memory.)*

Bergson's theory of attention depends upon this notion of a dynamic circuit between object and memory. An increase in attention or concentration, he argues, involves widening the scope of the memory images that come into play.[30] This broadening involves a work of embedding, that is, of interpreting, the perceived image through an act of contextualization.[31] Thus the deeper the memory layers we tap into, the more we actually perceive of reality, and the more meaning we can give to the real. It is as if the real, and the interpretation of the real, were almost the same thing. With "a greater expansion of memory" (in the larger and larger circuits of memory brought into play) "reflexion attains deeper layers of reality" (*MM* 114 [105]). The specific tension (or degree of focus of attention) determines the range of the memory images (the breath of the circle of memory, according to the schema Bergson provides) that are brought to bear on the perception. Attention involves a degree of mental, or psychic, tension that correlates with a more or less extensive appeal to the contextualizing power of memory images.

Memory images can serve action, then, by affecting the interpretation of the incoming perception, which in turn affects the choice of action to be voluntarily undertaken. Or, they can be quite detached from action. On this level, memory images carry more detail from the past; they are more embedded in the concrete moment of their past occurrence. Such are the images that return to us in dream.

Useful memory images, those that come forward from the past to be inserted into an act of perception that serves action, lose detail and concreteness. This is what enables them to match up with the incoming perceptual data, to fit into the framework produced by the motor impulses that operate in automatic recognition. The memory, as it approaches its interface with action, "contracts or rather sharpens [*s'affile*] more and more, until it presents only the cutting edge of its blade [*le tranchant de sa lame*] to the experience which presents itself" (*MM* 116–117 [106]). But even this narrow, or tightly focused, intercalation of memory image into perception transposes what would have been a purely automatic ac-

---

30. We see that Bergson did not give up trying to characterize what the expansion [*grossissement*] of the intellect might mean. He could not explain it earlier, when he backed off from this formulation, because it involved launching a general theory of psychology that, in turn, required the elaboration of attention.

31. See figure 3 of Bergson's text, provided here on page 153.

tion (impersonal, as on the model of Pure Perception) into a voluntary action. Perception starts out on the motor level. This provides a kind of blueprint, which is then fleshed out by memory images that provide color and detail.

We see how important the figure of reading has been for Bergson's analysis of memory. It enables him to distinguish between two types of memory. It also enables him to confirm the spontaneity of the production of memory images. Finally, the issue of language enables him to address cognitive operations of giving meaning to the world.

Once again, Bergson confronts his model empirically with clinical evidence. Again, it will be a question of studies that concern brain lesions and their relation to memory dysfunctions, such as problems of recognition (psychic blindness or deafness) and various forms of aphasia.[32] Bergson argues against the view that brain lesions *cause* dysfunction because they erase memories that were somehow stored in a particular area of the brain.

Bergson first considers the reception of spoken language because this kind of aphasia has been extensively studied, clinically. It has been demonstrated that speech recognition involves a specific area of the brain. This example thus provides a good test case for the position that Bergson is arguing against, namely, the theory that the brain stores memories, and that aphasia can be causally explained by brain lesions.

Bergson looks at the experience of auditory word recognition to see if he can locate the two moments of perception and memory he has presented in his interactive theory. Can he isolate (1) an automatic sensorimotor process and (2) a moment of active projection of memory images? The specific example concerns hearing a foreign language, a language one does not understand because one has never learned it. This would be comparable to the experience an aphasic has in relation to his or her own language, since the aphasic has no memory of ever having heard it. In this instance, then, no memory can come into play. Sound occurs on a purely physical level. It is experienced as mere noise, as a sonorous mass [*une masse sonore*].[33]

"The question is," Bergson asks, "how knowledge of a language, which is only memory [*n'est que souvenir*] can modify the materiality of a present perception?" (*MM* 120 [109]). How is this usually explained?

32. As F.C.T. Moore points out, Bergson "made extensive reference to contemporary work by Charcot and Freud" on questions of amnesia and aphasia: *Bergson: Thinking Backwards*, 5.

33. See Worms, *Introduction*, 124 n. 1, for a discussion of relations between the analysis of Bergson and the linguistics of Saussure.

The brain lesion effaces memories, interrupting contact between perception of the sound and memory of the word. But, Bergson objects, this leaves out an intermediary step: the detour through the body. What really happens when one hears spoken language is that repetition enables the body to respond. The body attempts to imitate the sounds automatically, and in so doing, it begins to parse the sounds it receives. It breaks them down into parts, thereby differentiating the noise—the *masse sonore*—into distinct sounds, or what Roman Jakobson calls "distinctive features."[34] "Thus there occurs in our consciousness, in the form of nascent muscular sensations, what we will call the motor schematism [*schème moteur*] of the spoken language" (*MM* 121 [111]). In other words, the body (or its motor tendencies) disarticulates the sounds of the foreign language. This process involves coordinating the impressions of the ear with the muscles of the voice; it is a question of perfecting a kind of motor accompaniment. According to this analysis, then, the brain lesion would impact the motor schematism [*schème moteur*] (*MM* 127 [115]), but not the memory images themselves. This is the crucial point. Bergson does not want to minimize the important role the brain plays in perception and memory. He simply wants to insulate memory images from the brain, which, he believes, has nothing to do with them. This was the whole point of the postulate of Pure Memory.

Next it is a question of exploring the second step, the question of the projection of memory images. Bergson's premise is that for memories to become activated, they need a "motor support [*adjuvant moteur*]" (*MM* 133 [120]). He is against the theory that comprehension proceeds from the sound image (or perception) to the memory and from the memory to the idea (*MM* 136 [124–125]). The common approach is to separate these three elements, and to localize them in the brain, reducing them to physical causes and operations. Bergson maintains that it is not a question of things that can be located, but of a dynamic process through which one thing, perception, becomes another, memory—and the other way around! Again, we have to think in terms of a current and a circuit. Attentive (conscious) perception involves two currents: a centripetal one, which starts from the external object and appeals to memory, and a centrifugal one, which starts from Pure Memory and interacts with the body to help constitute the object of perception (*MM* 142 [130]).[35]

34. Roman Jakobson, *Essais de linguistique générale*, vol. 1.
35. Ultimately, in relation to the recognition of verbal images (i.e., in the case of reading) the centrifugal movement is privileged: "Whatever the number and the nature of the terms interposed, we do not proceed from the perception to the idea, but from the idea to

Pure Memory: The Virtual

In the last pages of the second chapter Bergson develops the notion of the virtual, introduced casually in the first chapter. He identifies Pure Memory with ideas and with intention.

> Ideas, pure memories, called forth from the depths of memory, develop themselves into memory images more and more capable of inserting themselves into the motor schema. As these memories take on the form of a more complete representation, more concrete and more conscious, they tend to become increasingly confused with the perception that attracts them and whose frame they adopt. Therefore . . . there cannot be a place in the brain where memories congeal [se figent] and accumulate. The supposed destruction of memory images by brain lesions is only an interruption of the continual progress by which the memory actualizes itself. (MM 140 [125–126])

Memory images cannot be lodged in the brain because Pure Memory is virtual! Memory does not exist until it is actualized through interaction with perception, or in the mode of dream.

The great mistake that psychologists have made, according to Bergson, is to think in static terms. As we saw in the Essai, this invariably results in a tendency to position all terms of discourse in space. What is important, when it comes to thinking memory, is to remember to think dynamically—to think in time! Speaking of theories of brain localization of memory functions, Bergson writes: "One envisages distinct perception and memory images statically, as if they were things, such that the first would be already complete without the second, instead of considering the dynamic progress through which the one becomes the other" (MM 142 [127]).

Pure Memory has no material existence. It is pure idea or intention, pure virtuality. It only actualizes itself as it comes into contact with perception (which serves action) through the intermediary of the motor schematism. "In other words, the centers where elementary sensations are born [naissent] can be activated [actionnés] from either the front or the back. From the front, they receive impressions from the sense organs

---

the perception, and the characteristic process of recognition is not centripetal but centrifugal" (MM 145–146 [130]).

and therefore from a real object. From behind they undergo, from one intermediary to the next, the influence of a virtual object" (*MM* 145 [129]).[36] From this perspective, attentive perception occurs in the reverse order from what is usually held.

The virtual image evolves toward a virtual sensation, and the virtual sensation evolves toward the real movement. "This movement, in realizing itself, also realizes the sensation of which it is the natural extension and the image that wanted to become embodied in the sensation [*faire corps avec la sensation*]" (*MM* 146 [131]). In other words, as action occurs, both the sensation and the image become actualized (*MM* 146 [131]). The past actualizes itself. Memory does not proceed from the present back into the past. It proceeds from the past into the present, by actualizing itself. If this is hard to imagine, it is because one is thinking statically, instead of dynamically. Try again, thinking in time.

4.3. Chapter 3 of *Matter and Memory*
"The Survival of Images, Memory, and Mind [*esprit*]"

In passing from the second to the third chapter of *Matter and Memory*, Bergson links the question of memory to the issues elaborated in the *Essai*: duration, immediate consciousness, and freedom. Here it will be a question of "how *l'esprit* can define itself through the act of memory."[37]

The Present

Thought is a movement. It includes three elements: Pure Memory becomes memory image, which then enters into perception. Each of these three terms—Pure Memory, memory image and perception—exists in interaction with the other two. None exists in isolation. All are involved in a process—the process of the circuit presented to us schematically in the preceding chapter. Now Bergson will reintroduce the ongoing force of duration into that schema, linking time to memory, and both to immediate consciousness.

36. Here "front" and "back" refer to the temporal dimensions of the future and the past in a dynamic movement of irreversible becoming.
37. Worms, *Introduction*, 139.

How does Bergson help us understand the *virtuality* of Pure Memory? He asks us to think about the actual experience of trying to retrieve a memory.[38] What happens? We pull our awareness back from the actual present moment and place ourselves in the past, the past in general. We then try to localize a particular moment in the past. This is a matter of trial and error [*un travail de tâtonnement*] that Bergson compares to the act of focusing a camera (*MM* 148 [134]). But the memory remains in a virtual state.[39] We still haven't grasped it in the form of an image, that is, of an actual memory. "Little by little it emerges as a nebulosity that would condense [*qui condenserait*]; from a virtual state it passes to an actual one" (*MM* 148 [134]). In the process of its actualization it "tends to imitate the perception" that animates it (*MM* 148 [134]). Yet, Bergson adds, "it remains attached to the past by its deepest roots" (*MM* 148 [134]). The most important point is the flow of this process. This is just what the difference between the virtual and the actual requires that we think. It is also just what is neglected by the psychological theories Bergson criticizes, specifically by the associationist psychologists who tend to reduce process to fixed elements, sacrificing "the instability of the real to the stable, the beginning to the end" (*MM* 149 [135]).[40]

The constant error of associationism is that it substitutes a discontinuous multiplicity of inert elements in juxtaposition for the continuity of becoming, which is the living real [*le réel vivant*] (*MM* 148 [134]). In so doing, it reduces perception to two elements: the sensation and the image (*MM* 149 [134]). Having simplified the *process* of perception, having arrested it, these theorists then consider memory to be just a weaker version of perception. The difference between perception and memory is considered simply a difference of degree, not a difference in kind. This misunderstanding is inevitable, given that the associationist psychologists have completely neglected the temporal process of actualization, that is, the passage from Pure Memory to memory image. As a result, both memory and perception are considered representations. Perception of the present is simply considered a stronger representation

---

38. One thinks of Proust's episode of the *madeleine* in *Remembrance of Things Past*.
39. Here "virtual" suggests something roughly parallel to "unconscious."
40. Here the primary reference is to Taine's *De l'intelligence*. See Worms, *Introduction*, 143, concerning the pertinence of the issues discussed in this chapter, especially the critique of associationism, to contemporary issues in the cognitive sciences. Worms alludes to Jerry Fodor and Daniel Dennett.

than memory. As a representation of the past, memory is considered to be just like perception, only a weaker representation.

Bergson insists that this way of thinking completely obscures the past and the becoming of time. One cannot find the past if one looks for it in the present. This would be like looking for darkness in light. The only way to make contact with the past is to enter into its obscurity, or in this case, its virtuality. "But the truth is that we will never reach the past if we don't place ourselves in it from the start. Essentially virtual, the past cannot be grasped as past unless we follow and adopt the movement by which it opens [s'épanouit] into a present image, emerging from the shadows into the light of day [émergeant des ténèbres au grand jour]" (MM 149–150 [135]).

Memory and perception are *different in kind* because the past is fundamentally different from the present. As we have seen, Bergson defines the present as the time of action. The body, we remember, has been defined as a center of action. It cuts into the future from the past, marking the point of the present. Whereas the present is action, the past is powerlessness to act. Since present and past are different in kind, so must be perception and memory. If memory is not just a weaker form of perception, then it must be something quite other (MM 151 [136–137]). Since perception has been defined (through the limit idea of Pure Perception) in relation to matter (i.e., as material action) we can see that Bergson's theory of memory is leading us to the phenomenon of *esprit*.

But it is not enough to distinguish the past from the present; we must introduce duration into the present itself. This, we remember, is what accounted for the difference between Pure Perception, on the one hand, and real perception on the other. In the same way, it is crucial to the difference between Pure Memory and real memory. What then, is "present"? We can think about it abstractly as a geometrical point. But the real present, the present we live or experience, is not a stable or fixed point. It is more like a moving target that moves through the temporal circuit of past present and future: "What I call 'my present' impinges both on my past and on my future. On my past first of all, for 'the moment I speak is already far from me'; on my future next, for this moment leans toward the future. I tend toward the future, and if I could fix this indivisible present, this infinitesimal element of the curve of time, it would show the direction of the future" (MM 153 [138]). Thus, "it is necessary that the psychological state I call 'my present' be both a perception of the immediate past and a determination of the immediate future" (MM 153 [138]). In practical terms, the immediate past is what we call sensation and the immediate future is action or movement. My present, in other words, is sensori-motor.

> My present consists in the consciousness I have of my body. Extended in space, my body experiences sensations and at the same time executes movements. Sensations and movements become localized at determinate points in this extension; at any given moment, there can only be one system of movements and sensations. . . . Situated between the matter that acts on it [*influe sur lui*] and that which it influences, my body is a center of action, the place where received impressions intelligently choose their way of transforming themselves into accomplished movements. It thus represents the actual state of my becoming, that which, in my duration, is in the process of formation [*en voie de formation*]. More generally, in this continuity of becoming which is reality itself, the present moment is constituted through the quasi-instantaneous cut that our perception operates in the mass in the process of flow [*en voie d'écoulement*] and this cut is precisely what we call the material world. Our body occupies the center of this. Of this material world it is what we directly feel flowing by [*sentons directement s'écouler*]. The actuality of our present consists of its actual state. Considered as extension in space, matter, in our opinion, should be defined as a present that is always beginning again. Conversely [*inversement*], our present is the very materiality of our existence, that is, nothing but an ensemble of sensations and movements. (*MM* 153–154 [138–139])

Here Bergson returns to his point of departure, the body as center of action, and gives it new meaning. The body is also a center in relation to a process of becoming. As center, it situates the temporal horizon, giving us the distinction between present, past, and future. Moreover, it also implies that the very notion of materiality is identified with the one temporal horizon, the present, which is tied to the body as center of action and to perception as that which occurs in the service of action.

The Past

My present consists in the consciousness I have of my body (*MM* 153 [138]). Matter "considered as extension in space, should define a present that continually begins again; conversely, our present is the very materiality of our existence, that is, a mixture of sensations and movements and nothing else" (*MM* 154 [139]). In other words, my present is sensori-motor.

If the present is defined in relation to the body as center of action— i.e., in terms of sensation and movement—then the past can be defined as that which has nothing to do with the body. "Pure Memory . . . does not concern any part of my body." Pure Memory, we remember, is the counterpart of Pure Perception. It is completely immaterial, in both senses of the word. It is not matter, and it does not matter in the sense that it is powerless to act, until it is actualized into memory images through association with the body and its actions and perceptions, until it mixes with them and contributes to them.

The importance of the heuristic notion of Pure Memory is that it brings home the radical difference (the difference in kind) between memory and perception. Memory is not a weaker version of perception. Perception (this was the lesson of the theory of Pure Perception) is not a representation at all but an action. Memory is pure, that is, virtual representation. It does not participate on the horizon of the present except as it is actualized, brought into contact with the present through a transformation that embeds or materializes Pure Memory as an image. Memory lives elsewhere and must be called forth to come into play in the present, to materialize itself as image and enter into the circuitry, or interaction, of memory and perception associated with consciousness and duration.

Most psychologists get it wrong, because they materialize memory (as image) from the start and neglect the process of actualization that lets it become an image. They also idealize perception as representation (*MM* 155 [139]). The present is imminent action (*MM* 156 [140]). When memory becomes memory image, it connects with this imminent action, because it enters into the present. "The image is a present state. The memory image leaves pure memory, leaves the past (characterized by powerless to act, non-extension, etc) to enter into the present" (*MM* 156 [140–141]).

The present is what is in the process of happening—*ce qui se fait* (*MM* 166 [150]). But because of the constant flow of time "nothing *is* less than the present [*rien n'est moins que le présent*], if by that you mean an indivisible limit that separates the past from the future" (*MM* 166 [150], emphasis added). And because of the constant flow of time "in actuality [*pratiquement*] we only perceive the past" (*MM* 166 [150]).

Unconsciousness

We now face this question: where, or how, does Pure Memory conserve itself? Where, so to speak, does it live? We remember that Bergson asked an analogous question in the *Essai* concerning time. The answer is in unconsciousness. "If consciousness is the characteristic mark of the present . . . of what is acting [*agissant*], then what does not act [*n'agit pas*] can cease belonging to consciousness without ceasing to exist altogether" (*MM* 156 [141]). Consciousness has been tied to the body—to its motor schematisms and pre-formations—and therefore to action in the present. Bergson now presents inaction, or powerlessness to act [*impuissance*], as an "unconscious psychological state" (*MM* 156 [141]). The past is an unconscious psychological state. The unconscious is the past!

We tend to consider only conscious psychological states and to think they are the only ones that exist. But once we consider the flow of time, we must also take into account the past. When we do so, we realize that consciousness is only the characteristic mark of what acts in the present. That which does not act—i.e., the past—also exists. Bergson has to conclude that the past exists because, in a sense, the present exists just as little as the past appears to do. As we cited earlier, "nothing is less than the present [*rien n'est moins que le présent*]" (*MM* 166 [150]) because of the dynamic flow of time. In a sense the present is always already past, since we are situated within duration, that is, within a real temporal flow.

In the psychological realm, consciousness is not synonymous with existence, only with real action, or immediate efficacy. When we limit the term in this way, we can accept the idea of an unconscious psychological state, one that is "powerless to act [*impuissant*]" (*MM* 157[141]). "The primary role of consciousness is to preside over action and illuminate a choice" (*MM* 157 [141]), i.e., to enable voluntary action. The important point, then, is that Bergson can ask us to think unconscious psychological states because he has redefined consciousness or perception in terms of action, not knowledge. To this extent, as we have seen, consciousness, by definition, only illuminates a part of the real, that part which pertains to the interests of its imminent action. For consciousness, everything real is actual. The rest is virtual. It falls into obscurity, perhaps, but it does not, for this reason, cease to exist or to be real. "There is no more reason to say that the past effaces itself once it has been perceived, than there is to suppose that material objects disappear when I cease to perceive them" (*MM* 157 [142]).

Bergson constantly reminds us to consider time to be as real as space. We acknowledge the existence of material things that fall outside the range of our immediate perception or consciousness. I know my daughter is sleeping in the next room, even though I cannot perceive her. I know New York City is there, even though I now live in California. Why is it, Bergson asks, that we acknowledge the existence of things that lie outside our consciousness when it comes to objects in space but not when it comes to the subject (*MM*, 158 [142]) or to being in time? It is because we attribute powers of conservation to space that we are not willing to grant to time. We accept a horizon of objectivity because we consider space to be its guarantee. We consider that space holds things, whereas we are not willing to believe that time holds the psychological states that occur in succession there.

When we reintroduce the perspective of action, however, space becomes a translation of time.[41] We perceive at a distance what we will act upon, or what will act upon us in a particular interval of time.

> Space thus provides us all at once [*tout d'un coup*] with the schema of our immediate future. And, since this future will flow indefinitely, the space that symbolizes it has the property of remaining indefinitely open in its immobility. . . . But whereas we feel attached [*suspendus à*] to these material objects that we endow with present reality [even though they may be out of our sight], on the contrary, our memories, as past, are so many dead weights that we drag around with us and that we would rather pretend to be rid of. The same instinct, by virtue of which we open up space indefinitely before us, makes us close up time behind us as it flows on. And whereas reality, in the mode of extension, seems to us to extend infinitely beyond our perception . . . in our inner life, only that seems real to us that begins in the present moment. The rest is practically abolished. So, when a memory reappears to consciousness, it seems to us like a ghost, whose mysterious appearance we have to explain by means of special

---

41. This marks a slight shift from the perspective of the *Essai*.

causes. In reality, the adherence of this memory to our present state is absolutely comparable to that of the objects we don't perceive to those that we do perceive, and the *unconscious* plays the same sort of role [*un rôle du même genre*] in both cases. (*MM* 160–161 [144–145], original emphasis)

Bergson emphasizes the resemblance between objects that we place next to one another simultaneously in space and psychological states that develop in time.

What does Bergson mean by "unconscious"? Quite literally anything that falls outside the range of our immediate consciousness. To this extent, objects elsewhere in space and memories elsewhere in time are both unconscious in the same way, and to the same extent—"the *unconscious* plays the same sort of role in both cases" (*MM* 161 [145]). Bergson argues that we need to pay more attention to the structural similarities between the domain of objects that present themselves to us simultaneously in space and the series of successive states that develop in time (*MM* 161 [145]).[42]

The fundamental difference between the two series is that the order of objects in space is necessary—it follows the laws of Euclidean geometry—whereas in time, the order of successive states is contingent. This is the difference that comes into play when we speak of the existence of something that falls outside our direct conscious perception. We attribute existence only to the necessary ordering. Bergson argues, however, that in inner experience there is an analogy to the necessary ordering of things in space. He calls this "character" (*MM* 162 [146]), which he explains in terms of the order that our past history gives to our own identity. Our character, he writes, is the actual synthesis of all our past states (*MM* 162 [146]) and it conditions, without determining, our present state (*MM* 164 [148]). Our previous psychological states live on in this condensed manner because we carry them with us all the time. The past is always with us. It informs everything we do.[43]

But we have strayed from our guiding question of how the past conserves itself. "We are so subject to the obsession with spatial images," Bergson writes, "that we cannot avoid asking *where* memory is con-

42. The photographic notion of development is implied, as a figure for the passage from the virtual state of pure memory to the embodied state of memory image.

43. Once again, we recognize an evolutionary perspective in this discussion of the past that conditions, but does not determine, the present. Character, in this sense, would enable and orient adaptation.

served" (*MM* 165 [148]). But by asking "where?" we have already spatialized the problem. Where *is* the past? The easiest answer is, "in the brain." We are accustomed to conceptualizing everything spatially, to thinking in terms of what contains things, since we see everything as being contained within space. This answer appears almost inevitable. "The fundamental illusion consists in transposing to duration itself, in the mode of becoming [*en voie d'écoulement*] the form of instantaneous cuts [*coupes*] that we perform on it" (*MM* 166 [149])—the cut, most notably of the present which we tend to situate in space.

> But how can the past, which, by hypothesis, has ceased to be, conserve itself? Is there not a real contradiction here? [. . .] We answer that the question is precisely to know if the past has ceased to exist, or if it has only stopped being useful. You define the present as that which is, when it is simply what is happening [*ce qui se fait*]. Nothing is less than the present moment, if you mean by that the indivisible limit that separates the past from the future. When we think of this present as what ought to be [*devant être*], it is no longer, and when we think of it as existing, it is already past. . . . All perception is already memory. (*MM* 166–167 [150])

All perception is already past. I repeat this passage so that we have time to take this message in: "In the fraction of a second that the shortest possible perception of light lasts, trillions of vibrations have taken place, the first separated from the last by an interval that is enormously divided. Your perception, however instantaneous, consists in an incalculable multitude of remembered elements, and, in fact, all perception is already memory. Actually [*pratiquement*], we only perceive the past, the pure present being that ungraspable progress whereby the past bites into [*ronge*] the future" (*MM* 167 [150]).

When it comes to our habits of thought (our tendency, for example, to ask where memory conserves itself) it is not just a question of metaphysical illusion. There is also an ideological factor at play. Or perhaps we should call it a biological factor. To the extent that the law of life is action, we have a very real *interest* in paying attention only to the immediate future, which unfolds for us and becomes our immediate past. This is the horizon of action and this is what social life requires us to attend to, in order to meet the challenges that we face. In other words: we think the way we do in order to adapt to our surroundings and to survive. We have an interest in keeping the future open, not in what has already taken place.

L'esprit (Mind)

By problematizing the question of where the past might be stored, and by giving the dimension of time an autonomous value commensurate with that granted to space, Bergson has opened up the domain of subjectivity. He has given subjectivity comparable value to objectivity, in parallel with it. Through the notion of unconsciousness, Bergson has rendered the existence of past time a viable notion. He has opened up the idea of existence, precisely by calling into question the presumed geometric status of the present construed as a point in linear time. He has reformulated the present as a perpetual re-beginning, in motion toward the immediate future and, at the same time, toward the immediate past. The elaboration of the real in terms of duration (that is, as a continuity of becoming) reminds us that the horizon of space is an abstraction.

Instead of asking where memory is stored (a question he has effectively invalidated), Bergson explores *how* it might be stored, returning to his dual theory of memory which includes a memory of the body (of habit and repetition) and a spontaneous memory of images. He pursues the question of their interaction from a temporal perspective that concerns the relation between the two types of memory. This enables him to keep both present and past (and body and consciousness) in play in his discussion—an essential move, as we are replacing a static spatial model that locates isolated objects (memories) in things (brains) with a model of the real as temporal becoming—the real as duration. From this perspective, Bergson can turn the whole question around. "It is a chimerical undertaking," he remarks, "to want to localize past, or even present, perceptions in the brain: they are not there, it [the brain] is in them" (*MM* 169 [151]).

It is precisely in this revised account of the interaction between the two modes of memory in recognition that Bergson will be able to theoretically locate the universe of subjectivity—or *esprit*. So far, Bergson has only spoken of the activity of consciousness, which he has related to the law of life (action) and to the body as center of action. The notion of character has given him an organizing principle for the idea of a unified temporal horizon of the living individual. We now have a conception of an agent (to avoid for a moment, the issue of the subject) which includes both a horizon of spatial positioning and of temporal depth, i.e., a temporal circulation between present and past.

Bergson returns to the two types of memory he distinguished in the last chapter in order to investigate their interaction. "The two terms we separated at first are going to be welded together [*souder ensemble*]" (*MM* 168 [151]), Bergson says, as he explores the active relation between the two.[44] In other words, what he presented to us on a static model in the last chapter, he now returns to and embeds in the real, in the continuous becoming of duration, now understood as "universal becoming" (*MM* 168–169 [151]).[45] He can do this, having demystified the present as a static point and having introduced duration into the present.

Bergson figures "the totality of memories accumulated in my memory" (*MM* 169 [152]), that is, the ensemble of the two memories (the memory of the body and the image memory) by the schema of an inverted cone.

"The point of the cone, S, makes contact with a plane P. The point S figures my present, but it is to be thought as a moving point, always advancing in time. Here we find the image of my body; this image is limited to receiving and returning [*rendre*] the actions which emanate from all the images of the plane" (*MM* 169 [152]). We see that Bergson has returned to the language of the opening page of *Matter and Memory*, where we read:

> Here I am in the presence of images, in the vaguest possible sense of the term, images that are perceived when I open my senses and are not perceived when I close them. All these images act upon and react to one another . . . in accordance with the laws of nature. (*MM* 11 [17])

S marks the moving site of action (or, if we consider the figure statically, it marks the site of Pure Perception). The base of the inverted cone, labeled AB, stands for "the totality of memories accumulated in my memory" (*MM* 169 [152]); it is "situated in the past [*assise dans le passé*]" (*MM* 169 [152–153]). Thus the base is fixed, though virtual or unconscious, and the point S is mobile, "operating a transversal cut of universal becoming" (*MM* 169 [152–153]). This figure renders a com-

44. Recall that the subtitle to *Matter and Memory* is "Essay on the Relation of the Body to the Mind [*esprit*]."

45. We see here that, contrary to what many critics have suggested, Bergson does not wait until *Creative Evolution* to evoke duration as an ontological fact.

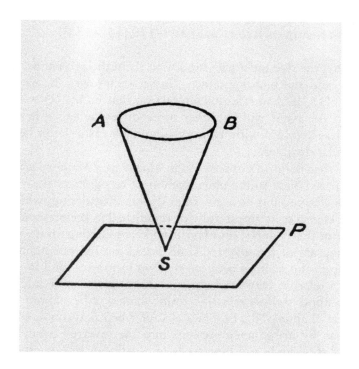

posite of the memory of the body and the memory of images. When one activates the figure, one can evoke the "mutual support [*mutuel appui*]" that each lends the other in their perpetual interaction.

On the one hand, the memory of the past [figured as AB, at the inverted base of the cone] presents to the sensori-motor mechanisms all the memories capable of guiding them in their task and of directing the motor reaction in the direction suggested by the lessons of experience: these are the associations by contiguity or similarity. But on the other hand, the sensori-motor mechanisms furnish the powerless, that is, unconscious memories with the means to become embodied, to materialize themselves, that is, to become present. For a memory to reappear to consciousness, it would have to descend from the heights of pure memory to the precise point where action occurs [S] . . . the call to which the memory responds comes from the present, and the memory borrows from the sensori-motor elements of the present action the warmth that gives it life. (*MM* 169–170 [152–153])

In this way, the two memories (and with them the present and the past, the body and the mind) interact, "insert themselves in one another" (*MM* 170 [153]). And it is this interaction that influences what we call character. An agent will be either more or less engaged in action, or more or less involved with memory—in which case, she or he might be considered a dreamer.

We see that Bergson's exposition in *Matter and Memory* is not linear. He has circled back to the phenomenon of recognition analyzed in the preceding chapter and now gives it a dynamic rendering, which recomposes the elements he so carefully distinguished in the previous analysis. Throughout this chapter, his exposition keeps circling around.

The diagram of the inverted cone, which on the one hand could be said to figure the relation between the two memories (and to this extent to figure a relation between body and mind) can also be interpreted to figure the mind itself—*l'esprit*—a term which will be elaborated further in the next chapter. This becomes clearer when Bergson adapts his initial schema by introducing sections into the inverted cone, where we now find "thousands and thousands of repetitions of our psychological life, figured by as many sections A*B*, A**B**, etc. of the same cone" (*MM* 181 [162]).[46]

With the introduction of a virtually unlimited number of intermediary levels, the cone comes to stand for *l'esprit*, which has two extreme moments or activities: action on the one hand and dream on the other. Considered in this light, the base of the inverted cone, AB, now stands for the dream function of the mind, whereas S stands, once again, for action—useful action in the present. To the extent that dream is disengaged from action, memory images are free to circulate and to attract one another in the absence of any requirement for usefulness in relation to action. Once again, action and dream are regulatory ideas. In its usual operations, the energies of the *esprit* move between the various planes of consciousness indicated by the various conic sections. What distinguishes these sections are differences in tension (or in focus of attention) which are greater as we approach S, the locus of action, and looser as we approach AB, the psychic level of dream.

---

46. The relation to the title of Deleuze and Guattari's *A Thousand Plateaus* [*Mille plateaux*] is self-evident.

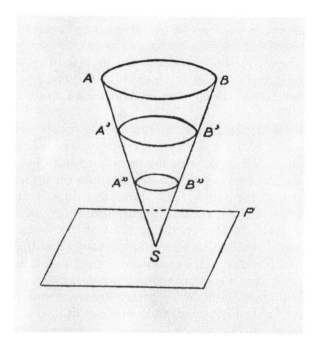

Once again, one has to animate this diagram for it to become meaningful. It is the double movement up and down across the various levels of mental tension that operates the interaction between memory and perception, already spoken of in Bergson's theory of recognition in the last chapter. From this perspective, the level AB associated with dream also stands for Pure Memory and S stands for Pure Perception. This is also to say that AB stands for pure disembodied idea and S stands for images, in the sense introduced by Bergson in the opening pages of the book.

The "double current" that goes both up and down the cone, between the base AB and the inverted summit, S, stands for the circuit of perception and memory already theorized. It produces a kind of mix of idea and image (or mind and matter), as well as a mix of signifier and signified on the level of language.[47] This double current now operates in the context of a generalized psychology whose principal feature is "the

---

47. Page 180 is particularly important in terms of the theory of language implied by Bergson's analysis of memory, which in many respects suggests the structural linguistics of Saussure.

double movement of contraction and expansion through which consciousness tightens or enlarges the development of its contents" (*MM* 185 [166]). It is as if the mind were figured as a virtual keyboard instrument, which gives a variety of tones to our psychic life. Depending on which level you find yourself on at a particular moment, you get a different *tonus* of mental life, which takes on a different set of tonalities.[48]

> On the one hand, the sensory motor state S orients memory, of which it is the actual and active extremity, and, on the other hand, this memory itself, with the totality of our past, exerts a kind of pressure or push forward to insert into the present action the greatest possible part of itself. From this double effort there results, at every instant, an indefinite multitude of possible states of memory, states figured by the sections of our schema A*B*, A** B**, etc. These are, so to speak, so many repetitions of our total past life. But each of these sections is more or less ample, depending on whether it is closer to the summit or the base. What is more, each of these complete representations of our past only brings to the light of consciousness what can fit into the sensorimotor framework, that which . . . resembles the present perception from the point of view of the action to be accomplished.[49] (*MM* 87 [168])

What moves from level to level, across the planes of consciousness? *L'esprit.* "We have supposed that the *esprit* is constantly crossing the intervals, or levels, between its two extreme limits, the level [*plan*] of action and the level of dream" (*MM* 192 [172]). And what about the body? "The body is what fixes our *esprit*" (*MM* 193 [173]). It is "only a place of rendez-vous between the excitations received and the movements accomplished" (*MM* 193 [173]). To maintain its own balance, the mind [*esprit*] requires the anchoring of the body and its pragmatic attention to life.

Dream

Dream is the state of mind that occurs when one's attention is not anchored by the sensori-motor equilibrium of the body (*MM* 194 [174]).

---

48. Bergson speaks of the "various 'tones' of our mental life" (*MM* 188 [169]).

49. A more detailed analysis of this argument would consider the relations of resemblance and contiguity that come into play in the operation of recognition as it is analyzed in these pages.

Since memory is not directed toward the specific demands of the present (or of imminent action), there are no longer any constraints on the associations that take place between images, since ultimately "everything resembles everything else [*tout se ressemble*]" (*MM* 187 [168]).[50] In the dream state (which does not require actual sleep) images are particularly vivid, for, as we go back into the past, memories carry more concrete detail. They have not been generalized or abstracted by the constraints of the present moment, which select images that resemble or fit the perceptual demands of that encounter. Dream, then, involves a level of psychic activity in which vivid and detailed images circulate freely.

Bergson expresses a number of different attitudes toward dream. Sometimes he evokes it as a liberation from the constraints of useful action and the social world that suppresses duration. To experience duration, he writes, "one must want to dream [*il faut vouloir rêver*]." Dream is also linked to the activity of the artist, and will be identified with instinct as opposed to intelligence in *Creative Evolution*. Sometimes it is associated with mental alienation or madness. It is clear, however, that for Bergson dream validates the argument that memory exists in its radical difference from matter. The function of the brain or nervous system (that is, of the body) is to orient memory toward the present, and to bind it to the real world of action. Memory is something absolutely independent from matter (*MM* 198 [177]). The brain functions to recall memories that are useful, but also to reject all the others. It wants nothing to do with them. "We do not see how memory could be lodged in matter" (*MM* 198 [177]).

4.4. Chapter 4 of *Matter and Memory*
"On the Delimitation and Fixation of Images: Perception and Matter: Soul [*âme*] and Body"

We recall that Bergson's broader subject in *Matter and Memory* concerns relations between body and mind [*l'esprit*]. The theory of memory orients this broader analysis. The first three chapters of the book have established the function of the body in relation to perception and memory. The body limits the life of the mind [*esprit*] in view of action. It acts as a mechanism of selection, pulling toward perception those memory images that can be useful to it, that fit into the frame sketched out by

---

50. This refers us to the ultimate unity of duration, which implies the concrete singularity of every event that occurs in irreversible time, each of which is linked to all the others through broader and broader fields of potential contextualization.

movements of the body. All of this underscores Bergson's main point: the body neither engenders representations, nor stores them in some particular part of the brain. It merely selects them. However, in so doing, it also materializes them, pulling memory images from Pure Memory and engaging them in the process of recognition through which perception occurs on its way to action.

In this last chapter of *Matter and Memory* Bergson returns to the question of metaphysical dualism, evoked in his first chapter, but initially set aside. We recall the opening words: "We are going to pretend for a moment that we know nothing of the theories of matter and the theories of mind or spirit [*esprit*], nothing of the discussions concerning the reality or ideality of the external world" (*MM* 11 [17]).

These are the metaphysical questions to which Bergson returns here. Now he can start from the premise that matter and mind are radically different in kind, that one cannot be reduced to, or explained in terms of, the other. The challenge at this point is to articulate the relation [*union*] (MM 201 [180]) of body and soul, considered as two utterly independent entities.[51]

In this chapter, then, Bergson returns to the metaphysical question on the basis of the psychological investigation he has just undertaken. He has confronted clinical studies concerning aphasia, clinical evidence concerning the impact of brain lesions, and come up with his own theory of perception that involves the interaction of mind and body, considered in their radical independence from one another. Body and mind encounter one another in action and, as we have seen, lend one another mutual support.

At this point, then, Bergson transposes the elements of his psychological analysis back into metaphysical terms. In case we had not already noticed, he reminds us explicitly that the terms "Pure Perception" and "Pure Memory" have already inscribed the metaphysical dualism of body and soul, although as virtual terms. "Pure Perception would place us quite truly in matter, and with memory we would already actually [*réellement*] penetrate into the mind [*esprit*]" (*MM* 200 [180]). What is more, he hints, "the same psychological insight that revealed the distinction between matter and mind stages their union for us [*nous fait as-*

---

51. Bergson uses the words "âme" and "esprit" almost interchangeably, although the former tends to be used in the context of metaphysical dualism and the latter of clinical psychology.

sister à leur union]" (*MM* 201 [251]). Bergson accepts neither the materialist nor the idealist solution to the problem of metaphysical dualism. Each tries to subordinate one term to the other, or to derive one from the other.

> Of the two opposing doctrines the one [materialism] attributes to the body and the other to the mind, a gift of veritable creation. The first [materialism] holds that the brain engenders ideas or representations, the second [idealism] that our understanding constructs the contours of nature. Against both these doctrines we invoke the same testimony, that of consciousness. It shows that our body is an image among others and that our understanding is a faculty of dissociating, and of logically distinguishing opposing terms, but not one that creates or constructs. (*MM* 201–202 [181])

What has Bergson's psychological analysis accomplished? By taking the metaphysical dualism to the extreme, it has paved the way for a *rapprochement* between the metaphysical oppositions such as quantity/quality and extended/nonextended, which have complicated any resolution of the problem of metaphysical dualism (*MM* 202 [181]).

This chapter of Bergson's book suggests a gloss, or interpretation, of the analysis given in the previous chapters, where the theory of Pure Perception appeared a bit perplexing. We might have wondered why, for example, Bergson would want to start off with the notion of Pure Perception (which appears to imply absolute instantaneity) when we know his commitment is to duration, a radical temporality of becoming? He shows us here that the theory of Pure Perception was not crucial to the psychological analysis he has presented. But it was crucial to the metaphysical issues that the psychological analysis was meant to clarify and displace. Pure Perception, Bergson affirms here, puts perception back in the things themselves [*dans les choses mêmes*]. Thus the perceived images of things are no longer situated within the body (or the brain) as representation; they are located squarely in the external world itself. We remember that this was the book's point of departure: "Here I am in the presence of images, in the vaguest possible sense of the term, images that are perceived when I open my senses and are not perceived when I close them" (*MM* 11 [17]). The images, he continues to insist, are out there—not in my mind.

Here, where it is a question of trying to embed the psychological argument made earlier concerning perception into a broader metaphysical framework, Bergson will plug in the core argument of the *Essai*. The development is complex. Let's try to follow it.

First, Bergson criticizes the traditional metaphysical positions: materialism, idealism, empiricism, and dogmatism. He then turns to Kant. Our knowledge of things, he suggests, is not, as Kant would have it, "relative to the fundamental structure of our mind, but only to the superficial habits it has acquired, that is, to the contingent form that it takes from our bodily functions and inferior needs" (*MM* 205 [184]). This insight grounds the method Bergson proposes to adopt in addressing the metaphysical problem at hand, the relation between mind and body. It is a question of the same critical method he established in the *Essai*, namely, not to mistake mere contingent adaptation for fact (*MM* 203 [183]) and to "go look for experience at its source" (*MM* 205 [184]).

It is a question, in other words, of what Bergson called "immediate consciousness" in the *Essai*. It is a question of direct contact with the real: "We must place ourselves back in pure duration, whose flow is continuous, and where one passes, by minute gradations, from one state to another: a truly lived continuity . . . artificially broken up for the convenience of ordinary knowledge" (*MM* 207 [186]).

Just where does *Matter and Memory* meet up with the *Essai*? At the crucial point where Bergson has substituted action for knowledge (or speculation/contemplation). For action means voluntary action (otherwise it would be referred to simply as movement) and voluntary action means freedom—this was the central point of the *Essai*. To understand "the intimate nature of action" a "theory of freedom" (*MM* 208 [186]) is necessary. It is a question of critically separating out a false duration, one in which "we see each other acting," from real duration, "where we act" (*MM* 207 [186])—a duration in which our states melt into one another as we have seen in the *Essai*.

The challenge to philosophy is this: can we place ourselves within duration through thought? (*MM* 207 [186]). What is at stake, once again, is a kind of *dépassement* of Kant. What would a return to the immediate mean? "[T]o detach oneself from space without leaving extension [*se dégager de l'espace sans sortir de l'étendue*]" (*MM* 208 [187]). Here Bergson returns to the problem of language. "And could not immediate consciousness find its own justification and proof in itself, if one could establish that these difficulties, these contradictions, these problems arise primarily from the symbolic figuration that covers them over, a figuration that we have come to identify with reality itself and whose thickness can only be pierced by an exceptional, intense effort?" (*MM* 209 [187]). Bergson draws back from undertaking a critical theory of matter, a theory that would start from a critical analysis of the difference between space and extension. But he does sketch out the direction such a theory might take. The rest of this chapter is taken up with elaborating four major points.

(1) Movement Is Indivisible

All movement, as passage from rest to rest, is absolutely indivisible (*MM* 212 [190]). The first thing that is needed in order to displace metaphysical questions from the perspective of immediate experience (or the experience of duration) is a reconsideration of movement—a dynamic, nonspatialized, understanding of it. This is the point Bergson made in the *Essai* in connection with the image of the shooting star. "The indivisibility of movement implies the impossibility of the instant" (*MM* 212 [190]). The illusion that we can divide movement up into constituent parts occurs because we expect to be able to map movement into space. Bergson recapitulates the argument made in the *Essai*. The mistake is to expect space to be able to give an integral representation of duration (*MM* 212 [189–190]). When you try to map movement onto space you "substitute the trajectory for the movement itself [*vous substituez la trajectoire au trajet*]" (*MM* 211 [190]). One can only map the trajectory after the fact, once movement has ceased and nothing is moving! Since the movement itself, as it is happening, does not yet have a designated end point, it cannot be mapped or divided. It is this illusion, this confusion between the ongoing event and the re-presentation of it after the fact on a spatial horizon that lies behind Zeno's paradox.[52] What this amounts to, Bergson claims, is transposing becoming into a useful thing—a representation that gives us information. When we think about what is useful, or when we think about things in a way that is useful to us, this usually means mapping events onto space and then taking the movement for a thing (*MM* 213 [191]). To think about the move-

---

52. The paradox concerns the infinite divisibility of movement such that the infinite regress of its divisibility conflicts with its progress as movement; it arises, Bergson argues, when ongoing time and movement are confused with space. This was a fundamental insight in Bergson's philosophical career.

ment itself is not useful. That is why we are "no more inclined to think about the inner organization of movement, than the worker is to think about the molecular structure of his tools" (*MM* 213 [191]).[53]

(2) Real Movement

The second fact concerning movement is this: *There are real movements* (*MM* 215 [193]). To appreciate this fact it helps to shift one's perspective from mathematics to physics. The mathematician expresses movement in terms of variation of distance (*MM* 215 [193]). Physics, on the other hand, concerns concrete movement (*MM* 216 [193]). It recognizes that movement is real. The difference is important. For the mathematical, or geometrical, treatment of movement (derived from Descartes) will consider movement to be relative and (although Bergson does not say this explicitly here) reversible. To the extent that physics deals with concrete time, it can more easily recognize the fundamental irreversibility of movement and of time.[54]

Bergson concludes that the best way to make contact with movement as such is "when it appears to me from within, as a change of state or quality" (*MM* 219 [196]). The mistake, then, is to translate movement into quantity, as in the case of the quantity of distance covered. "I touch the reality of movement when it appears to me, inside myself, as a change of state or of quality" (*MM* 219 [196]). Even external movement can be perceived directly through change in qualities: "Between light and darkness, between colors, between nuances, the difference is absolute" (*MM* 219 [196]). To perceive movement, then, we must have what Nietzsche referred to as "fingers for nuance."[55]

53. The allusion to "molecular structure" is perhaps a key to Bergson's interest in getting beyond the spatial configurations of ordinary knowledge by what he calls "immediate intuition." See my chapter 2.

54. As discussed previously, this issue is fundamental for modern physics. The distinction between the mathematical treatment of movement and the physical treatment became dramatically clear with Boltzmann's mathematical reformulation of the second law of thermodynamics. This translation erased the "arrow of time." Stengers has suggested that it was Boltzmann's refusal to acknowledge the importance of concrete movement (and the irreversibility of temporal processes) that convinced Bergson that only philosophy could think time, not science. See Ilya Prigogine and Isabelle Stengers, *Entre le temps et l'éternité,* 34.

55. Friedrich Nietzsche, *Ecce Homo,* trans. Walter Kaufmann, 223.

(3) Artificial Divisions

The third fact is the following: *Any division of matter into individual bodies with absolutely determinate boundaries is an artificial division* (*MM* 220 [196]). Duration implies what Bergson calls a "moving continuity [*une continuité mouvante*] . . . where everything changes and remains at the same time [*à la fois*]. How does it happen that we dissociate these two terms, permanence and change, in order to represent permanence by bodies and change by homogeneous movements in space?" (*MM* 221 [197]).

Bergson is quite clear. The appeal to immediate experience is not an extreme subjectivism. Both immediate consciousness (consciousness free of metaphysical illusion) and science "return to the idea of universal continuity" (*MM* 221 [197]). "Science and consciousness [*science et conscience*] are, at bottom, in agreement, as long as we envisage consciousness in terms of its most immediate data [*données*] and science in relation to its most distant aspirations" (*MM* 221 [197]).

Given some of Bergson's statements concerning the opposition between science and philosophy,[56] his *rapprochement* of science and consciousness is striking. It helps us grasp that the appeal to immediate experience (and subsequently to intuition) is made in the context of developments in science that problematize the ordinary framework of experience. "Next to consciousness and science," Bergson writes, "there is life" (*MM* 221 [198]). Yet it is also life, considered in terms of biological imperatives concerning need and adaptation, that moves us ordinarily to disregard the continuity of the real and to consider matter in terms of separate units. Speaking of the way in which need influences perception, Bergson writes: "To establish such specific relations between portions of sensible reality cut out from the whole [*entre des portions ainsi découpées*] is precisely what we call *living* [*vivre*]" (*MM* 222 [198], original emphasis).

Bergson is concerned here with the relation between biology and epistemology—the need to construct knowledge along particular lines for the purposes of adaptation. This is not simply an individual tendency. Whole sciences are constructed according to intellectual habits derived

---

56. Concerning the opposition between philosophy and science see *Creative Evolution* and the short text "Qu'est-ce que la métaphysique," in *La pensée et le mouvant;* in English: *The Creative Mind: An Introduction to Metaphysics.*

from biological need. Thus Bergson laments contemporary trends in the field of chemistry that insist on conceiving of matter in terms of particles. "More and more," he insists, "the materiality of the atom is dissolving under the gaze of the physicist" (*MM* 223 [199]).[57]

The pages that follow are of great interest not because they develop the metaphysical argument, but because they reveal the extent to which Bergson's thought is in dialogue with developments in contemporary science. There are notes in these pages to scientific papers by Maxwell and Lord Kelvin's theories on vortex atoms and the molecular mobility of gases. What is the lesson of modern (i.e., nineteenth-century) physics? Scientists "show us, modifications, perturbations, changes in tension or energy running through concrete extension and nothing else" (*MM* 226 [201]). To this extent scientific developments meet up with the thrust of the psychological analysis of movement Bergson has just given us, one that proposes movement as an absolute. Movement is an independent reality, not a mere change of state in previously given things (or an accidental change in relations between objects). They present movement as an independent reality. In scientific terms, matter is considered more and more in terms of force: "We see force materializing itself, the atom idealizing itself and these two terms converging toward a common limit, the universe thus finding its continuity again" (*MM* 225 [200]).

For the physicist, Bergson writes, "vortices [*tourbillons*] and lines of force . . . are only convenient figures, designed to schematize calculations. But philosophy must ask why these symbols are more appropriate than others and allow one to go further" (*MM* 226 [201]). "Could we," he asks, "by reworking them, reconnect with [*rejoindre*] experience, if the notions to which they correspond indicated, at least, a direction we might follow in pursuit of a representation of the real?" (*MM* 226 [201]) This is perhaps the clearest statement one can find of Bergson's ambitions for philosophy in its close proximity to the radical investigations currently under way in the physical sciences.

(4) Changes of State

Here is the last proposition concerning movement: *Real movement is the transport of a state not a thing* (MM 226 [202]).

---

57. It is a question, no doubt, of the wave—particle theory of light and of adumbrations of the mysteries of quantum mechanics.

What is the thrust of these propositions? The rapprochement of the terms quality (which implies heterogeneity) and movement (which implies homogeneity) (*MM* 226 [202]). This is the point where Bergson begins to go beyond the analysis of the *Essai*, proceeding on the basis of the psychological analysis of perception he presented there. In the *Essai* his goal was to underline the difference between qualities and quantities, between the heterogeneous and the homogeneous, between inside (where sensation of qualities is experienced) and the outside (which we represent and know in spatial, homogeneous terms).

But just what is the shift? Bergson still maintains the radical difference between quality and quantity. He now wants to suggest, however, that to identify quality and quantity with an absolute difference between inside and outside is perhaps not exactly right. He now implies that the heterogeneity he identified with duration in the *Essai* (and limited to consciousness and to the inner experience of sensation) pertains to matter itself! This is the first step toward the ontology of duration that Bergson will explicitly introduce in his next major work, *Creative Evolution,* where he extends duration to being in general. "The question is precisely to know whether real movements only present quantitative differences among themselves, or whether they might not be quality itself, vibrating from within so to speak and scanning [*scander*] its own existence in an incalculable number of movements" (*MM* 227 [202]).

The movement of matter in the external world, Bergson now suggests—taken in itself and not projected onto space, and thereby transposed into quantity—must bear some analogy to the continuity of our own consciousness in the experience of duration. This is precisely the analogy that Bergson will pursue and develop explicitly through the notion of the *élan vital* in *Creative Evolution.* For "the movement studied by mechanics,[58] is nothing but an abstraction, or a symbol . . . a common denominator facilitating comparisons between all real movements. But these (real) movements, considered in themselves, are indivisibles that occupy duration, presuppose a before and an after, and bind together successive moments of time by a variable qualitative thread" (*MM* 227 [202–203]).

In *Matter and Memory* Bergson introduces a new feature into the thinking of duration. There is no longer a single duration, there are multiple rhythms of duration.

---

58. Once again, Bergson is very likely alluding to Boltzmann's mathematization of the second law of thermodynamics.

In reality, there is not one unique rhythm of duration; one can imagine many different rhythms, which, slower or faster, would measure the degree of tension or relaxation [*relâchement*] of consciousness, and, in that way, would fix their respective places in the series of beings. This representation of durations of unequal elasticity is perhaps painful for our minds to entertain, because our minds have contracted the useful habit of substituting a homogenous and independent time for the real duration experienced by consciousness. (*MM* 233 [207])

So what has become of memory in all this? So far, Bergson has been speaking only of matter and perception. Perception divides up the real continuity of matter as concrete extension—continuity of sensible qualities—according to the rhythms of our action.[59] Here is where memory comes in. "Memory (re)solidifies the continuous flow of things into sensible qualities" (*MM* 236 [210]). Memory "prolongs the past into the present, because our action will dispose of the future in exact proportion to how much our perception, enlarged by memory, will have contracted the past" (*MM* 236 [210]).

At this point, both necessity and freedom are defined in terms of rhythms of duration. Necessity implies a response, or reaction, to an action (or movement) on the same wavelength, so to speak, of duration. It involves accommodating the rhythm of matter: "To respond to an action one receives by an immediate reaction that condenses [*emboîte*] the rhythm and continues in the same duration, to be in the present, and in a present that always begins again, that is the fundamental law of matter; in that consists its necessity" (*MM* 236 [210]). This amounts to action as automatism. Freedom implies a change in rhythm from the rhythm of matter. "If there are free actions, or, at the very least, partially free ones, they can only belong to beings who are able to fix becoming from afar [*de loin en loin*], the becoming to which their own becoming attaches [*s'applique*], beings who are able to solidify it into distinct moments, to condense its matter in this way, and, by assimilating it, to digest it in movements of reaction that will slip through the mesh [*mailles*] of natural necessity" (*MM* 236 [210]).

Kantian critical philosophy was a reaction against metaphysical dogmatism, which held that homogeneous space and time were part of

---

59. Bergson has reworked Kant's notion of the transcendental esthetic in relation to a philosophy of action (*MM* 237 [211]).

things themselves. For Kant, of course, we can know nothing of things in themselves, but only our representations of them. And here is where space and time enter in; they order our representations of things, ostensibly according to the structure of the operation of our minds. Space and time are said to be the *a priori* forms of our sensibility. True to his method, Bergson's move is to show what the two opposing positions (dogmatism and critical philosophy) have in common, namely the assumption that perception serves contemplation, that space and time have a speculative interest (*MM* 238 [212]). Bergson proposes a vitalist alternative to both positions: homogeneous space and time are principles of division and solidification (as previously outlined) introduced into the real in relation to the form of our action, not our knowledge. Time and space, Bergson writes, "are the schemas of our action on matter" (*MM* 237 [211]).

Real duration and real extension [*étendue*], Bergson argues (against Kant), pertain to things in themselves. They reveal themselves immediately to our minds through intuition. Beneath duration and real extension there are the schemas of homogeneous space and time that we introduce in order to impose our actions on the real, in order, that is, to divide up the continuity of the real, to stabilize becoming, and to provide "points of application [*points d'application*]" for our actions (*MM* 238 [212]).

Failure to appreciate the conceptual difference between space and concrete extension has lead to a number of misunderstandings. These result in dead-end metaphysical dualisms and the inability to account for the correspondence, or interaction, between mind and external reality.

Bergson sets out to expose the misunderstanding that has led to this impasse. He essentially deconstructs the positions of metaphysical idealism and realism by showing that both share the same assumption: the assumption that homogeneous space underlies the experience of sensible qualities. Idealism, he says, "sees nothing but sensations in sensible qualities, and nothing in sensations but states of mind [*états d'âme*]" (*MM* 238 [212–213]). Realism also separates extension from sensible qualities. It simply pushes extension beyond perception altogether. Both positions hold that there is a radical discontinuity between what is extended (matter) and what is not (mind).

In order to appreciate what concrete extension might be, as it differs from the concept of homogeneous space, it is necessary to hold (as Bergson does) that extension is not to be understood only in relation to our sense of touch, but that all our senses participate in extensions. When we do this, we can more readily appreciate that instead of thinking of sensible qualities (or concrete extension) as being somehow in space, we should consider space something we impose on concrete extension, something like a grid that helps us map out our actions.

Traditional metaphysics, with its dualism between mind and body, has performed what Bergson calls an "inversion of the real" (*MM* 245 [218]). This involves the belief that stasis is prior to movement [*mobilité*], that immobility is the fundamental point of reference against which we plot our movement as a trajectory in space. From this perspective, movement is nothing but variation in distance, pure quantity that appears to have nothing to do with sensible quality. It is this "inversion of the real" that results in the radical separation of matter from mind, or what Bergson calls movement from quality. Qualities are then parked in the mind and movement (or quantity) is parked, as matter, in space. There is no adequate way to explain any connection or correspondence between them.

But all of this, Bergson suggests, is merely a myth, a certain construction of thinking. Immediate experience shows us that there is no essential difference between movement and quality, between the thing perceived and our perception of it (*MM* 218 [245]). According to the theory Bergson has outlined in the preceding chapters, perception itself (Pure Perception) is in things, not in the mind. If this is only a virtual category, it is because there is no instantaneity in the actual world. There is no Pure Perception to the extent that memory always participates in concrete perception. It is memory that adds subjectivity to our experience of qualities to the extent that it synthesizes different moments of time.

In concrete perception, as Bergson has analyzed it, matter (i.e., concrete extension) and consciousness (i.e., memory) interact. To this extent Bergson has demonstrated an interactive dualism between the metaphysical terms of body and soul.

Bergson's proposal is radical. It affirms that matter, in itself, is not so different from consciousness: "Extended matter, considered as a whole, is like a consciousness where everything is in equilibrium, compensates for itself [and] neutralizes itself . . . it truly offers the indivisibility of our perception" (*MM* 247 [219]).

What really separates matter from consciousness is space, which acts "like an insurmountable barrier" between the two terms. But space is merely an abstraction, merely a symbol or a schema. On the level of immediate experience (which is the horizon of philosophical intuition) consciousness and matter approach one another in continuity. It is only the requirements of action that impose the abstract framework of space, which does not pertain to the real as it really is. Space, Bergson summarizes, "interests the activities [*démarches*] of a being that acts on matter, but not the work of a mind that speculates on its essence" (*MM* 247 [219–220]).

Bergson returns to the fundamental question of his study: the question of the relation (or union) between body and soul [*âme*] or matter and mind [*esprit*]. He returns to the axiom announced earlier, to the effect that relations between subject and object (or mind and matter) should be considered in relation to time, not space. As he has already demonstrated in his analysis of the two extreme states of the mind—dream and action—mind touches concrete extension (matter) at the moment of action, that is, as it actualizes itself. To this extent the mind "can make contact with matter in the act of Pure Perception" (*MM* 248 [220]). Mind is radically distinct from matter. But it is distinct from matter *temporally,* that is, as memory, as an operation of temporal synthesis of the past and the present with a view toward the future. Memory "contracts the moments of . . . matter in order to put it to use and to manifest itself through *actions* that are the *raison d'être* of its union with the body" (*MM* 248 [220], original emphasis).

Thus, on the one hand, it is useful action that prevents us from appreciating the union, or interaction, of mind and body. Useful action invites us to conceptualize concrete extension as space. It inserts the concept of homogeneous space as a buffer between matter and mind. On the other hand, it is action itself that performs the union (the contact or interaction) between matter and mind—or matter and memory.

In this last chapter Bergson has analyzed his own psychology of memory to reveal its metaphysical implications. He has shown how it resolves the vulgar dualism that could never explain how mind acts on matter or matter on mind. All this remained a mystery. One was left with only the vague notion of a parallelism between the two orders, or some form of pre-established harmony. Bergson has produced an account of the concrete interaction between the two terms. In his theory, body and mind remain radically distinct in principle, but in actuality, they interact. Bergson has solved the metaphysical conundrum by thinking in time instead of in space.

According to Bergson's analysis, mind [*esprit*] comes into contact with matter in the very act of temporal synthesis, the act of "linking the successive moments of the duration of things" (*MM* 249 [221]).[60] Thus there are two meanings of the word "memory." The first refers to this act of temporal synthesis, which gathers up successive moments of matter. This is the most primitive mode of contact, or interaction, between matter and mind. But once we acknowledge this point of contact we realize that there are infinite degrees of contact or interaction. In higher living organisms the subject has more and more independence *vis-à-vis* matter, precisely because the subject enjoys memory in the second sense of the term—i.e., memory as the capacity to store up past time, to retain it and engage it to influence the future. This is memory in the more limited, and more ordinary, sense of the word. Bergson holds, however, that this is merely a matter of difference of degree (or contraction) of different moments of duration. The rest is a question of intensities of memory and of rhythms of duration. Thus: "On the first hypothesis, the one that conceives of the difference between body and mind [*âme*] in spatial terms, body and soul [*esprit*] are like two railroad tracks that would cut across one another at right angles; in the second, the rails line up with one another on a curve, so that one can pass from one track to the other imperceptibly" (*MM* 250 [222]).

We now recognize the strategic importance of the various steps of the argument Bergson has outlined throughout his book. Pure Perception, which is mind without memory, has been presented as being "in matter." Actual perception adds memory to this interaction. But memory is not some strange other to matter, for matter has its own mode of memory: repetition, such that its past is given in its present. This is what Bergson understands by necessity.

4.5. Résumé and Conclusion of *Matter and Memory*

(1) The body is an instrument of action, not representation. It explains our actions, not our perceptions. It does not store representations or memories. Bergson appears to affirm a radical dualism, even pushing it to the extreme. To uphold the dualism as vigorously as possible, he argues, is the only way to ultimately rearticulate the two terms. This is the

---

60. Again, it is important to note that the very idea of a "duration of things" was absent from the *Essai* and will be theorized in *Creative Evolution*.

strategy he has pursued through the notions of Pure Perception and Pure Memory.

(2) Wrong thinking results when we consider mind and body to be duplicates of one another, two translations of a principle that remains mysterious. Dualism will always oscillate between idealism and materialism. When one thinks in this way, it is impossible to appreciate the reciprocal influence of mind and body. This results in the sacrifice of freedom. Once again, the fundamental mistake is to consider perception and memory to operate in the service of pure knowledge. Both perception and memory serve action, not knowledge. Memory contracts duration, releasing action from the rhythm of necessity.

(3) Consider perception, then, in terms of the force of action. Since perception is contingent upon the positioning of the body in the ensemble of the material world, my perception in a sense belongs to the objects themselves (MM 257 [228–229]). My perception is in things; things are not in my perception of them. Perception involves the selection of images according to the needs of action. Its role is to eliminate from the totality of images all those that do not concern my action or interest the needs of my body. This is the hypothesis of Pure Perception.

Bergson affirms that he has taken a position between realism and idealism (MM 257 [229]). He explains that when he initially called things "images," this was a concession to idealism. It implied that all reality bears a relation to consciousness. But he goes beyond idealism, he explains, to the extent that he holds that the real exceeds perception—images exceed perception on every side. Once again, this is explained by the fact that perception selects images in relation to the demands of action and of the needs of the body. It does not operate in a disinterested manner in relation to pure knowledge. Conversely, the problem with realism is that it cannot explain consciousness. Bergson argues that this is because realism interposes the barrier of homogeneous space between matter and consciousness. This keeps the two apart. Space is privileged. It is as if space were given first, and then things were added to occupy positions in space. As we have seen, Bergson has argued that space is added to material things *after* our perception of them. He maintains that what he has called "concrete extension" precedes space. Extension precedes space, which only concerns our action. Space is like "a net we throw under the material continuity of things in order to master it, to decompose it in the sense of our activities and our need" (MM 260 [231]).

When we consider extension prior to space, we no longer confront the barrier between extended things and our perception of them. In this case we can begin from a realist perspective and arrive at the same conclusion we were led to when we started from the idealist premise: perception is in things. Our perception involves the virtual action of things on us and of us on things. This is what is meant by Pure Perception. From this perspective there is no radical divide between mind and body. The brain is not the cause, the effect, or the double of perception. It serves as its continuation, since perception is virtual action and the cerebral state is the beginning of our action (*MM* 262 [232]). Perception would be in effect a fragment of the real. Such, at least, is the meaning of the hypothesis of Pure Perception.

(4) In actuality, the perceiving subject adds to perception both his or her affections (i.e., the perception it has of its own body from within) and his or her memories of previous moments. It is time to reintegrate into consciousness the subjective elements of affect and memory. Whereas previously the subject was considered on the model of a mathematical point, now it is opened up to include the dual horizon of subjectivity (the sensation of affect from within the body) and objectivity (the exteriority of images). Affect is then an "impurity" we add to perception, one that we project from our own bodies onto all the others. Subjectivity consists in the interiority of affective sensations (*MM* 263 [234]).

(5) We have considered the subject. We have even suggested that the material universe itself, defined as a totality of images, is a sort of consciousness where everything compensates for, or neutralizes, everything else. But we have not yet arrived at the mind [*esprit*]. For this we have to consider an individual consciousness that prolongs and conserves the past in the present, and in so doing, evades [*se soustrait à*] the law of necessity, which implies that the past only occurs as self-repetition. Thus in passing from Pure Perception to memory we leave the domain of matter for that of spirit or mind [*esprit*].

(6) Bergson states that the theory of memory at the core of his study was meant to be both the theoretical consequence of his theory of Pure Perception and the experimental verification of it (*MM* 265 [235]). First of all, memory is completely different from perception. The theory of Pure Perception tells us that the perceived object is the present object, a body that modifies our body. Memory, however, is a representation (not a thing)—the representation of an absent object (*MM* 265 [236]). Memory is not just a weaker form of perception. It is something radically different from perception, something that differs from it *in kind*. Contact between the present and the past does not take place through localizations in the brain, which stores memories, but rather through the

process of recognition that engages the act of perception with an act of recognition.

(7) The hypothesis that memory is just a weaker form of perception appears absurd when we consider what the corollary of this would be, perception would be just a stronger form of memory! This is the germ of the idealism of someone like Berkeley. The fact is that memory does not involve regression from the present into the past. On the contrary, it involves a progression from the past to the present. We always start out in the past. We start from a virtual state and then follow a series of planes of consciousness, until the point where Pure Memory actualizes itself in a memory image and materializes itself in an actual perception. It comes into a present and active state. From this perspective, we begin to understand that the present is a condition of our body and its action. "Our present . . . is what acts on us and what makes us act; it is sensory and it is motor" (*MM* 270 [240]). Our present is a state of our body. Our past, on the contrary, is that which no longer acts, but could act, or will act, by inserting itself into a present sensation whose vitality it will borrow. At this moment, the memory ceases to be a memory and becomes perception (*MM* 270 [240]).

(8) What associationism neglects (among other things) is the thought of various planes of consciousness between action, on the one hand, and dream, on the other. Memory presents itself in varying degrees of contextual meaning or detail according to the mental plane on which one finds it.

(9) When we consider memory in this way—i.e., in terms of planes of mental activity between the two extremes of action (or matter) and dream (or idea)—then we can confirm what has been said concerning the role of the body, while we prepare the way for a rapprochement between the body and the mind.

Concrete perception would then be a synthesis between Pure Perception (matter) and Pure Memory [*esprit*]. As such, it yields an answer to the problem of the union of body and mind.

Bergson draws three metaphysical conclusions from his psychology of memory:

(A) If one maintains a strict dualism between mind and body, one will find nothing in common between the two. But this opposition between perception and matter is artificial, the work of an understanding that constructs the real according to its own needs. What is given in the real is something intermediate between divided extension (matter) and the pure nonextended. Bergson calls this the *extensif* (*MM* 276 [245]).

(B) Take the opposition between quality and quantity, that is, the opposition between consciousness and movement. Consciousness does not look on to an inner parade of nonextended perceptions. Bergson proposes that there is no radical opposition between matter and consciousness, the thing and the sensation of it. Concrete movement (as he has argued in the previous chapter) is something very like consciousness. Ultimately there is only a difference of rhythm (of contraction of duration) between matter and consciousness, between things and sensations of them, between quantity and quality (*MM* 278 [247]). The opposition between quantity and quality is overcome by the dynamic term *tension* (*MM* 278 [247]).

(C) Ultimately the argument for the interaction between matter and spirit, and the rhythmic fluctuations of extensivity and tension, lead to the affirmation of an interplay between freedom and necessity. "Freedom presses its roots into necessity. The mind [*l'esprit*] borrows from matter the perceptions from which it nourishes itself, and returns them in the form of movement, onto which it has impressed [*imprimé*] its freedom" (*MM* 280 [249]).

5. Channels of Contemporary Reception

In 1950, Merleau-Ponty published a short essay in which he presented two Bergsons, the "audacious" Bergson of the early years, and the clichéd Bergson of the later ones, when the philosopher's thought, processed through various Bergsonisms, had become superficial and banal.[1] The second, he writes, has deformed the first and lead us to forget Bergson's "direct, sober, immediate, unusual way of reinventing philosophy [*refaire la philosophie*]."[2] It is now a question of returning to the old Bergson, the audacious one.

In 1966, Gilles Deleuze published a short book entitled *Le bergsonisme*[3] that reintroduced Bergson to a generation of readers who had more or less forgotten him. For Deleuze, in an emerging structuralist/post-structuralist intellectual context, Bergson was an anti-philosopher (along with Leibnitz and Nietzsche); he was a thinker of radical difference and a philosopher of affirmation in a new key. *Bergsonism*, the English translation of Deleuze's book, appeared in 1988. This edition includes an afterword in which Deleuze evokes a return to Bergson in the following terms: "A 'return to Bergson' does not only mean a renewed admiration for a great philosopher but a renewal or an extension of his project today, in relation to the transformations of life and society, in parallel with the transformations of science."[4]

1. Maurice Merleau-Ponty, *Éloge de la philosophie*, 238, my translation.
2. Ibid., 239, my translation.
3. Gilles Deleuze, *Le bergsonisme*. References will be to *Bergsonism*, trans. Hugh Tomlinson and Barbara Habberjam (New York: Zone Books, 1988).
4. Ibid., 115.

Since the 1990s a number of books on Bergson have appeared that, in one way or another, take up Deleuze's call.[5] As we can see from this activity, the return to Bergson is happening today, and in a number of quite different ways. We would do well to wonder why.

Perhaps it is because the limits of structuralist/post-structuralist discourse are being felt ever more strongly as interest turns to the domain of cultural studies and to questions opened up by new media and technologies. Perhaps the return to Bergson occurs now because of the delay produced by the fact that Deleuze's *Bergsonism* was not published in English until 1988. Or perhaps it is because many of Deleuze's major works did not appear in English until the 1990s.[6] In any case, today, the return to the old Bergson, the audacious one, occurs in the name of a new Bergson. When John Mullarkey published his volume by that name—*The New Bergson*—in 1999, he stated that the essays in his volume attempt to read Bergson "as a contemporary philosopher" instead

5. In 1996 F. C. T. Moore published *Bergson: Thinking Backwards,* a study that considers issues from Bergson's philosophy in relation to aspects of analytic philosophy, specifically the thinking of Wittgenstein. In 1997 there appeared *Bergson et les neurosciences,* ed. Gallois and Forzy. That same year, Philippe Soulez and Frédéric Worms's *Bergson: biographie* was published. Worms also published *Introduction à Matière et mémoire,* a rigorous analysis of that work, and I published *Literary Polemics: Bataille, Sartre, Valéry, Breton,* which rereads French modernist literary culture through the intertext of Bergson. Jonathan Crary's *Suspensions of Perception: Attention, Spectacle, and Modern Culture* includes a substantial discussion of Bergson. John Mullarkey published *Bergson and Philosophy* in 1999, and, that same year, he edited a volume of essays which was published under the title *The New Bergson.* Keith Ansell Pearson's *Philosophy and the Adventure of the Virtual: Bergson and the Time of Life* appeared in 2002. That same year Brian Massumi published *Parables of the Virtual: Movement. Affect. Sensation,* which proposes a redirection of cultural studies from a Bergsonian perspective. Most recently, in 2004, Mark B. N. Hansen has published *New Philosophy for New Media,* which appeals to a "Bergsonist vocation" of new media. In France, 2004 saw the publication of Frédéric Worms's synthetic study of Bergson's œuvre, *Bergson ou les deux sens de la vie,* as well as of a new edition of Bergson's *Les deux sources de la morale et de la religion,* ed. Arnaud Bouaniche, Frédéric Keck, and Frédéric Worms. See also Frederick Burwick and Paul Douglass, eds., *The Crisis of Modernism: Bergson and the Vitalist Controversy;* Mark Antliff, *Inventing Bergson: Cultural Politics and the Parisian Avant-Garde;* Manuel De Landa, *Intensive Science and Virtual Philosophy;* Dorothea Olkowski, *Gilles Deleuze and the Ruin of Representation,* which discusses Bergson at some length; and *Becomings: Explorations in Time, Memory, and Futures,* ed. Elizabeth Grosz. In the context of the renewed interest in Bergson, note also the following on time or virtuality: Philip Turetzky, *Time (The Problems of Philosophy),* and Pierre Levy, *Becoming Virtual: Reality in the Digital Age,* trans. Robert Bononno.

6. Two of Deleuze's most important works, *Différence et répétition* and *La logique du sens,* published in France in the 1960s and early '70s, respectively, did not become available in English until the 1990s. *Mille plateaux,* published in France in 1980, appeared in English in 1988.

of a "historical curiosity."[7] More often than not, Bergson becomes "contemporary" today in relation to Deleuze.[8]

If there is a "return" to Bergson today, then, it is largely due to Gilles Deleuze whose own work has etched the contours of the New Bergson. This is not only because Deleuze wrote about Bergson; it is also because Deleuze's own thought is deeply engaged with that of his predecessor, even when Bergson is not explicitly mentioned.[9]

From the point of view of reception, however, it was probably the two volumes devoted to film that had the greatest impact on the revival of interest in Bergson.[10] The cinema books function on various levels. For philosophers who have been following Deleuze's thought, they carry important philosophical developments and would have brought out more clearly the Bergsonism that had been running through Deleuze's work (and not received much attention) since the 1950s. For others, the books provide an interesting history of French film, and an introduction to Bergson to the extent that Deleuze enters into substantial commentaries on specific passages from *Matter and Memory* that concern notions of movement, image, recognition, and time. We could say that with the cinema books Deleuze cross-pollinated Bergson to a whole new community of readers interested in film, film theory, and cultural studies. It is probably not by chance, then, that Zone books decided to publish an English translation of Deleuze's *Bergsonism* in 1988, two years after the English translation of *Cinema 1*.

7. Mullarkey, *The New Bergson*, 12.

8. Pearson writes: "How should the new be thought? This question remains at the forefront of philosophical disputations and, interestingly, has once again taken the form of an encounter between Bergsonism and its critics, with the agon between Alain Badiou and Gilles Deleuze echoing the complaints made in the 1930s by Bachelard contra Bergson." See *Philosophy and the Adventure of the Virtual*, 70. We should also remember that Deleuze is contemporary for English speakers, and hence for readers of *The New Bergson*, given that *Difference and Repetition* published in France in 1968 appeared in English just five years before *The New Bergson*.

9. Some have suggested that Bergson had more impact on Deleuze than any other philosopher—a very strong claim given the evident significance for Deleuze of Nietzsche, the subject of an important book he published in 1962, *Nietzsche et la philosophie*, translated by Hugh Tomlinson as *Nietzsche and Philosophy*. Badiou, a critic of Deleuze, makes this claim. Pearson cites the claim without disputing it and I have not seen anyone contest it. John Marks agrees, affirming that, "The importance of Bergson for Deleuze cannot be overestimated." See *Gilles Deleuze: Vitalism and Multiplicity*, 67.

10. *Cinéma 1: L'image mouvement*, trans. Hugh Tomlinson and Barbara Habberjam as *Cinema 1: The Movement Image*, and *Cinéma 2: L'image-temps*, trans. Hugh Tomlinson and Barbara Habberjam as *Cinema 2: The Time Image*.

The more than twenty-year lapse between the publication of *Le bergsonisme* in France (where it was largely ignored) and the English edition published by Zone is symptomatic of issues that need to be addressed if we are to try to situate the forces that transmit and block current interest in Bergson in the United States and Great Britain. The delay produces interesting effects, given that these two decades correspond, roughly, with the years of structuralism and post-structuralism in France.[11] One scholar, for example, has suggested that Deleuze retroactively turned Bergson into a precursor of post-structuralism in *Le bergsonisme*.[12] Others seem to turn first to Deleuze and then to Bergson as a way to get beyond post-structuralism.[13] A certain number of writers have created an entirely new entity—a peculiar hybrid character in the history of thought: "Deleuze Bergson."[14]

The Bergsonism of Deleuze

Given the extent to which current interest in Bergson is embedded in the Deleuzian context, and given what Pearson has called the "highly innovative character of Deleuze's Bergsonism,"[15] I would like to sketch out certain features of the Bergsonism of Deleuze.

Deleuze's interest in Bergson goes back at least to the mid 1950s. Among the articles included in *The New Bergson* is an English translation of "La conception de la différence chez Bergson" ["Bergson's Conception of Difference"], an article that Deleuze published in *Les études bergsoniennes* in 1956, six years prior to his important *Nietzsche et la philosophie* [*Nietzsche and Philosophy*], published in 1962. Where are we, in France, in the 1950s? We are on the cusp of structuralism as it turns against the existential phenomenology (Sartre, Merleau-Ponty)

11. Of course, post-structuralism continued beyond the late eighties. Its importance in France, however, began to decline around this time, whereas a number of major works representing these movements (those of Deleuze, in particular) appear in English for the first time in the 1990s.

12. Paul Douglass, "Deleuze's Bergson," in *The Crisis in Modernism: Bergsonism and the Vitalist Controversy,* 377.

13. Here I would include Brian Massumi and Elizabeth Grosz.

14. D. Olkowski uses this compound name repeatedly in *Gilles Deleuze and the Ruin of Representation.* Marks also uses it in *Gilles Deleuze: Vitalism and Multiplicity.* Pearson's book, whose subtitle reads, "Bergson and the Time of Life," devotes a good number of pages to Deleuze but does not conflate Bergson with Deleuze. In fact, his study is helpful in delineating the two.

15. *Philosophy and the Adventure of the Virtual,* 88.

that holds sway.[16] In 1947, Kojève's *Introduction à la lecture de Hegel* is published. That year Merleau-Ponty, who had attended Kojève's lectures in the 1930s, writes: "Hegel is the source of everything great that has been accomplished in philosophy for the last hundred years."[17] Kojève himself had written: "It is possible that the very future of the world, and therefore the meaning of the present and the significance of the past, depend ultimately on the way we interpret the writings of Hegel today."[18]

It will not take long for Deleuze to rebel and to seek another path. He is not alone in this gesture. As Lévi-Strauss reveals in *Tristes tropiques*, his own turn to anthropology was at least partially prompted by his desire to escape the relentless Hegelianism of the French university context. Lévi-Strauss publishes *The Elementary Structures of Kinship* in 1949. The first volume of *Structural Anthropology* will follow nine years later. According to Descombes, the philosophical reaction against Hegel and Husserl occurs after 1960 (the first issue of the review *Tel Quel* appears that year) when a turn to Nietzsche inspires a philosophy of difference.[19] As we shall see, Deleuze was ahead of the game. By the mid-fifties he is already looking for an alternative to Hegel, and he finds it in Bergson, whom he reads as a philosopher of difference. Bergson will orient the study of Nietzsche Deleuze will publish in 1962, *Nietzsche et la philosophie* [*Nietzsche and Philosophy*], a book that will have considerable impact.

In his 1956 essay, Deleuze champions Bergson as an alternative to Hegel, to the extent that Bergson presents "a great deepening of the concept of difference"[20] in a philosophy of internal difference, or self-differentiation, and of concrete, lived difference. Deleuze carefully distinguishes this thinking of vital difference from the abstract opposition of identity and difference he finds in Hegel. In Bergson, he writes, difference operates as an affirmation of novelty and indetermination. According to Deleuze, the internal difference Bergson presents

16. This existential phenomenology owes a lot to Bergson. Indeed, Julian Benda, who became an unremitting enemy of Bergson's thought, argued in his *Tradition de l'existentialisme ou les philosophies de la vie* that existentialism was nothing but a rehash of Bergsonism (see my *Literary Polemics*, chap. 7).

17. Cited in Descombes, *Le même et l'autre*, 23. All translations from this book are mine.

18. Ibid., 21.

19. Ibid., 13.

20. Deleuze, "Bergson's Conception of Difference," in *The New Bergson*, 62. Hereafter cited in-text as *CD*.

will have to be distinguished from contradiction, alterity, negation. This is where the Bergsonian theory and method of difference is opposed to that other method, to that other theory of difference that is called the dialectic, as much Plato's dialectic of
alterity as Hegel's dialectic of contradiction, both implying the
power and presence of the negative. . . . To think internal difference as such, as pure internal difference, to reach the pure concept of difference, to raise difference to the absolute, such is the
direction of Bergson's effort.[21] (*CD* 49)

Deleuze thus finds in Bergson (before Nietzsche) a philosophical alternative to Hegel. For Deleuze, Bergson deepens the thought of difference because he thinks it as self-difference in relation to biological processes of evolution. "Life is the process of difference" (*CD* 50). By
contrast, difference in Hegel is abstract. It is derived from, and constrained by, principles of logic: positing and negating. In Hegel the work
of negation is determination, whereas in Bergson "vital difference [is]
not a determination. . . . [I]t will lean toward indetermination itself.
Bergson always insists on the unpredictable character of living forms:
'indeterminate' i.e. unforeseeable" (*CD* 50). It is in relation to these two
features of Bergson's thought, internal difference and indetermination,
that Deleuze situates the notion of the virtual that will become so important in his own thinking: "self-differentiation is the movement of a
virtuality which actualizes itself" (*CD* 51). In Bergson, "thanks to the
notion of the virtual, the thing differs from itself in the first place, immediately" (*CD* 53). No dialectical opposition is required. It is thus the
notion of the virtual, in Bergson, that renders difference "more profound than negation, than contradiction" (*CD* 53)—and Bergson more
profound than Hegel.[22] What is the virtual? "The virtual becomes the
pure concept of difference. . . . [S]uch a concept is the possible coexistence of degrees of nuance. Memory is the name of this possible coexistence" (*CD* 55). In short, for Deleuze in this early essay, "duration is the
virtual" (*CD* 55), which "now defines an absolutely positive mode of
existence" (*CD* 55).

21. One cannot help noticing the residual Hegelianism of this formulation, which invokes opposition, "the pure concept" and "the absolute."
22. Again, we see how Deleuze develops his own notion of the virtual, through Bergson, against Hegel. "The negation of a real term by the other is only the positive realization of a virtuality, which contained both of them at once. It is thus by virtue of an igno-
rance of the virtual that we believe in contradiction, in negation. The opposition of two
terms is only the realization of the virtuality which contained them both" (*CD* 53).

I linger over this essay not only because it provides an exceptionally clear presentation of certain features of Deleuze's interpretation of Bergson's thought, but also because it offers a kind of virtual origin of ideas that Deleuze will subsequently develop in his own philosophical thinking. "Not only do duration and matter differ in nature," Deleuze writes in this essay, "but what so differs is difference itself and repetition. . . . Our guiding thread is the idea that (internal) difference differs (in nature) from repetition. . . . Bergson makes an effort to show us that difference is still a repetition and repetition already a difference" (*CD* 57). We could say that Deleuze's reading of Bergson directs the movement of his own thought, insofar as his next major work (after the study of Nietzsche) will be *Difference and Repetition*. This might be considered a kind of rewriting of *Matter and Memory*, oriented by the perspective of a certain Nietzsche—oriented, of course, from the perspective of a certain Bergson.[23]

Ten years later, in 1966, Deleuze publishes an expanded, and considerably altered, version of this essay in *Le bergsonisme*. Where are we in 1966? Now we are on the cusp of post-structuralism. Although Derrida does not publish *L'écriture et la différence* [*Writing and Difference*] until the following year (1967), many of the essays included in that volume have been in print individually since the early sixties. *La voix et le phénomène* [*Speech and Phenomena and Other Essays on Husserl's Theory of Signs*], Derrida's important critique of Husserl's phenomenology, will be published in 1967. *De la grammatologie* [*Of Grammatology*] will also appear in 1967, one year before Deleuze's *Différence et répétition* [*Difference and Repetition*].

In *De la grammatologie* [*Of Grammatology*], in which Derrida offers his critique of linguistics and displaces the linguistics of the sign to a theory of writing, we find the following statement, of considerable interest after the fact: "The whole field associated with the cybernetic program will be the field of writing. Assuming cybernetic theory can rid itself of all the metaphysical concepts—those of the soul/mind [*âme*], life [*vie*], value, memory choices [*choix de mémoire*]—that once served to oppose the machine to man."[24]

It is as if, in *Le bergsonisme* (1966), Deleuze had carefully edited out all those features of Bergson's thought that might appear "metaphysical" (the soul, life, value, memory choice) all those features that distin-

---

23. Pearson writes that "in *Nietzsche and Philosophy* Deleuze is reading eternal return through a Bergsonian lens." See *Philosophy and the Adventure of the Virtual*, 201.
24. *De la grammatologie*, 19 n. 3 (my translation).

guish the human being from the machine, that suggest an appeal to experience and a phenomenological perspective. It is perhaps this gesture that most clearly delineates the contours of the New Bergson.

Deleuze's second presentation of Bergson is sensitive to the discursive context of an emerging post-structuralism, as well as to the fact that, in the official university world, Bergson's thought still suffered from marginalization due to the lingering impact of old charges of irrationalism. In a remarkably dry tone (given the rhetorical enthusiasm of much of his later work) *Bergsonism* presents a more systematic—or rationalized—version of the earlier essay.[25] It analyses Bergsonian intuition as a fundamental method of his philosophy, and of its exposition. Deleuze's *Bergsonism* de-emphasizes precisely those features of Bergson's thought that his earlier essay had invoked against the abstraction of Hegel's dialectical machinery: notions of immediacy, concreteness, and lived experience. "Duration is not merely lived experience," we read here, "it is also experience enlarged or even *gone beyond*; it is already a condition of experience."[26] *Bergsonism* steers away from issues of subjectivity, consciousness, or the psychological experience of duration, all important features of Bergson's first work, *Essai sur les données immédiates de la conscience.*[27]

Deleuze's *Bergsonism* opens with the following assertion: "Duration, Memory, *élan vital* mark the major stages of Bergson's philosophy. This book sets out to determine, first, the relationship between these three notions and, second, the progress they involve" (*B* 13). Two important features of Deleuze's study leap out. First, whereas Bergson affirmed unapologetically that "I have no system,"[28] Deleuze presents Bergson's philosophy as systematic. Second, he affirms a progress in the development of Bergson's thought, which appears to self-correct as it proceeds by moving away from the phenomenological cast of the early work, toward the purely ontological character of *Creative Evolution*.

Deleuze separates duration from psychological experience and subjectivity as much as possible. It will be construed in terms of the process of self-differentiation elaborated in the earlier essay. Memory will be

25. A rationalist style (or tone) was valued in the structuralist context. This will shift, to a certain extent, with the challenges of post-structuralism.

26. Deleuze, *Bergsonism*, 37 (my emphasis). Hereafter cited in-text as *B*.

27. This tendency is to be situated in the context of both structuralism and post-structuralism's critiques of the subject, of humanism, and of phenomenology. "Psychological duration," we read here, "should be only a clearly determined case, an opening onto an ontological duration" (*B* 49).

28. Quoted in French "(*Je n'ai pas de système*") in *The New Bergson*, 5.

identified almost exclusively with Pure Memory, which is entirely virtual. Much less attention will be paid to actual memory, which involves, as we have seen, memory images that play a supplementary role in perception. "What Bergson calls 'pure recollection,'" Deleuze writes in *Bergsonism*, "has no psychological existence. This is why it is called *virtual*, inactive and unconscious" (*B* 55). Memory is cut off from any notion of subject, body, or agency.[29] Deleuze refers to "recollection" in this abstract sense and writes: "Only the present is 'psychological;' but the past is pure ontology; pure recollection has only ontological significance" (*B* 56). He then invokes what he calls Bergson's "leap into ontology" (*B* 57), which he characterizes as "a case of leaving psychology altogether" (*B* 57).[30] On this basis, duration can be redefined as "virtual coexistence" (*B* 60). "It is as if Life were merged into the very movement of differentiation, in ramified series. . . . Duration, to be precise, is called Life when it appears in this movement" (*B* 94–95).

We arrive at the following conclusion: "Differentiation is never a negation but a creation, and . . . difference is never negative but essentially positive and creative" (*B* 103). Once again, and even more bluntly than in the earlier essay, Deleuze focuses his presentation of Bergson's thought upon its perceived challenge to Hegel: "We see, therefore, how all the critical aspects of Bergsonian philosophy are part of a single theme: a critique of the negative of limitation, of the negative of opposition, of the general idea" (*B* 47).[31]

29. I am not claiming that Deleuze's interpretation is incorrect. However, in the *Essai*, Bergson does speak in terms of subjective consciousness. Here, and in *Matter and Memory*, memory is the site of subjectivity, since actualized memory (real memory as distinct from Pure Memory) pertains to the concrete singularity of lived experience. Part of the problem is the attempt to characterize Bergson's thought as a whole, when it was not intended to be systematic. Later formulations sometimes vary from earlier ones. However, Bergson never dissociates himself from the *Essai*. On the contrary, he cites it in his later work and explicitly states that, when he extends duration to life in *Creative Evolution*, he is extending his model of consciousness. See my "The 'Zig-zags of a Doctrine': Bergson, Deleuze and the Question of Experience," *Pli* 15 (2004): 34–53.

30. Deleuze insists upon this erasure of the subjective and the psychological. "Here again," he writes, "one must avoid an overly psychological interpretation of the text." He goes on to emphasize that "there is therefore a 'past in general' that is not the particular past of a particular present but . . . is like an ontological element" (*B* 56).

31. Clearly this is the single theme that most appeals to Deleuze in 1966. In 1988, in the afterword to the English edition, he invokes a different theme. His call for a "return to Bergson" rests on three main features: "Intuition, Science, and Metaphysics" (or the close proximity of the two in the work of Bergson where "duration becomes the metaphysical correlate of modern science") and multiplicities—"the constitution of a logic of multiplicities in accord with the physico-mathematical notion that derives from Riemann" (*B* 116).

Is Deleuze "re-imagining Bergson as a precursor of the 'poststructural turn,'" as Paul Douglass suggested?[32] Perhaps, only I would re-phrase this observation and say that Deleuze accommodates the conditions of reception in 1966. He thinks from within the discursive field of an emerging post-structuralism, one that is not in search of precursors, but pressures what can be said and how.

Douglass's formulation raises an interesting question, however. Why, if Deleuze could rewrite Bergson in a post-structuralist idiom, do we hear no more about Bergson in the context of post-structuralism? Why is he not taken up in this context as, for example, Levinas was taken up by Derrida and Blanchot? Although rereadings of Freud (Lacan), Nietzsche, Heidegger, and Marx (Althusser) take place in the context of post-structuralism, the rereading of Bergson does not occur until Deleuze, whose *Bergsonism* had little, if any, impact until the 1990s and, unlike the rereadings of Marx and Freud, did not become part of a discursive field shared by other thinkers.[33]

This raises yet another question: why would a New Bergson attract interest in the 1990s, just as a certain post-structuralism is losing some of its theoretical authority? It is certainly the case, as Douglass reminds us, that Deleuze had a great deal in common with post-structuralist thinkers like Derrida and Foucault. But it is important to consider what distinguishes him as well. This will make it easier to see how one might turn to Bergson today as a way *out* of post-structuralism, rather as Deleuze turned to him for a way out of the impasse of Hegelian dialectic in 1956.

Indeed, instead of serving as a precursor of the post-structural turn, it seems that Bergson was buried (again) by post-structuralism, even as he had been buried in the 1930s by the discourse of Hegel, popularized by the famous lectures of Kojève. In the context of the new rationalism of structuralism, Bergson carried the stigma of irrationalism, an effect of the attacks by Bertrand Russell and Julian Benda, and even the Catholic Church, which had put his works on the Index in 1914.[34] More importantly, perhaps, Bergson was perceived

32. Paul Douglass, "Deleuze's Bergson," in *The Crisis in Modernism*, 377.

33. Some gestures are being made in this direction retroactively. Ann Game's *Undoing the Social: Towards a Deconstructive Sociology* has sections on Foucault, Freud, and Irigaray, along with Bergson in a chapter titled "Towards a Materialist Semiotics" and has sections on Bergson and Freud in a chapter on time.

34. Guerlac, *Literary Polemics*, 197. For further discussion, see Grogin, *The Bergsonian Controversy in France*.

as a phenomenologist at a time when Derrida's critique of phenomenology carried the day.

The issue is complicated. In the context of *Tel Quel*, Derrida's critique of phenomenology served as a barrier against the existential humanism of Sartre, and his ideology of literary engagement. Sartre and Merleau-Ponty, however, as Lyotard has pointed out, had themselves been eager to dissociate themselves from Bergson.[35] Ironically, this was largely because they found Bergson to be not Hegelian (or Husserlian) enough, which is also to say, not phenomenological enough. Sartre complains that in Bergson's thought the subject is not an intentional consciousness; he criticizes the "melodic syntheses without a synthetic act, organizations without an organizing power."[36] In other words, Sartre laments what Deleuze admires.

Bergson is interesting to read today precisely because of the ways in which his thinking escapes the critique Derrida carried out so effectively against Husserl. The philosophy of Bergson appeals to immediate experience (this is never recanted) and to intuition. In this sense, it could be called phenomenological. Yet his thinking displaces the presuppositions attacked in Derrida's critique of Husserl. For in Bergson, as we have seen, perception itself is not an immediate experience (it requires attentive recognition and an appeal to memory that is regulated according to various degrees of tension or preparedness for action). Nor does perception occur in the service of knowledge; it pertains, as we have seen, to action. Finally, in Bergson, it is never a question of self-presence, not even in the act of intuition. What Bergson calls Pure Perception could hardly be called an experience at all and real perception is not immediate. Bergson's shift from a model of cognition to a model of action sig-

---

35. See Lyotard, *La phénoménologie*. Pearson also makes this point, referring to Lyotard's study. He writes: "For Sartre the problem centred precisely on what he took to be the *lack* of a 'positive description' of the *intentional* character of thought within Bergson's account of the subject. . . . In his 1953 study Lyotard notes that phenomenology separates itself from Bergsonism precisely on the question of time." See *Philosophy and the Adventure of the Virtual*, 169. The key text here is Sartre's *L'imagination* (1936) [*Psychology of Imagination*] that includes a critical reading of Bergson from a Husserlian perspective.

36. Cited from Sartre's *Psychology of Imagination* by Pearson. See *Philosophy and the Adventure of the Virtual*, 169. Concerning the question of time, Pearson concludes that there has been an "inadequate reading" of Bergson in the context of phenomenology. There are, of course, additional reasons why Sartre would want to keep Bergson at bay. As mentioned above, Benda's *Tradition de l'existentialisme* (1947) had charged that existentialism was nothing but warmed-over Bergsonism. See my *Literary Polemics*, 194–197.

nificantly displaces a number of the issues involved in Derrida's critique of Husserl.

Husserl's phenomenology represents an attempt to found the truth of science in immediate lived experience. As Lyotard wrote, it is above all "a meditation on knowledge [*la connaissance*], a knowledge of knowledge. . . . It knows that knowledge occurs as concrete or 'empirical' science, it wants to know what grounds this scientific knowledge."[37] Husserlian phenomenology develops a philosophical method that would yield essences through perception. In a radical gesture against neo-Kantian philosophy, Husserl proposes that truth is embedded in empirical experience itself. The method of Husserl's phenomenology involves a reflection that can purify empirical experience so as to yield knowledge of the thing in itself. It represents an attempt to reconnect Kant's noumenal world (the world of the thing-in-itself) with the world of lived experience, the phenomenal world in Kant's sense.[38] It thus sought to give certainty to the objective world of experience and to demonstrate the absolute objectivity of the positive sciences. In this sense, it could be said to pursue the path established by Comte, Renan, and Taine.[39]

"Is not the idea of knowledge and of the theory of knowledge, in itself metaphysical?" asks Derrida.[40] Does it not, in Husserl's phenomenology, include a presupposition that objects in the world present themselves to consciousness in a mode of presence?[41] Ultimately, it is the presupposition of consciousness as something that can be present to itself—the Cartesian certainty of the Cogito—that Derrida labels metaphysical. He skillfully locates this gesture in Husserl's thought in spite of its professed temporal engagement.[42]

37. Lyotard, *Phénoménologie*, 4 (my translation).

38. Lyotard writes: "From the second volume of the *Logical Investigations* Husserl expands his theory of the essence, bringing it to the favored terrain of empiricism, perception. . . . The procedure of imaginative variation gives us the essence itself, the being of the object. . . . The essence is experienced in an immediate intuition." See *Phénoménologie*, 11–12 (my translation).

39. See chap. 2. As Lyotard explains, however, it also includes an ante-rational, if not anti-rational moment that was subsequently expanded upon by thinkers like Merleau-Ponty, who, to this extent, come much closer to the thinking of Bergson in the *Essai*. See *Phénoménologie*, 5–6.

40. Derrida, *La voix et le phénomène*, 3 (all translations from this work are mine).

41. Derrida, "The evidence that gives meaning has a full and original intuition." See *Voix et le phénomène*, 3.

42. Although Derrida acknowledges the radical nature of Husserl's thought, the fact that in many respects it performs a critique of metaphysics "that has certain specific affinities . . . with that of Nietzsche or that of Bergson," his aim is to demonstrate the ways in which Husserl's text remains inscribed within, or unwittingly reinscribes,

According to Derrida, "a determination of being as ideality becomes confused, in a paradoxical manner, with the determination of being as presence."[43] As a corollary, temporality is reduced to, or centered on, a "now," a mode of presence. In phenomenology, ultimately, Being is presence or a modification of presence.[44] Philosophy in general, Derrida concedes, "is . . . a philosophy of presence."[45] Derrida suggests only the possibility of a "thinking . . . not necessarily the opposite of philosophy [that] would be able to approach the real stakes [*le véritable enjeu*] . . . the concept of time."[46]

The real issue, then, is time.[47] This is the issue Derrida elaborates in terms of the difference between speech and writing, that is, in a philosophy of difference that will become known as grammatology. Grammatology will affirm the illusion of immediacy and the necessity of the mediation of the sign. Derrida, in other words, will elaborate a philosophy of time in semiological terms, that is, in relation to issues of signification that can be problematized in relation to Freud, Nietzsche, and Heidegger. Writing, for Derrida, inscribes temporality—*l'enjeu véritable* [what is really at stake]—as difference (or *différance*).

Derrida deconstructs Husserl by showing that time cuts into the attempt to establish self-presence, the presence of consciousness of itself. He thus deconstructs Husserl from a vantage point that, to my mind, is very close to Bergson's perspective: a critique of Western metaphysics for its suppression of time, a suppression reinforced by discursive language.

The paradox is that Bergson has been dismissed in the post-structuralist context as a phenomenologist.[48] The critique of phenomenology is a critique of the philosophy of presence. Yet it is Bergson, who, as we have seen, holds that any epistemology, and all rational phi-

---

metaphysical presuppositions of presence and self-presence. See, *Voix et le phénomène*, 27 n. 1.

43. Ibid., 60.

44. Ibid.

45. Ibid., 70. Derrida adds that it is also "a thinking of non-presence, which is not necessarily its opposite."

46. Ibid.

47. For an appreciation of Bergson by Levinas, see Emmanuel Levinas, *Time and the Other*, trans. Richard Cohen, 127–133. Concerning relations between Bergson and Heidegger and Bergson and Husserl, see 130 n. 5, 131 n. 6.

48. At a conference on *Tel Quel* at the University of London, I tried to introduce Bergson into the discussion. This intervention was summarily dismissed—Bergson, everyone agreed, was a phenomenologist, in other words, of no interest.

losophy, will necessary suppress time as duration, that is, as a dynamic force of becoming and of difference. Derrida evokes a "thinking of non-presence" that would not necessarily be the *opposite* of metaphysics, and yet speaks of a confrontation between phenomenology and a thinking of time.

"Does getting beyond a 'logic of identity' involve a dialectical getting beyond, or is it a question of getting beyond dialectic?" asks Vincent Descombes, who adds: "but this question is also the [question] Derrida asks himself: the beyond dialectic [*l'au-delà de la dialectique*], is it not inevitably a dialectical beyond [*un au-delà dialectique*]?"[49] Descombes concludes: "No one can say if dialectical identity and difference are one and the same or not . . . in this game . . . if you say 'identity' it changes right away into difference, and if one locates a difference, it metamorphoses into identity, so that in the end the victory of Hegel is as indiscernible as his defeat. The game is endless."[50]

This question of identity and difference is the one Deleuze takes up in *Difference and Repetition*, published the year after Derrida's *Speech and Phenomenon*. One might conclude that it was Deleuze's sense of the undecidability of the dialectical play of identity and difference, as subsequently diagnosed by Descombes, that prompted his turn to Bergson and the insistence with which he read Bergson in opposition to Hegel.

There is an important difference, however, between Derrida's approach to a critique of representation and that of Deleuze. Unlike Derrida, Deleuze was not committed to a semiological formulation of the question of difference, i.e., to the elaboration of difference in relation to the question of signification. Deleuze, we might say, follows up on the Bergsonian features of the Derridean critique of phenomenology, addressing the *real stakes* of time as duration, which he reads in terms of pure self-difference and theorizes in terms of the virtual. What remains to be explored, and I cannot undertake this here, is the proximity of Derrida's notion of deconstruction as writing practice and Bergson's keen analysis of the limits of language in the face of time, as well as a comparative analysis of the writing strategies of Derrida and Bergson, given that both share a common lucidity as to the ideological pressures of language.[51]

49. *La même et l'autre,* 172.
50. Ibid., 178.
51. For Bergson's analysis of writing (beyond the critique of language already encountered in the texts presented here), see "De l'intuition," in *La pensée et le mouvant: Essais et conférences,* in English, *The Creative Mind: An Introduction to Metaphysics,* trans. M. L. Andison. It is interesting that in *The New Bergson,* where it is ostensibly a

However compelling the force of deconstruction, and however fruitful it has shown itself to be in investigations of cultural studies, by the 1990s the textual paradigm (Derrida, Barthes) and discourse analysis (Foucault) appeared to have done much of the critical work that they could do. I would suggest that the interest in Deleuze increased because he was less limited by a textual/discursive framework and, as Bergson had been before him, more attuned to developments in science and technology. We have seen how Deleuze recast the appeal to Bergson in these terms in 1988.[52]

But it is also possible that interest in Deleuze, on the part of some, had to do with a significant ambiguity, caused by the double meaning that attaches to the word "virtual." On the one hand, virtual is to be understood in relation to the distinction virtual/actual; on the other, it comes into play in relation to "virtual reality" in the discourses of artificial intelligence and information technology.[53] The ambiguity can lead to significant misunderstandings when it is a question of passing from Deleuze to Bergson.

The Virtual

As we have seen, Bergson speaks of the past as virtual in *Matter and Memory*. By this he means that it really exists, only outside our consciousness. It involves a mode of being that is not actual in the precise sense that it cannot act in the present. The present is sensori-motor; it concerns the introduction of movement—or change—into the world. The past exists virtually in the sense that it is powerless to act materially in the present. It exists in the mode of that which no longer acts [*ce qui n'agit plus*]. The term "virtual" is to be thought in relation to the movement of time. "Virtual" involves a mode of existence of the past; it also participates in a process of becoming present, or of self-actualizing, in the process of attentive recognition.

---

question of considering Bergson in relation to contemporary issues of philosophy, no mention is made of Derrida, even when the two philosophers share fundamental concerns in relation to time and writing.

52. I am referring to the afterword in *Bergsonism* already mentioned.

53. Lev Manovich defines "virtual worlds" in the following way: "3-D computer-generated interactive environments [. . .] [V]irtual worlds," he adds "represent an important trend across computer culture, consistently promising to become a new standard in human-computer interfaces and computer networks." See *The Language of New Media*, 8 n. 4.

In *Creative Evolution*, Bergson extends the notion of duration and the temporality of becoming from a model of the individual, whose body is a center of action and whose consciousness is identified with memory, to life. The issue is evolution—what Bergson called *transformism*, that is, organic adaptation understood as a contingent creation of new forms.[54] Here time is given "positive reality"[55] as a force, a force of production or invention—in other words, a force of contingency. Life is portrayed in terms of the "energy that has not yet been expended" that Bergson evoked in his definition of the future in *Matter and Memory*.[56] Although it cannot act in the present, past time nevertheless exerts a certain force in *Creative Evolution*: "Our past manifests itself to us integrally by its pressure [*poussée*] and in the form of tendency."[57] Organic evolution (life) is portrayed on the model of duration: "the past presses up against the present and draws from it a new form, incommensurable with its antecedents."[58] In the unfolding of evolution there is a "zone of possible actions or of virtual activity that surrounds the action actually accomplished by the living being."[59] As we see here, the word "virtual" is invoked to mark a temporal difference within the event of an action; this temporal difference includes a difference between the multiple and the one, as well as the event of difference between past and present which occurs as the present becomes past.[60]

The virtual, in this sense, is characteristic of life itself, considered as a dynamic process: "a living being is a center of action. It represents a certain sum of contingency in the world."[61] This is the meaning of the virtual in Bergson. "It is necessary to adopt the language of the under-

54. "This is why we believe that the language of transformism now imposes itself on all of philosophy, just as the dogmatic affirmation of transformism imposes itself on science." See Henri Bergson, *L'évolution créatrice*, 26. All translations from this work are mine.

55. Pearson uses the expression "positive reality" of time. See *Philosophy and the Adventure of the Virtual*, 5.

56. See *Matière et mémoire*, 285.

57. See *L'évolution créatrice*, 5.

58. Ibid., 27.

59. Ibid., 145. Here Bergson identifies this moment of indetermination, hesitation, or choice with consciousness. This is a comparable moment to the one we find in the *Essai*, where it is a question of the distinction between the voluntary and the automatic. There affect plays an important role.

60. Ibid., 145. Here we find that "possible actions [*actions possibles*]," indefinite and plural, are distinguished from "the action performed [*l'action accomplie*]," which carries the definite article and whose full actualization is marked by its (already) being designated as past—*accomplie*.

61. Ibid., 262.

standing [*entendement*]," Bergson writes, "because only the understanding has one."[62] Images such as the *élan vital*, the *fusée* [flare or rocket] of becoming, along with the notion of the virtual, are strategies for conveying what concepts cannot say: the real force of time as production of novelty.[63]

Deleuze theorizes the virtual as a structure of self-differentiation.[64] He emphasizes that one question "becomes pressing": "What is the nature of this one and simple Virtual?" (*B* 6).[65] Deleuze goes on to speak of "the difference between the virtual from which we begin and the actuals at which we arrive."[66] We notice two important things here. First, the virtual has donned a capital V as it becomes the "one and simple Virtual." Second, in the passage just cited, the movement of actualization does not proceed from a virtual multiplicity to the singularity of the actualized real (as in the passage from Bergson cited above, which gives us a movement from "possible actions" to the "action performed"[67]). In the passage we have cited from Deleuze, actualization proceeds from a singular Virtual to the plural "actuals at which we arrive." The virtual has become a concept—a sort of *philosopheme*.[68]

---

62. *L'évolution créatrice*, 25. "Understanding [*entendement*]" is to be thought in terms of the Kantian distinction between the understanding and reason.

63. Bergson explicitly states that the *élan vital* is an image because no concept would be adequate to the task of discursively speaking the event of time. The virtual also is linked to the notion of tendency. Under the entry "Tendance," the dictionary *Le Robert* provides a citation from Maine de Biran (who influenced Bergson) and also links the word to the vocabulary of statistics.

64. Deleuze writes, "Virtuality exists in such a way that it realizes itself in dissociating itself, in such a way that it is forced to dissociate itself in order to realize itself. Self-differentiation is the movement of a virtuality which actualizes itself" (*B* 51). As we have already seen, the concept of the virtual performs a defense against Hegel: "In Bergson, and thanks to the notion of the virtual, the thing differs from itself in the first place, immediately" (*B* 53). In Hegel, on the other hand, "the thing differs from itself because it differs in the first place from all that it is not, such that difference goes to the point of contradiction" (*B* 53).

65. The citation continues: "How is it that, as early as *Time and Free Will*, then in *Matter and Memory*, Bergson's philosophy should have attributed such importance to the idea of virtuality at the very moment when it was challenging the category of the possible?" (*B* 6).

66. Ibid.

67. *L'évolution créatrice*, 145.

68. In the "agon" referred to earlier, between Badiou and Deleuze, Badiou charges that Deleuze turns the virtual into a transcendental term. I am not trying to make this argument. I am simply saying that the virtual becomes a concept (not necessarily a transcendental concept) in Deleuze. Henceforth it appears as a concept in titles, such as Pearson's *Philosophy and the Adventure of the Virtual* and Massumi's *Parables for the*

But this is not yet the most important misunderstanding which occurs when this concept of the virtual is conflated with the "virtual" of "virtual reality," that is, with cybernetics and cyborgs. Deleuze is perceived as a "theorist of cyber theory," and so, by way of association, is Bergson.[69] Why would Deleuze be considered a "theorist of cyber theory"? Because he elaborates a notion of the machinic, starting with the desiring machines in *Anti-Oedipus*. "The three errors concerning desire," he writes, "are called the lack, the law and the signifier. It amounts to one and the same error, idealism, that forms a pious conception of the unconscious."[70] Deleuze opposes to Lacan a materialist conception of the unconscious as machinic. The real difference in kind, he suggests, is not between the structurally distinguished realms of the Symbolic and the Imaginary, but between the Oedipal (or the structural) and the real, which he characterizes as machinic. "Wouldn't the real difference" he asks, "be between Oedipus, structural as well as imaginary, and something else that all the Oedipuses crush and repress . . . the machines of desire . . . that constitute the Real in itself, beyond and beneath the Symbolic as well as the Imaginary?" (*AO* 52–53).[71]

Virtual. See Pearson's interesting defense of Deleuze against Badiou in *Philosophy and the Adventure of the Virtual*, 70–77.

69. "The role of conceptual personae is to show thought's territories, its absolute deterritorializations and reterritorializations," write Deleuze and Guattari. They also speak of intercessors as "crystals or seeds of thought." See Gilles Deleuze and Félix Guattari, *What Is Philosophy?* trans. H. Tomlinson and G. Burchell, 69. Bergson is a key intercessor for Deleuze, to the point where philosophers such as Dorothea Olkowski and John Marks refer to a figure called Deleuze Bergson—so closely have the two been identified.

70. Deleuze and Guattari, *Anti-Oedipus: Capitalism and Schizophrenia*, trans R. Hurley, M. Seem, and H. Lane, 111 (translation modified). See the French edition, *L'anti-Oedipe,* 132. Subsequent references to this work will refer to the English edition and will be given in the text in parentheses, marked *AO.*

71. Deleuze adds: "For the Unconscious itself is no more structural than personal, it does not symbolize any more that it imagines or represents; it engineers, it is machinic. Neither imaginary nor symbolic, it is the Real" (*AO* 53). The metaphor of the machine in *Anti-Oedipus* neutralizes the question of the subject—the subject of desire whose story was being told, in the psychoanalytic framework of Lacan, through the figure of Oedipus. With the Oedipal reading of the unconscious, Deleuze complains, "the whole desiring production [*toute la production désirante*] is beaten down [*écrasée*], becomes submissive to the requirements of representation. . . . The unconscious ceases to be what it is, a factory, a workshop, to become a theatre. . . . The psychoanalyst is the director of this private theatre . . . instead of being the engineer or the mechanic that puts together the units of production" (*AO* 55, translation modified). Deleuze invokes, and criticizes, in the context of materialist psychiatry, Clerambault. For a discussion of relations between Lacan and Clerambault, see Soraya Tlatli, *La folie lyrique: Essai sur le surréalisme et la psychiatrie.*

Desiring machines.[72] The theoretical figure suits the post-structuralist intellectual parameters: anti-humanism, critique of the subject, refusal of phenomenology. We remember Derrida's provisional identification of writing with cybernetics, on condition that cybernetics divest itself of all the metaphysical terms used to distinguish man from machine.[73] And we noted Deleuze's omission of these terms in his reading of Bergson. In other words, the terms that Derrida asks cybernetics to shed—*âme* (or *esprit*), memory, choice, life, etc.—belong to the language of Bergson; Deleuze will formulate his notion of the machinic (in line with Derrida's requirements that would bring cybernetics into line with his theory of writing) on the basis of a reading of Bergson that edits out these terms. "What we term machine," Deleuze writes, "is [a] synthesis of heterogeneities as such."[74] The problem, of course, is the proximity of the machinic (a figure for radical difference in Deleuze) to the mechanical. For this is where Bergson draws the line. As we have seen, the difference between living being and machine is fundamental for him. It requires a strict division between the domains of science and philosophy.[75]

The Deleuzian sympathy for the machine (one that plays itself out in interesting ways in the cinema books—with a friendly challenge to Bergson), and the critical assimilation of the two philosophers (in the figure of Deleuze-Bergson) has lead to some serious misunderstandings.[76] One commentator, for example, characterizes both Bergson and Deleuze as

72. Deleuze's emphasis on desiring machines obscures the proximity of his critique of psychoanalysis (Freud and Lacan) to Bergson. As we have seen in chapter 4, Bergson lets us consider a dynamic unconsciousness (in lieu of a topographical Unconscious) in relation to a conception of the real. Bergson enables us to think Unconsciousness without the bar of repression associated with Oedipus. In *Anti-Oedipus,* Deleuze and Guattari only make an oblique mention of Bergson and "his grand conception of microcosm-macrocosm relationships. Bergson brought about a discreet revolution," they add, "that deserves further consideration" (*AO* 95–96). There is interesting work yet to be done on Bergson and psychoanalysis that would pursue the lines of Deleuze's critique of Freud and Lacan on the one hand and associations with Clerambault, Pierre Janet, and Ribot, on the other.

73. Derrida, *De la grammatologie*, 19.

74. Cited from *Mille plateaux* by Manuel De Landa, "Deleuze, Diagrams, and the Open-Ended Becoming of the World," in *Becomings*, 36.

75. We recall the critical line of separation Bergson draws between the living and the inert, which corresponds to a divide between science and philosophy, and, in a sense, between objectivity and subjectivity. These lines are drawn most clearly in the *Essai*, but remain in play, to a large extent, in Bergson's subsequent thought. They are at play, of course, in a different way, in the essay on laughter.

76. Bergson has criticized what he calls "cinematographic illusion" concerning time. Deleuze argues that Bergson simply had not yet envisaged the technical capacities of modern film to convey movement and time images.

"machinic materialists."[77] The label might have made Bergson laugh. But the misunderstandings become more acute, and perhaps more significant, when the machinic, as a structure or process, is identified with the machine of the computer and the lines that divide the human from the machine really do begin to break down.[78]

One feature of the computer revolution has been the creation of new media of art and communication, media that are fast replacing film, and in relation to which the very metaphor of the machine becomes outdated. "All new media objects, whether created from scratch on computer or converted from analogue media sources, are composed of digital code."[79] They originate in mathematical form and are subject to algorithmic manipulation. They can exist in potentially infinite versions thanks to techniques of transcoding.[80]

The capacity for transcoding, and the nature of the quantification involved in digitization, has lead to shifts in models used by cultural theorists who want to study them. Language-based semiotics no longer fit the units of meaning that are involved in digitization, where the units or samples involved do not always correspond to units of meaning as presupposed by linguistic semiotic models.[81]

One theorist of new media, Mark Hansen, finds in Bergson the philosophical ground for digitization as a process of embodiment. Whereas Paul Virilio despairs of a loss of the body in the cyber world,[82] Hansen has a quite different vision. From his perspective digitization puts an even greater premium on the creative and affective capacities of our bodies. Hansen turns to Bergson as a "theorist of embodied percep-

77. Marks, *Gilles Deleuze*, 50.

78. Marks writes, for example, that "human intelligence can be replicated, is more 'robotic' or machine-like than we usually think." See *Gilles Deleuze*, 53.

79. Lev Manovich, *The Language of New Media*, 27.

80. For more on transcoding, see *Language of New Media*, 45–48.

81. Manovich writes, "The key assumption of modern semiotics is that communication requires discrete units. Without discrete units, there is no language. . . . In assuming that any form of communication requires a discrete representation, semioticians took human language as the prototypical example of a communication system. A human language is discrete on most scales." However, he goes on to explain, "most semioticians came to recognize that a language-based model of distinct units of meaning cannot be applied to many kinds of cultural communication. . . . More important, the discrete units of modern media are usually not units of meanings in the ways morphemes are." See *Language of New Media*, 28, 29.

82. See Paul Virilio, *L'art du moteur* and *Cybermonde: La politique du pire*. Chapter 6 of this book discusses Virilio's concerns in relation to Bergson in more detail.

tion"[83] referring, in particular, to the early pages of *Matter and Memory*.

In his analysis of cinema Deleuze evoked a world of post-human disembodiment. Hansen reverses the direction of Deleuze's reading of Bergson and finds in Bergson's theory of perception an account of the relation between affection and perception that he develops into a theory of new media embodiment.

Hansen claims that "the digital image lays bare the Bergsonist foundation of all image technology, that is, the origin of the perceivable image in the selective function of the body as center of indetermination."[84]

This formulation refers us directly to the theory of perception in *Matter and Memory*, where Bergson defines the body, as we have seen, not only as a center of action, but as center of free or voluntary action to the extent that the body is a center of indetermination. Hansen's thesis, then, is that the digital image "demarcates the very process through which the body, in conjunction with the various apparatuses for rendering information perceptible, gives form to or *in-forms* information."[85] In other words, "information is made perceivable through embodied experience,"[86] the digital image requires an actualization of the image, just as in Bergson's account of attentive recognition, a memory image is actualized, which enables the cognitive act of perception to take place. We remember that in Bergson the image memory works together with the memory of the body and its sensori-motor diagrams. New media, according to Hansen, invite the performance of perception in Bergson's sense to the extent that they require the kind of interaction Bergson theorizes as an interaction between mind and body in order for an image to emerge.[87]

Hansen reads Bergson in a manner quite different from Deleuze. Is Hansen retreating from the frontiers of the post-human into an old humanism? I don't think so. For traditionally the claims of humanism—at

---

83. Mark B. N. Hansen, *New Philosophy for New Media*, 4.
84. Ibid., 10.
85. Ibid.
86. Ibid.
87. Hansen supports his reading of Bergson with contemporary work in cognitive science, referring to the work of Francisco Varela that reinforces Bergson's analysis of the importance of affect in perception and analyzes the importance of affect to time consciousness through contemporary clinical experiment.

least since Descartes—have been lodged in reason or cognitive consciousness. It is primarily *this* humanism that is challenged by poststructuralist theorists such as Derrida and Foucault. This was a humanism that claimed for itself a position of mastery over the world. In short, it was the humanism so deliriously invoked by Renan.

What Hansen, and the theorists he invokes, propose is something like an interactive embodiment in which it is less a question of a subject of consciousness than of agency, and less a question of cognition, than of affect. Hansen refers to the work of Gilbert Simondon who links affectivity, time, and embodiment to a horizon of the pre-individual. This, as Hansen suggests, would be an extension of Bergson's interactive ontology, "the universal interaction that is no doubt reality itself."[88]

The passage from film to digital media has occasioned a new reading of Bergson, one that explicitly reverses the Bergsonism of Deleuze. According to Hansen, "Deleuze's neo-Bergsonist account of the cinema carries out the progressive disembodying" of the human, reinforcing a notion of the machinic or the post-human. Hansen sets out to retrieve Bergson's embodied understanding of contingent agency from Deleuze's "transformative appropriation" of Bergson. Whereas Deleuze "wages an assault" on the "sensori-motor basis of the human body," Hansen sets out to "redeem" Bergson's fundamental insight into affective embodiment.[89]

As the previous discussion reveals, Bergson has become important for thinking about the cultural meanings—and the ethics and politics—that will come into play with the transformations brought about by the information revolution.[90] The point is not to defend one position or another in relation to this new agon, but to show that Bergson is now, more than ever, open for reading and pertinent to ongoing debates. To take a position in these matters it will be necessary to engage seriously with Bergson's texts. It has been the aim of this book to invite such an engagement.

In a recently published book, *Parables for the Virtual* (2002), Brian Massumi proposes to reorient cultural studies from a Bergsonist perspec-

---

88. Cited in Jacqueline Carroy, "Le temps intersubjectif et ses métaphores: Interaction ou endosmose? Une lecture de Bergson," *Connexions* 41:186 (my translation).

89. *New Philosophy* 6, 7, 1, 6.

90. Manovich writes, "The 1990s rapid transformation of culture into e-culture, of computers into universal culture carriers, of media into new media, demands that we rethink our categories and models." See *Language of New Media*, 6. One could say that Hansen's reading of Bergson opens onto an ethics to the extent that it places affect at the core of embodiment.

tive. For the last few decades, he argues, cultural studies has meant the analysis of cultural and ideological mediations in fundamentally linguistic terms. Discourse analysis prevailed. Real bodies could not be taken into account, only discursive ones, constructed according to a grid of predetermined binaries. Nature too was approached as constructed in discourse. It is time, he suggests, to "part company" with the linguistic model—or at least to become aware of its limitations.[91] There was so much that could not be thought in these terms: real bodies, nature, affect, sensation. What is more, largely concerned with analyses of ideological positioning, this approach to cultural studies was unable to account for change. After a certain point, it could not discover anything new.

Massumi sets out to explore the implications for cultural studies of reintroducing movement and sensation back into one's thinking about the body. He wants to redirect the focus to qualitative differences that occur as change. He frames his project in relation to Bergson, the philosophical precursor, he affirms, for the discussion of "paradoxes of passage and position."[92] He orients a new field of cultural studies in relation to what he calls the "Bergsonian revolution."[93]

In what does this revolution consist? First, it "turns the world on its head" to the extent that "position no longer comes first, with movement a problematic second. It is secondary to movement and derived from it."[94] This involves a mode of thinking in which passage precedes construction. It means thinking in terms of emergence—thinking not just ontologically but, as Massumi puts it "ontogenetically."[95] For Massumi, the "Bergsonian revolution" means the attempt to engage with the becoming of culture, instead of considering culture statically and mapping its geographies. It means being willing to think nature, the body, and even a certain mode of the subject.[96]

91. Brian Massumi, *Parables for the Virtual*, 5.
92. Ibid., 7.
93. Massumi is not alone in this move. The feminist philosopher Elizabeth Grosz has also engaged with Bergson and Bergsonian issues: time, evolution, embodiment, and emergence, all of which have provided her with a critical orientation toward identity politics. Ann Game links Bergson to feminist philosophy in *Undoing the Social: Towards a Deconstructive Sociology*. See also Dorothea Olkowski, *Gilles Deleuze and the Ruin of Representation*.
94. Massumi, *Parables for the Virtual*, 8.
95. Ibid.
96. Massumi cleverly writes "subject-" to convey the subject-in-relation, the incipient, or emergent, subject. His formulation fits Bergson's statement in *L'évolution créatrice* to the effect that, "The living being is above all a place of passage [*lieu de passage*]."

Massumi is unambiguous: "Ideas about culture or social construction have dead-ended because they have insisted on bracketing the *nature* of process." He points out the following paradox: "theoretical moves aimed at ending Man end up making human culture the measure of meaning of all things." From a Bergsonian perspective, Massumi develops a notion of affect based on the process of emergence. "Affect," he concludes, "holds a power to rethink postmodern power after ideology."[97]

Cultural studies, then, is renewed and reoriented by a thinking of emergence, a thinking of the force of time that engenders novelty. Massumi has taken from Bergson the clarity and the critical force needed to radically reorient cultural studies. Bergson is not reimagined as a precursor to post-structuralism here; he is appealed to in an effort to find a way out of the limits of post-structuralist cultural theory.

See *Parables for the Virtual*, 12. Elsewhere Bergson refers to the living being as a hyphen [*trait d'union*].

97. Ibid., 3, 13, 42.

6. Current Issues

T. E. Hulme proclaimed that Bergson had dispelled "the nightmare of determinism."[1] Perhaps he overstated the case. The quantitative mania Bergson diagnosed in his own day is more pervasive than ever in Western culture. The tools of statistical analysis dominate the social sciences as well as the computer sciences and related fields. Information and communication technologies are in the process of changing the way we live. Behaviorist psychology is thriving and behavior modification by pharmacological means has become a hugely profitable industry that is transforming social experience. Theories of rational choice not only inform the work of theoretical economists, they also find their way into marketing strategies that now have global reach. Cognitive science research, much of which concerns relations between humans and computers, relies on methods of psychophysics, the implications of which Bergson challenged over a century ago. Research in artificial intelligence and robotics uses sophisticated techniques of mathematical formalization to extend the participation of automaton agents on the scene of human experience (there is talk, for example, of robot companions for the aged). These developments, together with experiments in cloning and biomedical engineering (highlighted by the recent decipherment of the genome sequence) increasingly blur the distinction between the human and the inhuman, the animate and inanimate realms, the "real" and the artificial—or the virtual.

1. A. E. Pilkington, *Bergson and His Influence: A Reassessment*, 218.

"The theory of mutations," we read in *L'évolution créatrice*, "holds that at a certain moment, after a long period of time has passed, the entire species is affected by [*est prise de*] a tendency to change."[2] Taken together, the various transformations underway in our own historical period are so overwhelming that some theorists have turned to the language of evolutionary change to characterize them. In what terms can we begin to discuss these changes? With respect to what metaphysical or critical presuppositions will the conversation take place? How will the discussion be framed? We find ourselves rather in the position Valéry evoked in the passage cited at the beginning of this study—our world is being utterly transformed, and we only have immemorial ideas![3]

Bergson has much to say about a number of issues that concern us, most specifically how to think the human in relation to the machine, on the one hand, and nature, on the other. He has much to say about evolution, about mechanism, life, intelligence, and instinct. He offers a way to pose the question of the difference between the living and the inert— it is, as we have seen, a question of two registers of time.

Time

We have seen that the second law of thermodynamics posed the issue of time's arrow in the natural sciences. In his lifetime, Bergson's work was characterized as a prolonged meditation on the implications of this law.[4] We have seen that Boltzmann rephrased the law in a mathematics of probability that removed the directionality of time's arrow and that Bergson was defeated by Einstein in his attempt to keep indeterminacy (and duration) pertinent in the context of relativity, where time becomes absorbed within the fourth dimension, space-time.

In recent decades, some scientists have taken up Bergson's position concerning the irreversibility of time. "Present day physics," writes the Nobel Prize winning chemist Ilya Prigogine in the 1980s, "is rediscover-

2. Bergson, *L'évolution créatrice*, 86. All translations from this work are mine.
3. See chap. 2.
4. For one example of the link between the issues of evolution and thermodynamics see Bernard Brunhes, "L'Evolutionnisme et le principe de Carnot," *Revue de Métaphysique et de Morale* 5 (1897): 35–43. This essay makes reference to an earlier article in the same journal: L. Weber, "L'évolutionnisme et le principe de la conservation de l'énergie," *Revue de Métaphysique et de Morale*, 87. The issue that includes the essay by Brunhes also includes a review of Bergson's *Matter and Memory* by V. Delbos, 353–389.

ing time, not the old time, according to which the watch is eternally returning to its own past, but an internal time, which corresponds to activity and finally to creative processes."[5] Prigogine, who has revived explorations of the second law of thermodynamics in quantum mechanical
terms, studied dissipative structures that appear to validate the reality of
irreversible processes in nature and hence the affirmation of irreversible
time. According to Prigogine and Stengers, Bergson's critique of classical
physics has not only been vindicated by contemporary research in
physics, this research is only now catching up with his insights concerning the ontology of irreversible time. "Whereas the laws of classical
physics denied the arrow of time, we can affirm today that irreversible
becoming marks all living creatures."[6] Contemporary physics is, in the
words of Stengers and Prigogine, a "physics of becoming," a "process
physics."[7] These authors suggest that after Boltzmann translated the second law of thermodynamics (the law of entropy which had carried the
arrow of time) into the mathematics of a reversible process by attending
only to the state of equilibrium, Bergson despaired of physics ever engaging with irreversible time. Hence his decision to insist upon a sharp
separation between the projects of science, on the one hand, and metaphysics, on the other, and his belief that only a combination of the two
could yield true knowledge. Almost a century later, Prigogine reopened
the question of irreversible processes when he focused his research on
states of disequilibrium (known as dissipative structures) that he located
in the physical world.[8] Today, if one accepts the analysis of Stengers and
Prigogine, Bergson's conception of time has won out in the debate
among physicists.

This, of course, is open to discussion. One physicist has proclaimed

5. Ilya Prigogine, "Irreversibility and Space-Time Structure," in *Physics and the Ultimate Significance of Time*, ed. David R. Griffin, 249. He goes on to say that "this redis-
covery of time . . . makes . . . our period as exciting and full of promise for the future as
the great period between Galileo and Newton."
6. Prigogine and Stengers, *Entre le temps et l'éternité*, 143 (my translation).
7. Ibid.
8. Prigogine and Stengers have this to say concerning developments in chaos theory:
"Dynamic chaotic processes make it possible to construct this bridge, that Boltzmann
had not been able to create, between dynamics and the world of irreversible processes."
They add, "Dynamic systems that fit the classical (determinist) model can now be shown
to be a special case." "It is the arrow of time," they continue, "that dominates the evolution of the system" (115). See *Entre le temps et l'éternité*, 107, 115 (my translation). On
this point see also David Bohm on what he calls "the implicate order" in "Time, the Implicate Order and Pre-Space," in *Physics and the Ultimate Significance of Time: Bohm,
Prigogine, and Process Philosophy*, ed. David Ray Griffin.

the end of time in a book by that name;[9] it has prompted lively discussion. Some claim that to speak about an ontology of irreversible time, as Prigogine has done, is to slip into (mere) philosophizing. Perhaps for reasons of the "shortage of words" alluded to earlier[10] it is not possible to speak effectively about time across the gulf that separates scientific performance from discourse.

Another current development that pertains to elements of Bergson's thought is the trend within the history of science to investigate ideological pressures on the development of scientific knowledge. Thus it is now possible to speak, as Stengers does, of scientific "ecologies."[11] It is possible to undertake cultural histories of the development of science that question how various interests might pressure the directions that scientific experimentation takes and the view of the world it engenders.[12] This might be called a Bergsonian perspective to the extent that, in *Creative Evolution*, Bergson posed intelligence as an adaptive feature and affirmed that its use is guided by pragmatic needs. The biological, or adaptive, character of intelligence is an issue with renewed implications today in the context of artificial intelligence. From this perspective it is now possible to consider the interests that pressured Einstein's theory of relativity. As Stengers and Prigogine put it, "The dream of Einstein had always been the unification of physics, the discovery of a unique principle that would give intelligibility to physical reality. This dream relegated becoming to the status of obstacle, of an illusion to be demystified, for physics."[13]

Speaking of "how unstable processes modify the structure of space-time," Prigogine and Stengers write, "This question was at the heart of the debate between Einstein and Bergson. The outcome of this debate was disastrous for Bergson: it was generally agreed that he was mistaken in his interpretation of Einstein's theory of special relativity. And yet . . . the existence of unstable dynamic processes rehabilitates, up to a certain point, the idea of a *universal time* defended by Bergson."[14] The debate between Bergson and Einstein is perhaps not over yet.

9. Julian Barbour, *The End of Time, The Next Revolution in Physics*.

10. See the discussion in chapter 2. Pullman discusses the inadequacy of language to convey the complexities of quantum mechanics. See, *The Atom in the History of Human Thought*, 298.

11. Stengers speaks of an "ecology of practices [*écologie des pratiques*]." See Isabelle Stengers, *Cosmopolitiques 2: L'invention de la mécanique: Pouvoir et raison*, 7.

12. See, for example, Mara Beller, *Quantum Dialogue: The Making of a Revolution*.

13. *Entre le temps et l'éternité*, 15 (my translation).

14. Ibid., 195. See also Jimena Canales, "Einstein, Bergson, and the Experiment That Failed: Intellectual Cooperation at the League of Nations."

Determinism (Chaos Theory)

Central to the work of Prigogine on the dynamics of dissipative structures is the configuration of mathematical models and experimental procedures loosely known as "chaos theory."[15] Chaos theory studies dynamic systems, systems that change over time. It "enables us to understand how unpredictable behavior appears in simple systems" (K 81). It pertains to systems that exist on the micro-physical (or quantum) level, as well as to those that appear on the scale of ordinary measurement (the Newtonian level) and on the cosmic scale. It also pertains both to features of the physical world and to features of the social or cultural, world. Chaos theory can be applied to "chemical interactions, crowds or variations introduced by evolutionary change" (K 29).

These systems are simple and yet unusual in that an apparently negligible factor can end up having a huge impact on subsequent changes in the system over time.[16] This results in changes that do not fit the usual patterns of statistical analysis, since these, quite logically, anticipate that small factors in the initial state of a system will continue to have only a small impact on the development of the system as a whole over time. In relation to these unstable systems, predictability is challenged. "Two systems that start very close together can move very far apart" (K xi). Because it investigates change directly, chaos theory refocuses attention on the kind of qualitative issues that interested Bergson.[17] The emphasis on time, process, qualitative analysis, and complexity return us to central features of Bergson's thought.

Chaos theory challenges predictability, but it does not necessarily imply the breakdown of determinism; the instability of chaos systems can be observed locally within a larger deterministic system.[18] On the

15. I am relying on Stephen H. Kellert's characterization of chaos theory in *In the Wake of Chaos,* x. Subsequent references to this work will be abbreviated as *K.*

16. This is referred to as "sensitive dependence on initial conditions," ibid.

17. As Kellert indicates, it asks about "the general character of . . . [a system's] long-term behavior, rather than seeking to arrive at numerical predictions about its exact future state" (K 3, 4). It requires attention to qualities, which Bergson emphasizes in connection with the experience of duration in the *Essai.*

18. Kellert argues that chaos theory implies indeterminism, especially when it is theorized in tandem with quantum mechanics. But he acknowledges that other theorists identify chaos theory with determinism, since, in principle, if initial conditions could be accurately known, the rest would follow. In practice, as Kellert indicates, chaos theory is investigated and used in relation to what he calls "local determinisms." See, in this connection, the work of Daniel Dennett, *Darwin's Dangerous Idea: Evolution and the Mean-*

quantum level, however, it "leads . . . to grave doubts about determinism itself"(K 50). For prediction to be possible, chaos theory requires a rigorously accurate account of the initial state of the dynamic system, since the sensitivity to initial conditions can lead to extremely divergent developments (K 71). In the context of quantum mechanics, it is not possible to locate the initial state of a particle (remember the Heisenberg Uncertainty Principle); it is only possible to locate the general area in which the particle is *probably* located.[19] Thus it becomes all but impossible to derive any predictability when we are dealing with chaotic systems on the subatomic scale. "Chaotic dynamics," Kellert writes, "will take the tiny indeterminacies of quantum-mechanical systems and stretch them into huge variations, dilating the smallest patch until, at some sufficiently distant time in the future, almost anything is possible"(K 73).[20]

The implications for the field of cosmology are significant. As Kellert puts it, "Determinism is not so much proven false as rendered meaningless. . . . Where this all leads is to the notion that the historical evolution of the physical universe is fundamentally open" (K 75). Bergson made this very point against Spencer in *Creative Evolution*.[21]

This is not entirely surprising, given that the mathematics that enabled subsequent developments in chaos theory was developed by Bergson's colleague at the Académie française, Henri Poincaré.[22] To this extent we could say that Bergson and chaos theory are in a sense contemporaries.

Here is Bergson on Henri Poincaré in 1910: "In his two volumes *Science et hypothèses* [Science and Hypotheses] and *La valeur de la science* [The Value of Science] he launches a veritable critique of scientific knowledge whose symbolic and provisional character he demonstrates."[23] Bergson goes on to situate Poincaré's critique of science in the

---

ings of Life, discussed by Keith Ansell Pearson in *Philosophy and the Adventure of the Virtual: Bergson and the Time of Life,* 76–86.

19. See my discussion of the Heisenberg Principle in chap. 2.

20. This is the area in which Prigogine worked, i.e., with unstable and intrinsically random quantum states (*K* 72).

21. This is indeed the central argument of *Creative Evolution.* The contemporary version of this debate would take place with Dennett. See Pearson, *Philosophy and the Adventure of the Virtual,* 77–87.

22. "The investigation of qualitative aspects of a system's behavior began with the work of Poincaré" (*K* 4). Poincaré, a philosopher of science as well as a mathematician, had already problematized prediction on the basis of sensitivity to initial conditions.

23. Bergson, *Correspondances,* 349 (my translation).

context of other thinkers of contingency. Speaking of Félix Lacher Ravaisson, he writes: "He demonstrated simple habits of nature in the laws of physics and thus opened the way for a philosophy that would hold these laws to be contingent. Such is the idea [Émile] Boutroux presents in his remarkable work on 'The Contingency of the Laws of Nature.' The conclusions of a critique such as that of Poincaré will naturally meet up with this philosophy [*vont tout naturellement rejoindre cette philosophie*]."[24]

Kellert asks an important question: if the fundamental mathematical tools that underlie chaos theory have been in place since the 1880s, why the delay in the development of this theory? It is here that Bergson's critical authority takes on particular value. For Bergson did not just intuit subsequent developments in science and mathematics, he also analyzed a worldview, an epistemological and ideological framework that he characterized as an "obsession with spatial images."[25] He refers this worldview to social imperatives and to this extent suggests what we could call an ideological analysis that begins to account for what Kellert calls the systematic "prejudice in favor of linear systems" (*K* 138) and the neglect of chaos.

Some have explained the belated development of chaos theory in terms of technological development. Digital computers have made it easier to see chaos, since they can produce simulations of dynamic systems and visualizations of mathematical models. To Kellert, however, this is a minor factor. Just as Bergson argues that an obsession with space is a kind of defense against the reality of time, Kellert believes that physicists learned, or were taught, not to see chaos because of a "prejudice in favor of systems as regular and predictable as clockwork" (*K* 135).[26] He demonstrates how "science training made chaos very hard to see," not only in mathematics, physics, and engineering but also in fields such as population biology and economics (*K* 141). "Chaos is as com-

24. Ibid. Again, discussions of relations between new developments in science, mathematics, evolution, psychology, and linguistics were very much in the air in Bergson's day. See the *Revue de Métaphysique et de Morale* 5 (1897) which includes an article by Poincaré and a review (in two parts) of A. Hannequin's *L'hypothèse des atomes dans la science contemporaine* by Louis Coutrat, 87–113, 221–247. See as well the review of Ribot's *La psychologie des sentiments* by F. Rauh, 200–220.

25. Bergson, *Matière et mémoire* (Paris: PUF, 1939), 165. My translation.

26. Kellert writes that to present chaos theory "as a corollary of the computer revolution is a kind of defense." He cites James Gleick from *Chaos*. See *In the Wake of Chaos*, 129.

mon as daffodils in spring," he writes, "Yet even when looking right at it, scientists saw nothing of interest" (*K* 136).

What is at stake in this denial? Time. "Stable periodic behavior is clocklike behavior."[27] In short, Kellert attributes the historical delay[28] in the development of chaos theory to what he calls "the metaphysical comforts of determinism" (*K* 147).[29] Prediction, of course, means control.[30] Once again, it is a question of the particular kind of humanism endorsed by Renan and Taine over a century ago. To this ideology of humanism Bergson opposed a philosophy of time, life, and creative becoming. "The mechanistic view of the world," Kellert writes, "served as a legitimating ideology for the project of dominating nature, while at the same time functioning to secure a hierarchical social order" (*K* 156). The critical power of Bergson's thought contests the ideological framework that Kellert diagnoses. To say this is perhaps only to modify T. E. Hulme's more optimistic statement. Bergson may not have dispelled the nightmare of determinism, but his critical thinking challenges our comfort with respect to it.

Bergson appears to have anticipated the general direction of a number of important scientific developments. As a result, his thought strikes

27. The citation continues: "A mechanical clock is designed to display limit cycle behavior that mimics the motion of the idealized linear case. Exact closed-form solutions, which took the shape of routine mathematical expressions, received the label 'simple'" (*K* 144).

28. Kellert cites Prigogine and Stengers concerning chemical reactions that can undergo bifurcation and begin complex oscillatory behavior, and that "'could have been discovered long ago but were not.' Although the systems themselves were found in the nineteenth century, their study was 'repressed in the cultural and ideological context of those times'" (*K* 147).

29. He writes: "The metaphysical comforts of determinism begin to explain why apparently random or 'noisy' experimental results might be so easily dismissed as unsuitable for scientific investigation. . . . The notion that science should seek only straightforward causal mechanisms expressed in microreductionist, ahistorical language would obviously hinder the developments of chaos theory" (*K* 144). The "prejudice in favor of linear systems," he writes, "took the form of a kind of tyranny of selective example" (*K* 136). Kellert also addresses the importance of the question of gender in relation to these issues and to the culture of scientific institutions generally.

30. See Kellert for a discussion of the pedagogy of science in physics, engineering, and applied mathematics. "Textbooks," he writes, "usually treated only linear force laws in discussions of oscillations, for instance, thus assimilating all vibrational behavior to the motion of a mass on an ideal spring—what is known as simple harmonic motion. . . . The few that treated nonlinear force laws concentrated on mathematical techniques such as perturbation theory, which aim to transform the situation into simple harmonic motion or at least to reduce it to an easily solvable form." See *In the Wake of Chaos*, 137–138.

us as particularly well attuned to our present circumstances. This, in itself, would warrant careful reading of his work. Even more important, however, is the critical force of his thinking, which can orient a response to these conditions. To think duration, the irreversible time of becoming, Bergson wrote, requires the breaking of many frames. This remains the difficult task of philosophy today.

Artificial Intelligence: Cybernetics

Chaos theory is used in a determinist mode in the cognitive sciences, specifically in research in artificial intelligence where it is a question of the mechanization of thought. Once again, we seem to have arrived at the point of realizing Taine's dream—or perhaps Bergson's worst nightmare!

A fundamental feature of Bergson's early work, as we have seen, is the delineation of the animate from the inanimate. This is the basis for Bergson's critical distinction between science, which can know inert matter in a timeless manner objectively, and metaphysics, or the philosophy of intuition, which enjoys the wisdom of time.

Although Bergson extends duration to the ontological level in *Creative Evolution*, he never wavers concerning the difference between knowing inert things and experiencing living beings, which implies an experience of time. The ambitions of cognitive science, which aim at the mechanization and computer simulation of thought, obscure this limit. Once again Bergson's thought can help us ask important questions in the face of these developments. As we shall see, it also helps us recognize a certain ambivalence that seems to haunt the project of AI.

The premise of the field of artificial intelligence is that human intelligence is machine-like.[31] Research has already produced striking results in areas such as medicine and engineering (and even computer games) where a computer can be programmed to perform very specialized tasks of complex reasoning with concrete results. If the applications of this research remain somewhat limited,[32] its implications are vast. Lev Manovich, for example, describes the following experience: "I was playing against both human and computer controlled characters in a VR

31. John Marks, *Gilles Deleuze: Vitalism and Multiplicity*, 53.
32. "Computers can pretend to be intelligent only by tricking us into using a very small part of who we are when we communicate with them." See Lev Manovich, *Principles of New Media*, 1. www.Mediamatic.net/article-200.6026.html.

simulation of some sort of non-existent sport game. All my opponents appeared as simple blobs covering a few pixels of my VR display; at this resolution, it made absolutely no difference who was human and who was not."[33]

Voices ranging from Thomas Nagel to Paul Virilio warn of the imminent extinction of the idea of the human. "It is possible . . . that the very idea of a person . . . is a dying notion," writes Nagel, "not likely to survive the advances of scientific psychology and neurophysiology."[34] Virilio considers the collapse of the distinction between the human body and technology in a more dramatic tone. After two scientific revolutions, he writes, "The third revolution is the transplant revolution, the colonization of the body by biotechnology. . . . Cloning is the drama of the living. . . . Technology is colonizing the human body just as it colonized the body of the Earth. . . . Today it is the animal body that is being threatened with colonization by micromachines."[35]

Alarmist? Perhaps. But it gives pause. Cybernetics aspires to a mechanization of thought. Thought is assimilated to information, which is passed through the internet. Here it becomes possible to simulate not just intelligent operations, but also sensations of the body. The body itself is understood to function in relation to a computer program—the genome. It undergoes electronic interventions and becomes fitted with prostheses, or nanotechnological interventions that blur the limit between animate beings and inanimate ones, the limit between the human and the machine. "Organic heterogeneity," Virilio writes, is no longer a question of "an external body [*corps étranger*] attached to the living body [*le corps propre*] of the patient"—it is no longer a question of mere prosthesis—but of "a foreign rhythm [*rythme étranger*] able to make it [the body] vibrate in unison with the machine."[36] *Technogreffes*, this is Virilio's term for the "intra-organic intrusion of technology [*la technique*] and its micro-machines into the heart of the living [*au sein du vivant*],"[37] for the mixing of the technological with the living enabled by

33. Ibid.

34. Thomas Nagel, writing on Fodor, in *Other Minds*, 70. He goes on to say that "by giving the homunculus too much to do," Fodor "may have obscured the special character of what humans can actually be said to do." See *Other Minds*, 70.

35. Paul Virilio, *Politics of the Very Worst*, trans. Michael Cavaliere, ed. Sylvère Lotringer (New York: *Semiotext(e)*, 1999), 53–55.

36. Paul Virilio, *L'art du moteur*, 135–136 (my translation). "We are headed," he writes apocalyptically, "to the reduction of the living to less than nothing." See *Politics of the Very Worst*, 54.

37. *L'art du moteur*, 135. See chap. 5.

nanotechnologies. In Bergson's terms, *technogreffes* would be the epitome of the comic[38]—or would it mean the end of irony?

The attempt to mechanize mental activity (or to simulate mental activity through mechanized processes) has lead to some surprising developments. Increasingly, the effort to make the machine operate as we do leads beyond the rational operations of intellect associated with the earlier models of the computer and of the human mind.[39] More and more it is a question of trying to simulate the powers of invention that Bergson identified as the signature of living beings, as distinct from inert things.

Cutting edge work in the fields of media technologies, cognitive science, and artificial intelligence technologies involves the constitution of databases that would eventually be able to program common sense into computers—so that they will become more like us! Instead of conceiving of the human on the model of the machine, it is a question of producing machines that simulate the living.

In *The Mind Doesn't Work That Way* Jerry Fodor argued that the Computational Theory of Mind could not accommodate certain features of human mental activity, namely, global judgments of the simplest and most general kind that often tend to be context driven. Go to the web page of the Common Sense Computing Project at MIT and you will find the following statement:

> The purpose of this web site is unusual, but we hope you find it interesting and compelling, because we need your help! Our goal is to teach computers all those things an average person knows but takes for granted, because they are so obvious. This is known as the problem of giving computers "common sense." [. . .]

38. In his essay on laughter, Bergson characterizes the comic in just such terms, namely, as "mechanism inserted into nature [*un mécanisme inséré dans la nature*]." See Henri Bergson, *Œuvres,* 409.

39. See, for example, Jerry Fodor, *The Language of Thought* and *The Mind Doesn't Work That Way,* which summarizes the Computational Theory of Mind that holds that the mind works like a computer. From the moment of its emergence approximately fifty years ago, Fodor writes, cognitive science has "had as its defining project to examine a theory largely owing to Turing, that cognitive mental processes are operations defined as syntactically structured mental representations that are much like sentences." From this perspective, mental processes are considered computations, where computation is defined as "a causal process that is syntactically driven." Although he criticizes certain AI theorists for going too far, and underscores the limitations of CTM (it cannot, for example, adequately account for the mind's capacity to make global judgments), he nevertheless holds in this book that Computational Theory is "by far the best theory of cognition we've got." See *Mind Doesn't Work That Way,* 1, 4.

Computer scientists have been trying to find ways to teach computers all this knowledge for many generations now, but they have not been very successful. . . . We think this problem can be solved—by harnessing the knowledge of everyone on the internet![40]

Announcing gleefully that "Everyone has common sense, so everyone can participate!" the web site invites our participation, explaining that the goal of the project is to "Take the internet to the next level, beyond its current state as a giant repository of web pages, to a new state where it will be able to think about all the knowledge it contains, in essence, *to make it a living entity*."[41] The goal of the project, then, is to create software envisaged as a new kind of life form!

Another project that aims to breathe life into the information experience is the Ambient Intelligence Project, also at the MIT Media Lab. The home page of one participant in this project states that he works in "cognition-inspired computational modeling of . . . everyday reasoning, emotions, personality, and attitudes."[42] The goal of his work, he states, is "to build a psychologically and socially plausible AI capable of building and sustaining a social and psychological relationship with a person. The AI," he writes, "must be capable of intimacy."[43] If the comic, for Bergson, is defined as the insertion of the mechanical into the living, what would he call the insertion of the living into the mechanical (or the informatic)?

We see that researchers in the cognitive sciences and in artificial intelligence are not just interested in simulating linear logical operations; they are also engaged in exploring how machines might embody emotions and creativity.[44] It is not enough that machines can outperform us in a narrow domain of problem solving; we want them to be creative, so we investigate the computational modeling of creativity. Research is now being conducted into how to produce a child-like robot, by which is meant one that is capable of learning and inventing creatively.[45] In

40. http://commonsense.media.mit.edu.
41. Ibid., emphasis added.
42. http://web.media.mit.edu/%7Ehugo.
43. Ibid.
44. See *The Emotion Machine,* available on-line through the Marvin Minsky homepage in which Marvin Minsky characterizes emotion in terms of process and asks what it would mean for machines to embody such processes.
45. See "Bringing up RoboBaby," *Wired* 2 (12 Dec. 1994). http://www.wired .com/wired/archive/2.12/cog.html.

short, we want our robots to evolve—and to evolve creatively, as Bergson might have said. So we study creative mutation mechanisms.

What is clear, however, is that these efforts to artificially reproduce the human reveal something about the current sense of what it means to be human. Instead of seeing our reflection as the rational animal, we find, as on the walls of the Lascaux cave, values of movement, of life, and of immediate experience.[46] We find precisely the values Bergson defended in his challenge to determinism, and, specifically, to the psychophysics of Fechner. These are the very values Bergson attached to living creatures in their difference from inert ones, to the human as distinct from the machine. Although I have not yet seen Bergson named in this context, appeals are made precisely to the sense experience of qualities, embodiment, emergence or invention, evolution, freedom, intuition, and the concrete features of the context of experience, all key elements, as we have seen, of Bergson's philosophy of time.

The attempt to simulate these features of human beings—of their experience and behavior—pushes the technical means employed in this research further in the direction of complexity and of nonlinear operations—thereby reinforcing Bergson's view of indetermination, and ultimately, his open, or process, ontology.[47] Paradoxically, then, it tends to vindicate Bergson's challenge to Spencer's mechanistic evolution, that is, to vindicate the notion of creative evolution that Bergson linked to the force of time.

The paradox, then, is that investigations of virtual reality have brought us back to issues Bergson addressed in his earliest work, the *Essai*—issues of quality versus quantity, of affect and embodiment. They bring us back, in other words, to a notion of contingent experience. But this appeal to the affective, or subjective, dimension of experience is now made to the end of producing more complex automatons. "The living being," Bergson wrote, "is a human being, a person. The mechanical tool [*dispositif mécanique*] is, on the contrary, a thing. What provoked laughter, was the temporary transfiguration of a person into a thing."[48] The production of a child robot would perform, it seems, a reverse transfiguration.

Bergson was not blind to the possibilities of "mechanism inserted into nature" or of an "automatic ordering [*réglementation*] of soci-

46. I am alluding to G. Bataille's analysis of sacred transgression. See his "Lascaux ou la naissance de l'art," in *Œuvres*, vol. 9.
47. For a discussion of process ontology, see Nicholas Rescher, *Process Metaphysics: An Introduction to Process Philosophy*.
48. Bergson, "Le rire," in *Œuvres*, 414 (my translation).

ety."[49] This was for him the essence of the comic. But what appeared quintessentially comic to Bergson a century ago now strikes Virilio as tragic—the process is picking up speed.

"We are going to witness," Virilio writes, "the accident of accidents, the accident of time."[50] "Human beings," he continues, "exist in the three dimensions of chronological time—past, present, and future. It is obvious that the liberation of the present—real time or world time— runs the risk of making us lose the past and the future in favor of a pre- sentification, which amounts to an amputation of the volume of time. Time is volume."[51] What this postmodern philosopher laments, in this Proustian evocation of lost time, is a loss of "the volume of time," a no- tion that suggests Bergsonian duration. Virilio has framed the issue of postmodern alienation, tied to the information revolution, as a problem of speed; he has formulated it as a matter of time. To this extent he echoes Valéry, whose analysis of the crisis of modernity we took as the point of departure for this study of Bergson. Valéry characterized his own period as an age "completely formed by the sciences, in perpetual technological transformation."[52] He too analyzed the crisis of modern- ity as a crisis of time in acceleration.[53]

At the beginning of this study we situated Bergson, through Valéry, in the fold between a modern triumph and a crisis of modernism. It is thus a bit surprising to find Bergson's thought so pertinent to the post- modern dilemmas of the information age. The question remains, how- ever, whether AI research into interactive experience, ambient intelli- gence, and tangible user interfaces ("tangible bits")[54]—research that appears to reintroduce Bergson's concerns into our own cultural inter- faces—might be considered a response to the issues raised by Virilio, or simply part of the problem he somewhat frantically begs us to con- front? Does it represent a response to his call for more contact as a mode of resistance against the alienations—the appropriations and ex- propriations—of the electronic age, or does it simply render what Vir- ilio calls "the cybernetic society"[55] even more sinister through haptic

49. Ibid., 409.
50. *Politics of the Very Worst*, 81.
51. Ibid.
52. Valéry, *Œuvres*, 1:971.
53. On this point see my "Le symptôme de la mer et la 'folie de l'eau' chez Valéry," *Bulletin des Études Valéryennes* 91 (June 2002).
54. See the web page of Hiroshi Ishii, http://web.media.mit.edu/~ishii.
55. *Politics of the Very Worst*, 80. Virilio writes, for example, that "We are faced with a phenomenon of interactivity that is tendentiously depriving us of our free will so as to bring us to a system of questions/answers that cannot be evaded. When people

seductions that only serve to blur the boundary, as Hiroshi Ishii puts it, between "atoms and bits," thereby exacerbating the kind of acceleration and global closure that Virilio decries. Taine wrote gleefully in Bergson's day that science could now send its instrumental tentacles into the very depths of the human soul. Are we at a comparable moment, one in which bits intrude on, and contaminate, the very possibility of intimacy? Apparently Virilio thinks so.

Bergson is probably not the philosopher who will help us build a better robot, although his ideas inform this project in surprisingly interesting ways. He is, however, a philosopher who can help us think about the ambition to do so. The specific nature of his critique of the humanist ideology of his day (I am using the term in the sense of Renan) reveals how complex the issues of humanism, anti-humanism, post-humanism, and life are at the present time. The interest of Bergson today might lie in this: he can help us recognize the situation in which we find ourselves and remind us what it means to think in time.

------

vaunt the world brain by declaring that humans are no longer human but neurons inside a world brain, and that interactivity favors this phenomenon it is more than just a question of a society out of control—it's the cybernetic society. Taking the model of bees or some other self-regulated system, it's the very opposite of freedom and democracy." The work on delegated agency, by Pattie Maes of MIT implies an augmentation of intelligence through a systems interactivity that evokes the activity of ants or bees. Is it a solution to the problem Virilio diagnoses, or is it part of the problem?

Conclusion

Thinking in Time

"We come to know what it means to think when we ourselves try to think."
—HEIDEGGER, "What Is Called Thinking?"

William James writes to Bergson that *Matter and Memory* "fills *my* mind with all sorts of new questions and hypotheses and brings the old into the most agreeable liquefaction." He appreciates Bergson's ability "simply to *break away* from old categories, deny old worn-out beliefs, and restate things *ab initio*, making the lines of division fall into entirely new places!"[1]

We have considered the current reception of Bergson and various contemporary issues that invite a return to his thought. To conclude this study, I would like to simply recall a few of the "new lines of division" Bergson introduces into our thinking in the two works we have considered closely.[2]

Sensation is the beginning of freedom (*Essai*).

Time is a form of energy (*Essai*).

The past is a reality (*Essai*).

My perception is outside my body (*Matter and Memory*).

1. Quoted from A. E. Pilkington, *Bergson and His Influence: A Reassessment,* 217.
2. I attribute these thoughts, sometimes paraphrased, sometimes quoted, to the work in question, but I would like to let them float free of their page references. Most of them can be found in the respective readings of the works.

Perception is nothing but an occasion for remembering (*Matter and Memory*).

The same feeling, by the very fact of being repeated, is a new feeling (*Essai*).

Memory does not consist in a regression from the present to the past, but, on the contrary, in a progress from the past to the present (*Matter and Memory*).

Questions relative to the subject and the object should be thought as a function of time rather than space (*Matter and Memory*).

Nothing is less than the present (*Matter and Memory*).

Movement is quality, not quantity (*Essai*).

We only perceive the past (*Matter and Memory*).

The only effect produced by feeling is the fact of having been felt (*Matter and Memory*).

Time is invention or it is nothing at all (*Essai*).

Finally, here are some of the metaphysical frameworks that break when we think in time, and the shifts in perspective Bergson proposes to these metaphysical illusions:

❈❈❈

Metaphysical illusion separates mind and body, privileging one or the other, engendering realism on the one hand and idealism on the other.
Correction: think an interactive union of body and mind, as suggested in the subtitle of *Matter and Memory: Essay on the Relation between the Body and the Mind* [*esprit*]. The relation is a temporal one, as the term memory suggests.

❈❈❈

Metaphysical illusion holds that perception and memory are operations of pure knowledge.

Correction: consider perception to be in the service of action, not knowledge and see that memory is in part constitutive of perception.

❊❊❊

Metaphysical illusion leads us to consider the body (or the brain) as an instrument of representation.

Correction: it is an instrument of action; it serves the satisfaction of needs or practical interests. The world is not in the brain (as representation), the brain is in the world (as matter).

❊❊❊

Metaphysical illusion proposes an opposition between appearance (phenomenon) and thing (thing in itself or noumenon).

Correction: think instead in terms of relations between part and whole.

❊❊❊

Metaphysical illusion presents memory as regressive, i.e., as a movement from present to past.

Correction: memory involves a progress from past to present; it is a question of the actualization of memory images through their articulation with the present, construed in terms of action. "We place ourselves in the past from the start [*C'est dans le passé que nous nous plaçons d'emblée*]." Consciousness operates in the past and only in relation to the past.

❊❊❊

Metaphysical illusion holds that perception is disinterested and contemplative.

Correction: perception is always interested, because it serves action. It subtracts from a broader receptivity of the real only that which pertains to its incipient action.

When we read Bergson and we get stuck, it is because we've stopped thinking in time!

Bibliography

Al-Saji, Alia. "The Memory of Another Past: Bergson, Deleuze, and a New Theory of Time." *Continental Philosophy Review* 37 (2004): 203–239.

Ambient Intelligence Group. http://interact.media.mit.edu/.

Andrew, Dudley. "Tracing Ricoeur." *diacritics* (summer 2000).

Antliff, Mark. *Inventing Bergson: Cultural Politics and the Parisian Avant-Garde.* Princeton: Princeton University Press, 1993.

Arbour, Romeo. *Bergson et les lettres françaises.* Paris: José Corti, 1955.

Bachelard, Gaston. *La formation de l'esprit scientifique: Contribution à un psycho-analyse de la connaissance.* Paris: Vrin, 1999.

———. *Formation of the Scientific Mind: A Contribution to a Psychoanalysis of Objective Knowledge.* Manchester: Clinamen Press, 2002.

———. *La philosophie du non: Essai d'une philosophie du nouvel esprit scientifique.* Paris: PUF, 1962.

Badiou, Alain. *Manifesto for Philosophy.* Translated by Norman Madarasz. Albany: State University of New York Press, 1999.

Barbour, Julian. *The End of Time: The Next Revolution in Physics.* Oxford: Oxford University Press, 2001.

Bataille, Georges. *L'érotisme.* Paris: Minuit, 1957.

———. *Erotism: Death and Sensuality.* Translated by Mary Dalwood. San Francisco: City Lights Books, 1986.

———. *L'éxpérience intérieure.* Paris: Gallimard, 1978.

———. *Inner Experience.* Translated by Leslie Ann Boldt. Albany: State University of New York Press, 1988.

———. "Lascaux ou la naissance de l'art." *Œuvres.* Vol. 9. Paris: Gallimard, 1979.

Baudelaire, Charles. *Œuvres complètes.* Paris: Gallimard, 1961.

Beller, Mara. *Quantum Dialogue: The Making of a Revolution.* Chicago: University of Chicago Press, 1999.

Benda, Julien. *Le bergsonisme: Philosophie de la mobilité.* Paris: Mercure de France, 1912.

——. *Sur le succès du Bergsonisme*. Paris: Mercure de France, 1929.

——. *La tradition de l'existentialisme, ou les philosophies de la vie*. Paris: Grasset, 1947.

——. *La trahison des clercs*. Paris: Grasset, 1975.

——. *Une philosophie pathétique*. Paris: Cahiers de la quinzaine, 1913.

Benjamin, Walter. *Illuminations*. Edited by Hannah Arendt. Translated by Harry Zohn. New York: Schocken, 1969.

Bergson, Henri. *Aristotle's Concept of Place*. Translated by J. K. Ryan. In *Studies in Philosophy and History of Philosophy*, 5:13–72.

——. *Correspondances*. Paris: PUF, 2002.

——. *Creative Evolution*. Authorized translation by Arthur Mitchell. London: Dover Publications, 1998.

——. *The Creative Mind: An Introduction to Metaphysics*. Translated by M. L. Andison. New York: Wisdom Library, 1946.

——. *Les deux sources de la morale et de la religion*. Edited by Arnaud Bouaniche, Frédéric Keck, and Frédéric Worms. Paris: Ellipses, 2004.

——. *Duration and Simultaneity*. Translated by L. Jacobson and M. Lewis, with an introduction by Robin Durie. Manchester: Clinamen Press, 1999.

——. *Écrits et paroles*. Textes rassemblés par R. M. Mossé-Bastide. Paris: PUF, 1957.

——. *Essai sur les données immédiates de la conscience*. Paris: PUF, 2001.

——. *L'évolution créatrice*. Paris: PUF, 1941.

——. *Laughter: An Essay on the Meaning of the Comic*. Translated by Cloudesley Brereton and Fred Rothwell. Los Angeles: Green Integer Books, 1999.

——. *Matière et mémoire: Essai sur la relation du corps à l'esprit*. Paris: PUF, 1939.

——. *Matter and Memory: Essay on the Relation between the Body and the Mind*. Translated by N. M. Paul and W. S. Palmer. New York: Zone Books, 1990.

——. *Mélanges*. Paris: PUF, 1972.

——. *Œuvres*. Paris: PUF, 1959.

——. *Time and Free Will: An Essay on the Data of Immediate Consciousness*. Authorized Translation by F. L. Pogson. London: Dover Publications, 2001.

——. *The Two Sources of Morality and Religion*. Notre Dame: University of Notre Dame Press, 1977.

Blanchot, Maurice. "How Is Literature Possible?" In *A Blanchot Reader*, edited with an introduction by Michael Holland. Oxford: Blackwell, 1995.

——. *La part du feu*. Paris: Gallimard, 1949.

——. *The Work of Fire*. Translated by Charlotte Mandell. Stanford: Stanford University Press, 1995.

Bohm, David. "Time, the Implicate Order, and Pre-Space." In *Physics and the Ultimate Significance of Time: Bohm, Prigogine, and Process Philosophy*, edited by David Ray Griffith. Albany: State University of New York Press, 1986.

Bohr, Niels. "Conversations with Einstein." In *Albert Einstein: Philosopher-Scientist*. Cambridge: Cambridge University Press, 1949.

Botting, Fred, and Scott Wilson, eds. *The Bataille Reader*. Oxford: Blackwell, 1997.

Boyle, Robert. *The Works of the Honourable Robert Boyle*. Vol. 4. Edited by T. Birch. London, 1744.

Breton, André. *Œuvres complètes*. Paris: Gallimard, 1988.

Broglie, Louis de. "The Concepts of Contemporary Physics and Bergson's Ideas of Time and Motion." In *Bergson and the Evolution of Physics*, edited by P. A. Y. Gunter. Knoxville: University of Tennessee Press, 1969.

Brunhes, Bernard. "L'évolutionnisme et le principe de Carnot." *Revue de Métaphysique et de Morale* 5 (1897): 35–43.

Burwick, Frederick, and Paul Douglass, eds. *The Crisis in Modernism: Bergsonism and the Vitalist Controversy*. Cambridge: Cambridge University Press, 1992.

Caldwell, William. *Pragmatism and Idealism*. London: Adam and Charles Black, 1913.

Canguilhem, George. "Machine and Organism." Translated by Mark Cohen. In *Zone 6: Incorporations*, edited by Jonathan Crary and Sanford Kwinter. New York: Zone Books, 1992.

Čapek, Milič. *Bergson and Modern Physics: A Reinterpretation and Re-evaluation*. Dordrecht: Nijhoff, 1971.

Carroy, Jacqueline. "Le temps intersubjectif: Interaction ou endosmose? Une Lecture de Bergson." *Connexions* 41 (1986).

Comte, Auguste. *Cours de philosophie positive*. Paris: J. B. Baillière et Fils, 1864.

——. *General View of Positivism*. Translated by J. H. Bridges. New York: Robert Speller and Sons, 1957.

——. *Système de politique positive*. Paris: Librairie Scientifique-Industrielle de L. Mathias, 1854.

——. *System of Positive Polity*. New York: B. Franklin, 1968.

Coutrat, Louis. "Etude critique sur L'hypothèse des atomes dans la science contemporaine de A. Hannequin." *Revue de Métaphysique et de Morale* 5 (1897): 87–113, 200–220.

Crary, Jonathan. *Suspensions of Perception: Attention, Spectacle, and Modern Culture*. Cambridge: MIT Press, 1999.

Crary, Jonathan, et al., eds. *Zone 6: Incorporations*. New York: Zone Books, 1992.

De Landa, Manuel. "Deleuze, Diagrams, and the Open-Ended Becoming of the World." In *Becomings: Explorations in Time, Memory, and Futures*, edited by Elizabeth Grosz. Ithaca: Cornell University Press, 1999.

——. *Intensive Science and Virtual Philosophy*. London: Continuum, 2001.

——. "Nonorganic Life." In *Zone 6: Incorporations*, edited by Jonathan Crary et al. New York: Zone Books, 1992.

Delbos, Victor. "Étude critique de Bergson. *Matière et mémoire*." In *Revue de Métaphysique et de Morale* 5 (1897): 353–389.

Deleuze, Gilles. *Bergsonism*. Translated by Hugh Tomlinson and Barbara Habberjam. New York: Zone Books, 1991.

——. *Le bergsonisme*. Paris: Quadrige, 2004.

——. "Bergson's Concept of Difference." Translated by Melissa McMahon. In *The New Bergson*, edited by John Mullarkey. Manchester: Manchester University Press, 1999.

——. *Cinéma 1: L'image-mouvement*. Paris: Minuit, 1983.

——. *Cinema 1: The Movement Image*. Translated by Hugh Tomlinson and Barbara Habberjam. Minneapolis: University of Minnesota Press, 1986.

——. *Cinéma 2: L'image-temps*. Paris: Minuit, 1985.

——. *Cinema 2: The Time-Image*. Translated by Hugh Tomlinson and Robert Galeta. London: Athlone Press, 1989.

——. "La conception de la différence chez Bergson." In *Études bergsoniennes* 4 (1956): 77–112.

——. *Dialogues*. With Claire Parnet. Paris: Flammarion, 1977.

——. *Dialogues*. Translated by Hugh Tomlinson and Barbara Habberjam. London: Athlone Press, 1987.

——. *Difference and Repetition*. Translated by Paul Patton. London: Athlone Press, 1994.

——. *Différence et répétition*. Paris: PUF, 2000.

——. *The Logic of Sense*. Edited by Constantin V. Boundas. Translated by Mark Lester and Charles Stivale. New York: Columbia University Press, 1990.

——. *Logique du sens*. Paris: Minuit, 1969.

——. *Nietzsche and Philosophy*. Translated by Hugh Tomlinson. New York: Columbia University Press, 1983.

——. *Nietzsche et la philosophie*. Paris: Quadrige, 2003.

Deleuze, Gilles, and Félix Guattari. *anti-Oedipus: Capitalism and Schizophrenia*. Translated by Robert Hurley, Mark Seem, and Helen R. Lane. Minneapolis: University of Minnesota Press, 1983.

——. *Capitalisme et schizophrénie: L'anti-Œdipe*. Paris: Minuit, 1972.

——. *Mille plateaux*. Vol. 2 of *Capitalisme et schizophrénie*. Paris: Minuit, 1980.

——. *Qu'est-ce que la philosophie?* Paris: Minuit, 1991.

——. *A Thousand Plateaus: Capitalism and Schizophrenia*. Translated by Brian Massumi. Minneapolis: University of Minnesota Press, 1987.

——. *What Is Philosophy?*. Translated by Hugh Tomlinson and Graham Burchell. New York: Columbia University Press, 1994.

Delhomme, Jeanne. *Nietzsche et Bergson*. Paris: Éditions Deuxtemps Tierce, 1992.

Dennett, Daniel. *Darwin's Dangerous Idea: Evolution and the Meanings of Life*. London: Allen Lane, 1995.

Derrida, Jacques. *De la grammatologie*. Paris: Minuit, 1967.

——. *L'écriture et la différence*. Paris: Seuil, 1967.

——. *Of Grammatology*. Translated by Gayatri Chakravorty Spivak. Baltimore: Johns Hopkins University Press, 1976.

——. *Speech and Phenomena and Other Essays on Husserl's Theory of Signs*. Evanston: Northwestern University Press, 1973.

——. *La voix et le phénomène: Introduction au problème du signe dans la phénoménolgie de Husserl*. Paris: PUF, 1967.

——. *Writing and Difference*. Translated by Alan Bass. Chicago: University of Chicago Press, 1978.

Descartes, René. *Œuvres et lettres de Descartes*. Paris: Gallimard, 1952.

Descombes, Vincent. *La denrée mentale*. Paris: Minuit, 1995.

——. *Le même et l'autre: Quarante-cinq ans de philosophie française (1933–1978)*. Paris: Minuit, 1979.

——. *The Mind's Provisions: A Critique of Cognitivism*. Translated by Steven Adam Schwartz. Princeton: Princeton University Press, 2001.

——. *Modern French Philosophy*. Translated by L. Scott-Fox and J. M. Harding. Cambridge: Cambridge University Press, 1981.

de Visan, Tancrède. *Attitude du lyrisme contemporain.* Paris: Mercure de France, 1911.

Dupuy, Jean-Pierre. *Les savants croient-ils en leurs théories? Une lecture de l'histoire des sciences cognitives.* Paris: INRA, 2000.

Durie, Robin, ed. *Time and the Instant: Essays in the Physics and Philosophy of Time.* Manchester: Clinamen Press, 2000.

Fechner, Gustav. *Elements of Psychophysics.* Translated by Helmut E. Adler. New York: Holt, Rinehart and Winston, 1966. Excerpts translated by Herbert Sydney Langfeld available on-line at http://www.psychclassics.yorku.ca/Fechner/. Also in *The Classical Psychologist,* ed. Benjamin Rand, 562–572. Boston: Houghton Mifflin, 1912.

Fodor, Jerry. *The Language of Thought.* Cambridge: Harvard University Press, 1975.

——. *The Mind Doesn't Work That Way.* Cambridge: MIT Press, 2000.

Foucault, Michel. "Préface à la transgression." *Critique* 195–196 (1963): 751–769.

——. "A Preface to Transgression." Translated by Daniel F. Bouchard and Sherry Simon. In *Aesthetics, Method, and Epistemology: Essential Works of Michel Foucault, 1954–1984,* vol. 2, edited by James O. Faubion. New York: New Press, 1998.

Fraser, J. T., F. C. Hober, and G. H. Müller, eds. *The Study of Time II. Proceedings of the Second Conference of the International Society for the Study of Time, Lake Yamanaka, Japan.* New York: Springer-Verlag, 1975.

Freedman, David H. "Bringing Up RoboBaby." http://www.wired.com/wired/archive/2.12/cog.html. *Wired* 2 (12 Dec. 1994).

Freud, Sigmund. "Monograph on Aphasia." In *On the History of the Psychoanalytic Movement: Papers on Metapsychology and Other Works,* edited by James Strachey. London: Hogarth Press and the Institute of Psychoanalysis, 1955.

——. "An Outline of Psychoanalysis." In *Totem and Taboo and Other Works,* edited by James Strachey. London: Hogarth Press and the Institute of Psychoanalysis, 1955.

——. *The Standard Edition of the Complete Psychological Works of Sigmund Freud.* London: Hogarth Press and the Institute of Psychoanalysis, 1953–74.

——. "The Unconscious." In *On the History of the Psychoanalytic Movement: Papers on Metapsychology and Other Works,* edited by James Strachey. London: Hogarth Press and the Institute of Psychoanalysis, 1955.

Gallois, P., and G. Forzy, eds. *Bergson et les neurosciences.* Le Plessis-Robinson: Institut Synthélabo, 1997.

Game, Ann. *Undoing the Social: Towards a Deconstructive Sociology.* Milton Keynes: Open University Press, 1991.

Griffin, David Ray, ed. *Physics and the Ultimate Significance of Time: Bohm, Prigogine, and Process Philosophy.* Albany: State University of New York Press, 1986.

Grogin, R. C. *The Bergsonian Controversy in France: 1900–1914.* Calgary: University of Calgary Press, 1988.

Grosz, Elizabeth, ed. *Becomings: Explorations in Time, Memory, and Futures.* Ithaca, NY: Cornell University Press, 1999.

Guerlac, Suzanne. "Bataille in Theory: Afterimages (Lascaux)." *Diacritics* 26 (1996): 6–17.

———. *Literary Polemics: Bataille, Sartre, Valéry, Breton*. Stanford: Stanford University Press, 1997.

———. "Le symptôme de la mer et la 'Folie de l'eau' chez Valéry." *Bulletin des Études Valéryennes* 91 (June 2002): 27–47.

———. "The 'Zig-zags of a Doctrine': Bergson, Deleuze, and the Question of Experience." *Pli: The Warwick Journal of Philosophy* 15 (2004): 34–53.

Gunter, P. A. Y., ed. *Bergson and the Evolution of Physics*. Knoxville: University of Tennessee Press, 1969.

Hansen, Mark B. N. *New Philosophy for New Media*. Cambridge: MIT Press, 2004.

Hayes, Carleton J. H. *A Generation of Materialism, 1871–1900*. New York: Harper & Brothers, 1941.

Hegel, G. W. F. *Preface to the Phenomenology of Spirit*. Translated and edited by Yirmiyahu Yovel. Princeton: Princeton University Press, 2005.

Hénaff, Marcel. *Claude Lévi-Strauss and the Making of Structural Anthropology*. Translated by Mary Baker. Minneapolis: University of Minnesota Press, 1998.

———. *Claude Lévi-Strauss et l'anthropologie structurale*. Paris: Éditions Belfond, 1991.

Heidegger, Martin. *An Introduction to Metaphysics*. Translated by Ralph Manheim. New Haven: Yale University Press, 1959.

———. *On Time and Being*. Translated by Joan Stambaugh. Chicago: University of Chicago Press, 2002.

———. *What Is Called Thinking?* Translated by J. Glenn Gray. New York: Harper and Row, 1968.

Heisenberg, Werner. *Physics and Philosophy: The Revolution of Modern Science*. New York: Harper and Row, 1958.

Hiroshi Ishii Website http://web.media.mit.edu/~ishii.

Jakobson, Roman. *Essais de linguistique générale*. Paris: Minuit, 1963.

Janet, Pierre. *L'automatisme psychologique: Essai de psychologie expérimentale sur les formes inférieures de l'activité humaine*. Paris: Masson, 1989.

Kallen, Horace Meyer. *William James and Henri Bergson: A Study in Contrasting Theories of Life*. Chicago: University of Chicago Press, 1914.

Kant, Immanuel. *The Critique of Judgment*. Translated by J. H. Bernard. New York: Hafner Press, 1974.

Kellert, Stephen H. *In the Wake of Chaos: Unpredictable Order in Dynamical Systems*. Chicago: University of Chicago Press, 1993.

Kittler, Friedrich A. *Gramophone, Film, Typewriter: Writing Science*. Translated by Geoffrey Winthrop-Young and Michael Wutz. Stanford: Stanford University Press, 1999.

Kuhn, Thomas. *The Structure of Scientific Revolutions*. Chicago: University of Chicago Press, 1996.

Lapoujade, David. "Intuition and Sympathy in Bergson." *Pli: The Warwick Journal of Philosophy* 15 (2004): 1–17.

Le Roy, Édouard. *A New Philosophy: Henri Bergson*. Translated by Vincent Benson. New York: Henry Holt, 1913.

——. *Une philosophie nouvelle: Henri Bergson*. Paris: Félix Alcan, 1913.

Levinas, Emmanuel. *Time and the Other*. Translated by Richard A. Cohen. Pittsburgh: Duquesne University Press, 1987.

Lévi-Strauss, Claude. *L'anthropologie structurale*. Paris: Presses Pocket, 2003.

——. *The Elementary Structures of Kinship*. Translated by Rodney Needham. Boston: Beacon Press, 1969.

——. *Structural Anthropology*. Translated by Claire Jacobson and Brooke Grundfest Schoepf. New York: Basic Books, 1963.

——. *Les structures élémentaires de la parenté*. Paris: Éditions EHESS, 2000.

——. *Tristes Tropiques*. Paris: Presses Pocket, 2001.

——. *Tristes Tropiques*. Translated by Jonathan Cape. London: Penguin Books, 1992.

Levy, Pierre. *Becoming Virtual: Reality in the Digital Age*. Translated by Robert Bononno. London: Plenum Press, 1998.

Locke, John. *An Essay Concerning Human Understanding*. New York: Prometheus Books, 1994.

Lyotard, Jean-François. *La phénoménologie*. Paris: PUF, 1954.

Manovich, Lev. *The Language of New Media*. Cambridge: MIT Press, 2001.

——. Principles of New Media 2 Website http://mediamatic.net/article-200. 6027html.

Mallarmé, Stéphane. *Œuvres complètes*. Paris: Gallimard, 1945.

Marks, John. *Gilles Deleuze: Vitalism and Multiplicity*. London: Pluto Press, 1998.

Massumi, Brian. *Parables for the Virtual: Movement, Affect, Sensation*. Durham: Duke University Press, 2002.

Merleau-Ponty, Maurice. *Éloge de la philosophie et autres essais*. Paris: Gallimard, 1960.

——. *The Incarnate Subject: Malebranche, Biran and Bergson on the Union of Body and Soul*. Translated by Paul B. Milan. Edited by Andres G. Bjelland and Patrick Burke. Amherst, NY: Humanity Books, 2002.

——. *In Praise of Philosophy*. Translated by J. Wild and J. M. Edie. Evanston: Northwestern University Press, 1963.

——. *L'union de l'âme et du corps chez Malebranche, Biran et Bergson*. Paris: Vrin, 1997.

Minsky, Marvin. *The Emotion Machine*. New York: Simon and Schuster, 2007 (forthcoming).

——. http://web.media.mit.edu/minsky.

Missa, Jean-Noël. "Critique positive du chapitre II de *Matière et mémoire*." In *Bergson et les neurosciences*, edited by Philippe Gallois and Gérard Forzy. Paris: Institut Synthélabo, 1997.

——. *L'esprit-cerveau: La philosophie de l'esprit à la lumière des neurosciences*. Le Plessis-Robinson: Institut Synthélabo, 1993.

Moore, F. C. T. *Bergson: Thinking Backwards*. Cambridge: Cambridge University Press, 1996.

Mullarkey, John. *Bergson and Philosophy*. Edinburgh: Edinburgh University Press, 1999.

——, ed. *The New Bergson*. Manchester: Manchester University Press, 1999.

Murphy, Timothy S. "Beneath Relativity: Bergson and Bohm on Absolute Time." In

The New Bergson, edited by John Mullarkey. Manchester: Manchester University Press, 1999.

Nagel, Thomas. *Other Minds: Critical Essays, 1969–1994*. Oxford: Oxford University Press, 1995.

Newton, Isaac. *The Principia: Mathematical Principles of Natural Philosophy*. Translated by Andrew Motte. Revised by Florian Cajori. Berkeley: University of California Press, 1934. Available on-line at http://plato.stanford.edu/entries/newton-stm/scholium.html.

Nietzsche, Friedrich. *On the Genealogy of Morals* and *Ecce Homo*. Translated by Walter Kaufmann. New York: Vintage Books, 1989.

Olkowski, Dorothea. *Gilles Deleuze and the Ruin of Representation*. Berkeley: University of California Press 1999.

Open Mind Commonsense http://commonsense.media.mit.edu/cgi-bin/info.cgi.

Pais, Abraham. *Inward Bound: Of Matter and Forces in the Physical World*. Oxford: Oxford University Press, 1986.

Papadopoulo, Alexandre. *Un philosophe entre deux défaites (Henri Bergson entre 1870 et 1940)*. Cairo: Éditions de la Revue de Caire, 1942.

Papanicolaou, Andrew C., and Pete A. Y. Gunter, eds. *Bergson and Modern Thought: Towards a Unified Science*. New York: Harwood Academic, 1987.

Paulhan, Jean. *Les fleurs de Tarbes ou la terreur dans les lettres*. Paris: Gallimard, 1941.

Pearson, Keith Ansell. *Philosophy and the Adventure of the Virtual: Bergson and the Time of Life*. London: Routledge 2002.

Philonenko, Alexis. *Bergson ou De la philosophie comme science rigoureuse*. Paris: Editions du Cerf, 1992.

Pilkington, A. E. *Bergson and His Influence: A Reassessment*. Cambridge: Cambridge University Press, 1976.

Planck Lectures http://nobelprize.org/physics/laureates/1918/planck-lecture.html.

Poincaré, Henri. "Réponse à quelques critiques." *Revue de Métaphysique et de Morale* 5 (1897): 59–70.

——. *Science et méthode*. Paris: Ernest Flammarion, 1909.

Politzer, George. *Le bergsonisme: Une mystification philosophique*. Paris: Éditions sociales, 1947. First published under the name François Arouet as *La fin d'une parade philosophique*. Paris: Les Revues, 1929.

Poster, Mark. *Existential Marxism in Postwar France: From Sartre to Althusser*. Princeton: Princeton University Press, 1977.

Prigogine, Ilya. "Irreversibility and Space-Time Structure." In *Physics and the Ultimate Significance of Time: Bohm, Prigogine, and Process Philosophy*, edited by David R. Griffin. Albany: State University of New York Press, 1986.

Prigogine, Ilya, and Isabelle Stengers. *Entre le temps et l'éternité*. Paris: Flammarion, 1992.

——. *Order Out of Chaos*. New York: Bantam Books, 1984.

Proust, Marcel. *À la recherche du temps perdu*. Paris: Gallimard, 1954.

——. *Swann's Way*. Translated by Lydia Davis. New York: Viking, 2003.

Pullman, Bernard. *The Atom in the History of Human Thought*. Translated by Axel Reisinger. Oxford: Oxford University Press, 1998.

Quirk, Tom. *Bergson and American Culture: The Worlds of Willa Cather and Wallace Stevens*. Chapel Hill: University of North Carolina Press, 1976.

Rauh, F. "Étude critique. De l'usage scientifique des théories psychologiques. À propos de deux livres récents. II. Psychologie des sentiments, par M. Ribot." *Revue de Métaphysique et de Morale* 5 (1897): 200–220.

Renan, Ernest. *L'avenir de la science: Pensées de 1848*. Paris: Calmann-Lévy, 1890.

———. *The Future of Science*. Boston: Roberts Brothers, 1893.

Rescher, Nicholas. *Process Metaphysics: An Introduction to Process Philosophy*. Albany: State University of New York Press, 1996.

Ribot, Théodule. *Diseases of Memory; Diseases of Personality; Diseases of the Will*. Translated by W. H. Smith and M. M. Snell. Washington: University Publications of America, 1977.

Ricoeur, Paul. *La mémoire, l'histoire, l'oubli*. Paris: Éditions du Seuil, 2000.

Rosenfield, Israel. *The Invention of Memory: A New View of the Brain*. Translated by Anne-Sophie Cismaresco. New York: Basic Books, 1998.

Russell, Bertrand. *The Philosophy of Bergson*. London: Macmillan, 1914.

Sartre, Jean-Paul. *Critique de la raison dialectique*. 2 vols. Paris: Gallimard, 1985.

———. *Critique of Dialectical Reason*, vol. 1. Edited by Jonathan Ree. Translated by Alan Sheridan. London: Verso, 2004.

———. *Critique of Dialectical Reason*, vol. 2 (unfinished). Edited by Arlette Elkaïn-Sartre. Translated by Quintin Hare. London: Verso, 1991.

———. *Imagination*. Ann Arbor: University of Michigan Press, 1962.

———. *L'imagination*. Paris: Gallimard, 2005.

———. *L'imagination*. Paris: PUF, 2003.

———. *Nausea*. Translated by Lloyd Alexander. New York: New Directions, 1969.

———. *La nausée*. Paris: Gallimard, 1938.

———. *The Psychology of Imagination*. London: Routledge, 1995.

Shimojo Psychophysics Laboratory http://neuro/caltech.edu.

Simondon, Gilbert. "The Genesis of the Individual." In *Incorporations*, edited by Jonathan Crary et al. New York: Zone Books, 1992.

Sorell Tom. *Descartes*. Oxford: Oxford University Press, 1987.

Soulez, Philippe. *Bergson politique*. Paris: PUF, 1989.

Soulez, Philippe, and Frédéric Worms. *Bergson: Biographie*. Paris: Flammarion, 1997.

Spencer, Herbert. *First Principles*. New York: D. Appleton, 1904.

Stapp, Henry. "Einstein Time and Process Time." In *Physics and the Ultimate Significance of Time*, edited by David R. Griffin. Albany: State University of New York Press, 1986.

Stengers, Isabelle. *L'invention de la mécanique: Pouvoir et raison*. Vol. 2 of *Cosmopolitiques*. Paris: La Découverte, 1997.

———. *La thermodynamique: La réalité physique en crise*. Vol. 3 of *Cosmopolitiques*. Paris: La Découverte, 1997.

Sulloway, Frank. *Freud the Biologist of the Mind: Beyond the Psychoanalytic Legend*. New York: Basic Books, 1979.

Syrotinski, Michael. *Defying Gravity: Jean Paulhan's Interventions in Twentieth-Century French Intellectual History*. Albany: State University of New York Press, 1988.

Taine, Hippolyte. *De l'intelligence*. 2 vols. Paris: Hachette, 1870.

Thibaudet, Albert. *Le bergsonisme: Trente ans de la vie française*. Paris: Éditions de la Nouvelle Revue Française, 1923.

Tlatli, Soraya. *La folie lyrique: Essai sur le surréalisme et la psychiatrie*. Paris: Harmattan, 2004.

Turetzky, Philip. *Time (The Problems of Philosophy)*. London: Routledge, 1998.

Valéry, Paul. *Œuvres complètes*. 2 vols. Paris: Gallimard, 1987.

Varela, Francisco J. "The Reenchantment of the Concrete." In *Incorporations*, edited by Jonathan Crary et al. New York: Zone Books, 1992.

Vinson, Alain. "La fausse reconnaissance, le pressentiment et l'inquiétante étrangeté: Réflexions sur les conceptions respectives de Freud et de Bergson." *L'Enseignement Philosophique: 40e année* 6 (1990).

Virilio, Paul. *Cybermonde: La politique du pire*. Paris: Éditions Textuel, 2001.

———. *Politics of the Very Worst*. Translated by Michael Cavaliere. New York: Semiotext(e), 1999.

———. *L'art du moteur*. Paris: Galilée, 1993.

Weber, L. "L'évolutionnisme et le principe de la conservation de l'énergie." *Revue de Métaphysique et de Morale* 87.

Worms, Frédéric. *L'âme et le corps: Bergson*. Paris: Hatier, 1992.

———. *Bergson ou les deux sources de la vie*. Paris: PUF, 2004.

———. *Introduction à Matière et mémoire de Bergson*. Paris: PUF, 1997.

———. "Le rire et sa relation au mot d'esprit. Notes sur la lecture de Bergson et Freud." In *Freud et le rire*, edited by A. Willy Szafran and Adolphe Nysenholc. Paris: Editions Métailié, 1994.

———. *Le vocabulaire de Bergson*. Paris: Ellipses, 2000.

———, ed. *Annales bergsoniennes I: Bergson dans le siècle*. Paris: PUF, 2002.

———, ed. *Annales bergsoniennes II: Bergson, Deleuze, la phénoménologie*. Paris: PUF, 2004.

Index

The letter B stands for Henri Bergson.

action, in B's thought: automatic vs. voluntary, and choice, 107–10, 113; vs. dream, 154–55, 171; future action, 88; and indeterminacy, 119; and memory, 136–37; perception as, 111–15, 163, 214; and the present as time of action, 120–21, 142, 171; and recognition, 130, 152; vs. representation, 128–29; role of consciousness, 145; and space, 146; voluntary action, 53–54. *See also* body, the; consciousness; perception; recognition

affect, 4, 53, 54, 88, 90, 90 n45, 116

âme (soul): B's use of term, 156 n51; relation with the body, 156, 167. *See also* mind, the (*l'esprit*)

aphasia, studies of, 6, 23–24; B's use of, 123, 134 n27, 137, 156

Aristotle, 9 n27

artificial intelligence, 205; Ambient Intelligence Project, 208; B and, 82; computer science, 206, 207–8; the post human, 209. *See also* cybernetics

associationist psychology, 76, 81–82, 88, 129, 141, 171

attention, 133, 135, 136; to life, 154. *See also* recognition

Bachelard, Gaston, 17, 30 n50, 91 n46

Badiou, Alain, 175 n8, 175 n9, 189–90 n68

Balmer, Johann Jakob, 33

Baudelaire, Charles, 52, 101; "Correspondances," 50 n5

Bataille, Georges, 4, 91 n46

Benda, Julian, 12, 28 n42, 177 n16, 182

Benjamin, Walter, 1, 130 n23

Becquerel, Alexander Edmond, 34

Becquerel, Henri, 33–34

Bergson, Henri (B), life and career, 9–10, 12–13; vs. Einstein, 12–13, 198, 200; popular success, 10, 11–12; setting for, 14–16; and science of his day, 30, 42; special training, 30. *See also* Europe between 1890s and 1930s; Third Republic

Bergson, Henri, thought and philosophy: analysis of, interdisciplinary character of, 123; challenge to traditional positions, 88, 124, 158, 165, 213–14; criticism of, opposition to, attacks on, 9, 12–13, 28–29, 180, 181, 182; historical and scientific context, 16–20; influence on American artists, 11; influences upon, 2–3; intellectual context, 14–41; as pertinent today, 210; reaction against metaphysical dogmatism, 164–66; revival of studies on, 13, 174–76, 195–96; role in Symbolism, 11–12; stigma of irrationalism and phenomenology, 182, 183; task of, 71; threat to positivism, 28–29; view of indeterminism, importance of, 209; vitalist position, 165. *See also* current issues, B and

—works, general

    reception: in America, 11; dissemination of thought, 10; influence on cultural studies, 195–96; literary influence, 11–12, 74–75; philosophical influence, 76 n35, 175; since 1990, return to studies on, reasons for, 174–76. *See also* Bergonsism(s); current issues, B and; Deleuze, Gilles; Hansen, Mark; Massumi, Brian

    writing strategies, 123; use of examples, 56, 125, 129–30

—works, individual

    Creative Evolution (L'évolution créatrice), 6–7,

Bergson: works, individual (*continued*)
  109 n1, 161 n56; 180, 188; challenge to
  Spencer, 28, 202; and dream, 155; and duration, 5 n18, 163, 168 n60; energy of time,
  81, 205; and issues today, 198, 205. *See also*
  biology; *élan vital*
  Les deux sources de la morale et de la religion (*The
    Two Sources of Morality and Religion*), 8, 13,
    105
  Essai sur les données immédiates de la conscience
    (*Time and Free Will*): attack on psychomet-
    rics, 25; challenge to Descartes, 18; critique
    of Kant, 21, 44, 72 n29, 76, 92–94, 100–104;
    goal of, 163; significant role of, 4–5; think-
    ing about inner experience, 43, 44; title, 43
    Chapter 1, sensations and intensities (out-
      line): dancer, and role of movement,
      47–50; esthetics of art and process, 50–52;
      focus on inner experience, 60, 62–63 n13,
      98; freedom, 52–54; image of four can-
      dles, 55–57; quantity vs. quality, 54–57,
      58–60, 95 n90, concerning joy and es-
      thetic feelings, 45–50; role of time, 50
    Chapter 2, multiplicities of consiousness
      (outline): commentary on social life,
      75–76, 98; critique of language, 68–70,
      72–75, 98; divided self, 70–72, 82, 99; ho-
      mogeneity/heterogeneity, 64–66; image of
      shooting star, 67–68; kinds of conscious-
      ness and of multiplicities, 62, 109 n1;
      metaphor of melody, the musical phrase,
      66–67; time and duration, 62–63. *See also*
      consciousness; multiplicity, multiplicities
    Chapter 3 (outline): freedom vs. determin-
      ism, 77, 83–87, 98; matter vs. conscious-
      ness, 78; principle of identity, 90
    Conclusion: basic concepts, summary of,
      95–98; B's engagement with Kant,
      100–104
  L'évolution créatrice. See *Creative Evolution*,
    infra
  Matter and Memory: as current with the times,
    33, 40, 41; major ideas and content, 5–6,
    106–11, 155–56; and physics, 30 n49, 32 n53,
    33; theme of memory, 80 n38
    Chapter 1 (outline): action, not knowledge,
      111–12; the body, 113–14; images, 112,
      113; memory, 118, 119–24; perception,
      114–21; summary, 122–23
    Chapter 2 (outline): attention, 133–38; brain
      and, 124–25; image of telegraph operator,
      134; memory, two kinds, 125–28; Pure
      Memory, 127, 139–40; recognition, 129–33
    Chapter 3 (outline): dream, 154–55; the
      mind (*l'esprit*), 149–54; the past, 143–45;
      the present, 140–43; scheme of inverted
      cone, 151–54; unconsciousness, 145–49

Chapter 4 (outline): division of matter,
    161–62; link with *Essai*, B's development
    of, 158–59; movement, 159–60; problem
    of metaphysical dualism, 156–58, 167–68;
    rhythms of duration and role of memory,
    163–64
  Résumé and Conclusion, 168–72
  Le rire: Essai sur la signification du comique
    (*Laughter: An Essay on the Meaning of the
    Comic*), 7, 8, 207 n38, 208, 209–10
  Time and Free Will, translation of title, 43. See
    also *Essai sur les données immédiates de la con-
    science*
Bergsonism(s), 1–13, 64 n14; a selection of,
  212–14
biology, 111, 126, 148–49, 161
Blanchot, Maurice, 4, 74, 182
body, the: as center of action, 108–11, 113–14,
  120, 122, 126, 129, 144, 155, 168, 193, 214; and
  language, 138; living body, 122; as location for
  the mind, 154; and memory, 124; memory of,
  125–26, 150; and recognition, 129; role in perception and memory, 138, 155–56. *See also* action; brain; memory; mind/body dualism; perception
Bohr, Niels, and theory of atomic structure,
  29 n48, 30, 33, 34, 36; and conservation of
  matter, 39–40 n81
Boltzmann, Ludwig, 32, 35, 39, 160 n54, 198, 199
Born, Max, 39, 40
brain: B's characterization of, 108, 111–12, 114,
  122, 124, 128, 132, 135, 155, 214; and memory
  images, 138–39; and perception, 114 n5, 170.
  See also aphasia
Breton, André, 75
Broca, Paul, 23–24
Broglie, Louis de, 3, 29 n48, 36

Čapek, Milič, 41
Carnot, Sadi, 9, 31
Catholic Church, and B, 10, 12, 28–29, 182
chaos theory, 201–2; developments in, 199 n8;
  identification with determinism, 197, 201 n18,
  202, 204
character, 149; as synthesis of past states, 147
cinema: Benjamin on, 1 n1; Deleuze's analysis of
  and books on, 175, 193
Clausius, Rudolf, 31 n52
computer revolution, 194, 207–8; new media,
  192–93. *See also* artificial intelligence; cybernetics; cyborgs; virtual, the, virtuality
Comte, Auguste, 20–23, 28
consciousness: and duration, 163–64; immediate,
  62, 63, 64–65, 145, 158; vs. a "material unconscious," 110; and the material, 78, 97,
  166–67, 169, 170; and memory, 117, 122, 151,
  163–64; and movement, 172, 188 n59; and

perception, 117, 118, 122; role of, 145–46; two sorts of, 62
cultural studies, 195–96
Curie, Marie, 34, 39 n81
current issues, B and: artificial intelligence and humanization of machines, 205–10; chaos theory, 201–4; and crisis of modernity, 210–11; important scientific developments, 204–5; modern societal developments, 197–98; scientific changes and irreversible time, 198–201
cybernetics, cyborgs, 206; Deleuze and, 190, 191; Derrida and, 191

Darwin, Charles, 8, 27
Deleuze, Gilles, 29, 64, 91 n46; *Bergsonism*. 173–75, 180, 181; citing B on cinema, 68; and Derrida, 182, 186–87; interpretations of B as alternative to Hegel, 177–79; influence on reception of B, 173–75; and Nietzsche, 175 n9; reception in US, 179–80; "return to B," 181; and the virtual, 178, 189–92. *See also* cinema; Deleuze, Gilles, and Félix Guattari; duration; the virtual
Deleuze, Gilles, and Félix Guattari, *Anti-Oedipus*, 190; and cyber theory, 190–91; the machinic, 190 n71
Derrida, Jacques, 4, 182, 194; critique of phenomenology, 183–85; and cultural studies, 187; and Deleuze, 186–87. *See also* post-structuralism; time
Descartes, René, 25, 160; B's challenge to, 18
Descombes, Vincent, 3 n10, 4, 177, 186
determinism, as issue, 38–39; B's argument against and challenge to, 43, 77–78, 83–87, 98, 209; and freedom, 42–43, 77, 83–87, 98, 209; logic of, 86; and modern life, 197, 204; and psychology, 42–43; and science, 40, 77. *See also* freedom
Douglass, Paul, 182
dream, 76, 127, 139, 155; action and, 152, 154
duration, 5–7, 59, 63, 65–66, 89–92, 96–98, 103–5, 122, 149, 155 n50, 158, 161; in Deleuze, 178, 180, 181; as distinct from time, 69; and free action, 100; heterogeneous, 102, 104, 104 n56; homogeneous, or spatialized time, 71, 106; link to consciousness, 118; and mathematics, 2, 29; multiple durations, 163–65, 168, 172; as ontological fact, 149, 150 n45; and the present, 142, 145; Pure Duration, 97, 99, 101; Real Duration, 2, 32, 50, 56, 60, 63, 77, 80; and scientific discoveries, 38, 40; as temporal synthesis, 66–67; and thermodynamics, 32. *See also* *élan vital;* memory; time
Durkheim, Émile, 9, 20; B's dialogue with, 8

Einstein, Albert, 40 n83, 200; discovery of photon, 36; theory of relativity, 30, 34, and B, 13, 198, 200

élan vital, 7, 180; as force of time, 81, 163, 189
electrons: discovery of, 30, 34; theory of, 32
Eliot, T. S., 11
entropy, principle of, 31, 32, 37–38, 199; studies of, 35
Europe between 1890s and 1930s: changes in, 16–17; crisis of the sciences, 17–20, 37–38; mechanistic model, 18–20. *See also* Comte, Auguste; determinism; humanism; positivism; Renan, Ernest; Taine, Hippolyte
evolution: in B's thought, 7, 8, 188; Spencer's theory, 26–28. *See also* Creative Evolution *under* Bergson, Henri, works, individual; Darwin, Charles; Lamarck, Jean-Baptiste
experimental physics: B's attention to, 162; B's influence on, 29 n48; developments in, 30–32, 36–37, 41, 160 n54; different fields of, described, 31–40; quantum physics, 32, 34, 85; spectral analysis, techniques of, 33. *See also* Boltzmann, Ludwig; Broglie, Louis de; electrons; microphysics; Prigogine, Ilya; quantum mechanics; thermodynamics; Uncertainty Principle; wave theories
experimental psychology, 22–24; B and, 5, 76–77, 133. *See also* associationist psychology; Fechner, Gustav

Fechner, Gustav, 23–27; and psychophysics, 42, 57, 209
Fodor, Jerry, 206 n34, 207
Foucault, Michel, 4, 194
freedom, B's characterization of, 52–53, 92–93, 102, 105, 158; B's critique of Kant, 92–93, 95, 98, 101; vs. determinism, 5, 42–43, 77, 81–87, 98, 209; energies of, 82–83; free action, 82–83, 98, 100; free self, 99–100; link to sensations, 52–54, 212; logic of, 83–85; and necessity, 158, 164, 172; and pleasure and pain, 53; and rhythms of duration, 164, 172; within time, 104–5; and voluntary action, 158. *See also* determinism; memory; zone of indeterminacy
Freud, Sigmund, 65 n15, 76 n34; B's proximity to, 23 n27, 110 n3, 191 n72; Deleuze's critique of, 191 n72; rereadings of, 182, 185

Galileo, 18
Guattari, Félix. *See* Deleuze, Gilles, and Félix Guattari

habit, 125, 126 n120, 158; and motor memory, 127
Hansen, Mark, reading of B, 192–94
Hegel, Georg Wilhelm Friedrich: B as alternative to, 177–78, 181; influence and importance of, 3–4, 177; as replacement of B, 12, 182
Heidegger, Martin, 41 n87, 72 n29; and time, 2, 81 n39, 185

Heisenberg, Werner: Uncertainty Principle of, 17, 36–39, 40 nn83, 85; and B, 29 n48
Helmholtz, Hermann, 31 n52
Hulme, T. E., 197, 204
humanism: critique of, 211; 19th-century, 22–26; of Renan, 25–26; traditional claims of, 193. *See also* Comte, Auguste; mechanistic humanism; positivism; Spencer, Herbert; Taine, Hippolyte
Husserl, Edmund, phenomenology of, 184–85; Derrida's critique of, 179, 183–85; philosophical reaction against, 177

idealism vs. realism, 107, 111, 169; B's deconstruction of, 165
image(s): B's use of term, 112, 113, 117; conservation of, 124–25; dream images, 127; as external, 157; memory images, 119, 128, 136, 144, 149, 157; virtual images, 140. *See also under* memory in B's thought; perception; recognition
image memory. *See under* memory in B's thought
immediate experience, 5, 43, 47, 71; and immediate vs. reflective consciousness, 62; importance of, 104, 161; and intensity, 60; language as threat to, 69; as pure quality, 45; and qualitative multiplicity, 54; and radical heterogeneity, 64; as refutation of humanism, 98. *See also* intuition
inner experience: duration derived from 5, 163; as focus in *Essai*, 43, 44, 60, 62–63 n13, 98; as important in meaning of being human, 209–10; as irreversible and unrepeatable, 73, 78–79, 86, 89–90. *See also* immediate experience
intelligence, 7; as adaptive feature, 200. *See also* artificial intelligence
intensity, as quality, 62–63 n13, 67, 79, 90 n45, 95–96; linked to time, 73, 86
intuition, 63, 64, 69, 119, 120, 167; importance of, 63–64, 71
inverted cone figure, 150–54
Ishii, Hiroshi, 211

Jakobson, Roman, 138
James, William, 11, 28, 212
Janet, Pierre, 53 n9
Jaurès, Jean, 9

Kant, Immanuel, 50, 130 n22, 133 n26, 184; and practical reason, 21, 92, 99 n53, 100–103, 158; on representation, 72 n29, 76 n35, 93–94, 107, 111, 164–65; scientific work and causality, 38. *See also* freedom
Kellert, Stephen H., 201–5
Kelvin, Lord (William Thomson), 34, 162
Kojève, Alexandre, 3; lectures on Hegel, 12, 177

Lacan, Jacques, 4, 92 n47, 182, 190
Lagrange, Joseph-Louis, 19, 31
Lamarck, Jean-Baptiste, 27
language, 2, 76, 87, 192
  critique of: 68–70, 73–74, 85; and alienation, 2, 82, 85, 93; as inadequate, and problem for B, 80, 137, 158–59, 200 n10. *See also* Paulhan, Jean
  vs. immediate consciousness, 152
  memory and reading, 137–38
  motor schematism of, 138
  and "shortage of words" in science, 40–41
Lasserre, Pierre, 12
Le Roy, Édouard, 30 n50
Leibnitz, Gottfried Wilhelm, 173
Levinas, Emmanuel, 182
Lévi-Strauss, Claude, 177
Locke, John, 22–23 n23, 44
Lorentz, Hendrik Antoon, 32
Loschmidt, Josef, 32
Lovejoy, A. O., 11
Lukács, Georg, 12
Lyotard, Jean-François, 183, 184

machine, the: Deleuze's notions of, 190, 191–92; humanization of, 208–9; metaphor of, 190 n71
Mallarmé, Stéphane, 52, 72, 73
Manovich, Lev, 187 n53, 192 n81, 194 n90, 205–6
Maritain, Jacques, 12
Marx, Karl, rereadings of, 182
Massumi, Brian, *Parables for the Virtual*, 194–96
mathematics: B's advanced training in, 29, 30 n50; as influence, 2, 29, 203
material unconscious, the: in B, 110; in Deleuze, 190
matter: B's conception of, 108–9; critical theory of, 159, 163, 164; interaction with consciousness, 78, 166–67, 169; memory as independent of, 122–23; wave mechanical model and particle view, 3, 36
Mauriac, François, 11
Maurras, Charles, 12
Maxwell, James Clerke, 162
mechanistic humanism, 25–27; B's philosophical answer to, 204. *See also* Comte, Auguste; Renan, Ernst; Spencer, Herbert; Taine, Hippolyte
memory in B's thought, 5, 6, 79, 164, 167, 170–72
  characterized 118, 122–23, 149, 164, 213, 214
  vs. concrete memory, 142
  perception and, 118, 119–21, 122, 133–34, 142, 214
  Pure Memory, 127, 129, 135, 138–42, 144, 151, 153, 156, 171
  representation linked to, 108
  role in attention, 134–35, 168

two forms of, 125–28, 150; automatic or motor, 125–26, 150–51; of imagination (image memory), 125–29, 130–32, 136–37, 138, 144, 150–52, 156, 214; significance of, 128, 170–71 and virtuality, 139 *see also* body, the; duration; images; recognition; subjectivity

memory, Deleuze on, 180–81

Merleau-Ponty, Maurice, 5 n15, 173, 183

microphysics, 32–33, 34

mind, the (*l'esprit*): action vs. dream, 154–55; activities of, 152; B's description, 149–50; B's use of term, 156 n51; function of, 155. *See also* memory; mind/body dualism

mind/body dualism, 106, 107, 157; idealism and realism, 165, 169; and memory, 155; as metaphysical myth, 166; mind/body interaction, 107, 123, 128, 154, 166, 167; and present and past, 149. *See also* body, the; *and under* memory, in B's thought, two forms of

Minsky, Marvin, 208 n44

mobility (real movement), 67, 68

movement, B's concept: consciousness and, 172, 188 n59; dancer and, 47–50; as independent reality, 162; as indivisible, 159–60; real, 67–68, 160, 162–63; thought as, 140; and the virtual, 187

Mullarkey, John, 13 n44, 174–75

multiplicity, multiplicities: confused, 62, 66, 69–70, 91; distinct, 62, 68–70; as double notion, 62, 96; heterogeneous, 67; internal, and concept of number, 61; qualitative, 55, 56

Nagel, Thomas, 22 n23, 23 n27, 206

neurosciences: founding of, 24, neurophysiology, B's study of, 106, 123

Newton, Isaac, 18–19, 33, 38; concepts derived from, and influence, 22, 26

Nietzsche, Friedrich: Deleuze and, 173, 175 n9; rereadings of, 182, 185

number, concept of, 62; link to space, 61; link to time, 87

Pais, Abraham, 31 n52, 39 n81

Paulhan, Jean, *Les fleurs de Tarbes*, 74

Pearson, Keith Ansell, 13 n44, 175 n8

perception, B's theory of, 110–11, 114, 114 n5, 115, 132, 135, 148, 164, 193, 212; as action, 111–15, 163, 214; in action's service, 5, 107–111, 130, 169; consciousness and, 117, 118, 122; external, 115 n7; vs. feeling, 116 n8; framing of, 114–15; vs. memory, 109, 118, 119–21, 129, 142, 171, 213; and memory images, 132; Pure Perception, 109, 110, 115–17, 121, 123, 128, 156–57, 166, 168–70, vs. concrete perception, 122, 171. *See also* matter; recognition

phenomenology, 176–77, 182–85. *See also* Derrida, Jacques; Husserl, Edmund; Sartre, Jean-Paul

photometrics, 42, 57 n12. *See also* Fechner, Gustav

physics, philosophy and science of: classical laws, 38, 113, and B's critique, 199; as influence, 2–3, 29; and time, 3, 198–99. *See also* experimental physics

Planck, Max: Constant of, 34, 35; theory of energy quanta, 32, 35–36

Poincaré, Henri, 30 n50, 33–34, 40; B on, 202–3

Politzer, George, 12

positivism (positive philosophy), 21–26; B's breaking away from, 28; defined, 20; and evolution, 26–29. *See also* Comte, Auguste; Spencer, Herbert

post-structuralism: B and, 173, 174, 182, 185–86, 196; challenges to humanism, 193–94; and Deleuze's second presentation of B, 180, 182

Prigogine, Ilya, 198–200, 204 n28

Proust, Marcel, 9; B's links to, 125; *Swann's Way*, 69 n24, 73 n31

psychology: behavioral, 197; and human freedom, specific schools as threat, 42–43. *See also* associationist psychology; experimental psychology; Fechner, Gustav

psychometrics, theory of, 24–25

psychophysics, psychophysicists: B's arguments against, 57–58, 78, 88, 209; described, 42; methods used today, 197. *See also* Fechner, Gustav

Pullman, Bernard, 38 n74, 40, 200 n10

quantum mechanics: discoveries, consequences, 39, 40, 40 n83; problem of insufficient vocabulary to describe, 40–41

radiation, radioactivity: discovery of, 30, 33; experiments on, 34

Ravaisson, Félix Lacher, 203

reading, act of, and B's theory of memory, 135, 137

recognition, B's theory of, 124, 129–30, 134, 135, 149, 152, 171, 191, 193; attentive vs. automatic, 130–33

relativity, theory of, 30; B vs. Einstein, 12–13

Renan, Ernest, 21–22, 25–26, 27

representation, 109, 111, 120, 127, 141, 170

Ribot, Théodule, 23

Russell, Bertrand, 12, 13, 28, 63, 182

Sartre, Jean-Paul, 5 n15, 176, 183; *Nausea*, 66 n17

Schrödinger, Erwin, 36

science(s) in B's day: B's concern about automatism, 42; B's thought, and dialogue with, 160–61; crisis in, 37–38, 41 n87; and issue of certainty, 36–37, 38, 40 n83; and probability, 39

sensations: affective, tied to freedom, 52–54, 212; differences in, 44–45, 49; esthetic feelings, 47–50; influence of, 87–90; joy, quantity vs. quality, 45–47; kinds of sympathy, 50 n5; representative vs. affective, 58; sensation vs. perception, 116 n8; as unrepeatable, 73, 86, 89

Simmel, Georg, 10

Simondon, Gilbert, 194

Sorbonne Dispute, 8, 10 n29

Sorel, Georges, 10, 12

Soulez, Philippe, 30 n50

space: as abstraction, 149; as barrier between consciousness and matter, 166–67, 169; vs. duration, 96–97; vs. extension, 158; and number, 61; obsession with spatial images, 147; psychological discourse as positioned in, 139; and social life, 101–2, 104; and time, 64–65, 85, 87, 89, 103; as translation of time, 146

Spencer, Herbert, 8; B and, 27–28, 202; theory of evolution, 26–28

Stengers, Isabelle, 19, 160 n54, 199–200, 204 n28

structuralism, in France, 176–77

subjectivity, 149, 161; and memory, 121

sympathy, notion of, 50 n53

Synthetic Philosophy (Spencer), 26–28

Taine, Hippolyte, 23, 24, 26, 205, 211

technogreffes, 206–7

technology: blurring of distinction between animate and inanimate realms, 197; how to address, 198; technological changes in daily life, 14. *See also* artificial intelligence; computer revolution; current issues, B and

thermodynamics, 30, 160 n54; first law, 31, 34; second law, law of entropy, 31–32, and B, 198, 199; theories of and work in, 9, 35

Third Republic, changes and technological developments, 14–16

time: Derrida on, 185; characterizations of, 1–3; Valéry on, 1, 50

time, B's theory of
B on Kant's conception, 100–103
and current issues, 198–201, 209, 210–11
general characterizations
as "bastard concept," 65
as concrete, 4, 80
as force and form of energy, 2, 77–80, 188–89, 212
as invention, 213
key concepts tied to, 209
lived, as irreversible, 19, 78–79, 198–99
past, present, future, 142
temporal flow, 126, 144, 145

immediate future, importance of, 143, 148–49
linked to space, 64–65, 71 n26, 100, 146, 213
and memory, 126, 139
past, the, 187, 213
and the body, 144
immediate, 142–43, 148, 149
importance of, 147
memory and, 142, 171, 214
vs. the present, 120–21, 142
as reality, 212
see also unconscious
in physics, 198, 199, 204, 212
present, the
as action, 120–21, 128, 142, 171
described, 142–43, 187, 213
duration and, 142, 145
and memory process, 140–42, 144, 214
vs. the past, 120–21, 142
perception of, 141–45
relationship between intensities and, 73, 86
and sensations, 50, 213
universal time, 200
see also action; duration; memory; perception; recognition

Uncertainty Principle (Heisenberg), 17, 36–39, 40 n83, 40 n85; and B, 29 n48

unconscious, the: B's characterization, 110, 145, 147–48; in Deleuze, 170. *See also* Freud, Sigmund; material unconscious

Valéry, Paul: on changes in modern life and the sciences, 14, 15–17, 37, 210; on time, 1, 50

Varela, Francisco, 193 n87

Virilio, Paul, 1, 192, 206–7; time and modern crisis, 110–11

virtual, the, virtuality, 127, 139–42, 146, 181, 187–88; virtual reality, 190. *See also* Deleuze, Gilles

wave theories: consequences, 38–39; dual particle, 3, 29 n48, 36

Weil, Eric, 3

Wernicke, Carl, 24

Worms, Frédéric, 13 n44, 23 n27, 126 n20, 127, 130 n22, 132 n24, 135, 140, 141

X-ray, discovery of, 30, 33

Zeno's paradox, 68, 159

zone of indeterminacy, 108, 113, 122

Lightning Source UK Ltd.
Milton Keynes UK
UKHW011147170519
342846UK00001B/94/P

9 780801 473005

STATISTICAL METHODS
FOR RESEARCHERS
MADE VERY SIMPLE

Ronald R. Gauch

University Press of America,® Inc.
Lanham • New York • Oxford

Copyright © 2000 by
University Press of America, ® Inc.
4720 Boston Way
Lanham, Maryland 20706

12 Hid's Copse Rd.
Cumnor Hill, Oxford OX2 9JJ

Library of Congress Cataloging-in-Publication Data

Gauch, Ronald R.
Statistical methods for researchers made very simple / Ronald R. Gauch.
p. cm.
Includes bibliographical references and index.
1.   Statistics. I. Title.
QA276.12 .G38   2000   519.5—dc21   00-036441 CIP

ISBN 0-7618-1701-8 (pbk: alk. ppr.)